W9-AAO-529

ADVERTISING NEXT

ADVERTISING NEX

150 WINNING CAMPAIGNS FOR THE NEW COMMUNICATIONS AGE

TOM HIMPE

CHRONICLE BOOKS
SAN FRANCISCO

la glo
ba

AGÜERO
JOY

NIKE NEXT

Innovation is the lifeblood of the company. It drives us every day. We serve the world's greatest athletes and they are our most demanding consumers. We gain their insights and create products that give them an edge when they step out onto the court or the field. That belief has driven both innovative product solutions and our communications to connect better with our consumers.

In the 1970s, at track meets across the United States, we sold shoes out of the back of cars, creating one-to-one brand connections and propelling the brand forward one shoe sale at a time. In the '80s, we created new innovative products designed and inspired for world-class athletes. It was the era of Michael Jordan, and of athletes as icons, backed by big brand TV advertising. It worked. Fast-forward to the '90s and, with our growing global footprint, we added more surgical brand approaches, creating consumer experiences, and events with deeper local insights, allowing us to make more meaningful connections.

Since the turn of the century, the digital explosion has fundamentally changed the rules of consumer engagement. Today's young consumer is in the driver's seat and has a new set of expectations. Brands need to solve problems, enrich and entertain. Not

THE ABILITY TO NOT ONLY ENTERTAIN AND INSPIRE, BUT TO ENABLE NEW SOLUTIONS THAT ENHANCE EXISTING BEHAVIOURS IS THE EMBODIMENT OF THE 'JUST DO IT' SPIRIT.

just talk. We now have the opportunity (and responsibility) to engage in an ongoing conversation every single day.

The digital world permeates consumers' lives, but they never think of it as technology – it's just another tool of convenience. So rather than viewing it as 'new media' and a vehicle to fire messages at the consumer, we use it to service a need. As we move from passive one-way communications to a two-way conversation, we give our consumer a voice by listening, sharing, co-creating and, above all, by enabling meaningful solutions.

Nike+ is a great example of this. People need motivation. People like to run to music. And people want to keep track of their runs. So, together with Apple, we created the Nike + iPod system. Over 41 million miles have been logged in the first eighteen months, rapidly building the world's largest running club. The forum on nikeplus.com is packed with smart, interesting ideas that we can use to continuously improve the service for our runners much more quickly than if we were doing it all by ourselves.

The key point here is this: by creating a service and opening a direct channel to your consumers, you can form a very powerful relationship that enhances both the product and the service. Done right, this becomes a self-perpetuating relationship that doesn't depend on broad communications to drive interest. It gives the consumer a reason to return and re-engage with the brand over and over again, motivated by something that means more than anything else to them – their own achievements.

This ability to not only entertain and inspire, but to enable new solutions that enhance existing behaviours is the embodiment of the 'Just Do It' spirit.

STEFAN OLANDER
GLOBAL DIRECTOR OF BRAND CONNECTIONS AT NIKE

UNILEVER NEXT

As a leading global manufacturer of consumer goods, we have always prided ourselves on our consumer insights and understanding their relationships with our brands, from Dove, Lynx and Sunsilk to Lipton, Knorr, Magnum and Ben & Jerry's. In the rapidly changing media landscape, however, advertisers like us are having to radically rethink our strategies, communication ideas and traditional means of building those consumer relationships. We have started by embracing a new communications strategy that is based less on the old model of 'interruption' and more on 'engaging' consumers, by penetrating the culture, creating talkability and providing compelling opportunities for consumers to interact with our brands.

The Dove campaign is a case in point. We have taken a simple but personal approach and transformed the brand from a functional beauty product into something much bigger and more powerful: a brand idea that has sparked genuine debate about beauty and has been embraced universally by women around the world. The key word here is 'personal': we know that today's consumer has a voice and wants to express it, and with Dove we opened up a platform for those voices to be heard. You only have to read the Dove message board to see how deeply our core consumers care about self-esteem and modern society's definitions of beauty. The success of the Dove campaign also shows how important it is to remain true to a brand's values and bring them to life with every brand experience.

Our changing attitude towards media has been a fundamental part of this strategy. With the Lynx brand we knew that the traditional television format was probably not the most effective means of engaging with young males. It forced us to experiment with digital content long before many of our competitors did, and paved the way for later work on Dove and a number of our other brands. As a result, we now tend to let our ideas and objectives dictate the media we use, rather than vice versa. To launch the Dove Campaign for Real Beauty, for example, we opted for an outdoor campaign as we thought that it would have the most impact with that particular brand idea and would get people talking – much more so than television or digital media. With Dove Evolution, we went for a web video as this format gave us enough time to tell the story and allowed people to share it easily. These campaigns for both brands have been hugely successful.

Coupled with significant brand success, our experiences with Lynx and Dove have been instrumental in creating a company culture that has truly embraced the new attitude. Our successes spread naturally throughout the company and sparked renewed enthusiasm among brand marketers who were keen to contribute and push the boundaries further. One outcome of this is our Trendslator programme, launched a few years ago in the United States, which pairs senior executives with new marketers to advance our digital skills and knowledge. Our relationship with agencies has also been affected. We now bring our media agencies into the mix much earlier than in the past to better inform the overall communication strategy for the brand, and they often play an important role in bringing the campaign idea to life.

In this book, Tom Himpe suggests that small companies need to think big, and that big companies need to act small. This is quite a challenge for a company like Unilever, with over 170,000 employees and 300 brands in more than 100 countries around the world. In today's unpredictable climate, the mantras set out in this book offer invaluable guidance and inspiration for any marketing professional struggling with the challenges we all face as advertisers in the digital age, whether big or small.

LAURA KLAUBERG
VICE-PRESIDENT OF GLOBAL MEDIA AT UNILEVER

WE HAVE STARTED BY EMBRACING A NEW COMMUNICATIONS STRATEGY THAT IS BASED LESS ON THE OLD MODEL OF 'INTERRUPTION' AND MORE ON 'ENGAGING' CONSUMERS.

ON THINKING BIG AND ACTING SMALL

THE BOTTOM LINE IS THAT SIZE OR SCALE IS NOT THE REAL DISCRIMINATOR IN TODAY'S ALTERED COMMUNICATIONS LANDSCAPE; BEHAVIOUR IS. IT'S NOT SO MUCH ABOUT *BEING* SMALL OR *BEING* BIG; IT'S ABOUT *ACTING* SMALL OR *ACTING* BIG.

When you glance at the seventeen mantras in this book, you may think that a lot of them are only relevant to smaller brands. Mantras such as 'be transparent', 'be personal', 'be co-creative' or 'be experimental' seem to apply to small, agile, quirky brands rather than big, global, corporate ones. True, being small comes with a few natural advantages. It's easier for small companies to be transparent, as they are less structured and complex. They can approach their customers in a more personal way as they have fewer of them. And they can make quicker and bolder decisions as there are fewer decision-makers.

With a range of new communication tools at their disposal, small brands can now compete head-to-head with any big brand on the planet. The digital landscape has flattened media and marketing, creating equal opportunities for companies of all shapes and sizes. Hugh MacLeod, who turned Stormhoek from an unknown South African label into the unofficial wine brand of Silicon Valley through the power of blogging and social media (see pages 250–1), boldly claims that the company not only competes with all the other wine brands across the globe, but with the likes of Apple, Google and Microsoft. A strong believer in global micro brands, MacLeod has transformed a seemingly average product into a social object, spreading far beyond its traditional audience. After all, it costs the average small brand just as much to start a blog as it does a big company. The same goes for a profile on MySpace, Flickr, Facebook or any other such site. The internet has democratized communication and enabled small players, individual dare-devils and local entrepreneurs to play with the big boys.

But *being* small does not necessarily equal *acting* small. There are just as many small companies out there 'acting big', failing to embrace dialogue and conversation, shying away from open and transparent communication, clinging on to traditional ways of communication, being average rather than remarkable. The bottom line is that size or scale is not the real discriminator in today's altered communications landscape; behaviour is. It's not so much about *being* small or *being* big; it's about *acting* small or *acting* big.

Since the flattened media landscape is equally open to big companies, there are plenty of opportunities out there, provided they adopt the right behaviour. They have to start acting like an agile, small, authentic player, rather than a big, corporate giant. It may be easier for small brands to tell the truth on their blog, address their customers by name or involve them in the creative process, but nothing is stopping big brands from doing exactly the same. As always, some of the big boys seem to just 'get it' – generally the same ones that have always 'got it' right from the start. Brands such as Red Bull, Nike, MINI, Diesel, Virgin or Innocent Drinks – all represented in this book – have embraced innovation and change since their earliest days and have kept true to their original spirit while growing big and global. As a result, they seem to adopt the new marketing rulebook more flexibly and fluently than others.

American journalist Jeff Jarvis points out that 'small won't replace big, of course, but small will add up to considerable new competition. And that is because small can now succeed. The economies of scale must compete with the economies of small.' I would argue that the real competition is not between small and big companies; it's between companies that are acting small and acting big, between those who embrace the new landscape and those who don't, and between those who adopt the new mantras and those who are unable to do so. In the end, the digital revolution is not favouring small companies per se, but any company with the right attitude: flexible, agile, transparent and remarkable in actions, global in mindset. It has enabled small companies to think big and it has forced big companies to act small.

THE DIGITAL REVOLUTION HAS ENABLED SMALL COMPANIES TO THINK BIG AND FORCED BIG COMPANIES TO ACT SMALL.

THE CHANGING NATURE OF CAMPAIGNS

For decades, all advertising campaigns followed more or less the same pattern. However different the creative idea or message at the heart of them, campaigns were all expressed through the same mass channels and formats. In architectural terms, they were all built like prefab houses, with the real effort going into the interior decor rather than how the houses were put together.

Today, campaigns have become complex and custom-made constructions, with different subcontractors involved from a range of specialist disciplines. Brands want their communication to be more like a Frank Gehry building, remarkable and one-of-a-kind, and less like an ordinary house on the street, however attractive it might look on the inside.

As campaigns now tend to spread across a wider range of disciplines and channels, they have become increasingly complex and layered. Their construction requires the skills of an experienced architect, who is familiar with all the different building blocks and can make every aspect of the design fit together perfectly. It has become harder to summarize campaigns in a single catchphrase. They are more like riddles that have to be solved, or stories that have to be unravelled.

Contemporary campaigns are not as easy to grasp or decode, nor do they want to be. They are living and breathing entities that make sense to those who fully engage in them, but whose essence can sometimes be hard to convey to outsiders.

BRANDS WANT THEIR COMMUNICATION TO BE MORE LIKE A FRANK GEHRY BUILDING, REMARKABLE AND ONE-OF-A-KIND, AND LESS LIKE AN ORDINARY HOUSE ON THE STREET, HOWEVER ATTRACTIVE IT MIGHT LOOK ON THE INSIDE.

THE MOST FUNDAMENTAL EVOLUTION IN TODAY'S COMMUNICATIONS LANDSCAPE IS THE SHIFT FROM SHORT-TERM CAMPAIGNS TO LONG-TERM, STRUCTURAL INITIATIVES.

Campaigns have also become more diverse. They can take many different shapes and forms, from a one-off experience to a long-term service, from a series of webisodes to an online platform. Like Bram Stoker's Dracula, who could change shape in the right conditions, brands can adapt themselves to any environment, easily and comfortably switching across disciplines and channels. The wide range of campaigns showcased in this book highlights the breadth of options available to marketers today.

The most fundamental evolution in today's communications landscape is the shift from short-term campaigns to long-term, structural initiatives. The advertising industry has always thought in terms of short-term spikes rather than ongoing dialogue. Whenever a product is about to be launched, or awareness has to be increased or a competitor is on the up, there is a brief surge in communication efforts, after which there is often a return to radio silence. Anyone would admit that this is a strange way of building relationships. A good, solid relationship does not rely on brief appearances, but on ongoing conversation and interaction. And new tools and techniques allow brands to have that ongoing, permanent bond.

So brands are increasingly attempting to build long-term, often self-sufficient platforms, whether it's an online community (Nike+, see pages 260–1; Levi's, see pages 234–7), a permanent service (UPS Widget, see pages 348–9; HSBC cabs, see pages 334–5) or a physical space (Coca-Cola, see pages 166–9; Cartier, see pages 364–5; Louis Vuitton, see pages 366–7). All of the above initiatives have excelled at creating unique, permanent platforms that prevent the brand from simply making a string of sporadic appearances.

BE PLAYFUL

'Let my playing be my learning, and my learning be my playing,' wrote the historian and cultural theorist Johan Huizinga in his 1938 book *Homo Ludens* ('Man at Play'), which discusses the importance of the play element in culture and society. Today, it seems as if Huizinga's assertions are more relevant to marketers than ever. Their ever-growing appetite for playful brand experiences is partly fuelled by an increasingly mature and mainstream gaming industry.

Gaming, the immersive medium par excellence, has the ability to truly get under people's skin and engage them for a seemingly unlimited period of time, something that can hardly be said of many other media. 'Video games clearly have a powerful effect on gamers,' says David Walsh, president of the National Institute on Media and the Family.

'The really good ones tend to be very, very addictive. But these games can be good teachers. We just have to pay attention to what they are teaching.'

Because of its immersive nature, gaming has matured beyond the realm of pure entertainment, and is increasingly used as a learning mechanism in military, medical, educational and political spheres. 'We've known for a while that games can sharpen memory and improve hand–eye coordination, but they can also be used to teach problem-solving skills, increase our awareness of world issues, help with social phobias and can even treat those with serious illnesses,' says Ben Sawyer, co-founder and director of the Games for Health Project, an organization that brings together medical professionals, researchers and gamemakers to explore new ways to improve health care practice and policy.

As a result of its widening scope, gaming is becoming an interesting and viable route for almost every company or organization, beyond the predictable players, i.e., the cool brands aiming for the trendy or young audiences. The more 'serious' industries and domains, such as finance, government or b2b, are now also looking at games as a way to make their messages more digestible or sexy. The easiest way in is through in-game advertising, subtle and clever integration of messages in existing game properties. The more audacious and ambitious brands, however, create their very own game experiences from scratch. This chapter focuses more heavily on the latter category.

And it all seems to be just the beginning. The computer gaming industry is doubling in size every five years and is in constant transformation. Chris Swain, a professor of game design at the University of Southern California, predicts that 'games are the literature of the twenty-first century. When you look at games today, it may be difficult to see that. But the pieces are in place for this to happen.' According to Emory Rowland of Clickfire.com, games in the future will be increasingly social, multi-sensory, affordable, customizable and educational.

The true opportunity for computer or online games, however, lies in their ability to extend virtual playful experiences into the real world, or link them to real-world events. At the LeWeb3 conference in December 2007, Rafi Haladjian declared that 'the next frontier is not doing more things with bits, but with real things in the real world'. The true 'brand *ludens*' does not confine the notion of playfulness to an online experience or a gaming console, but incorporates it into its overall behaviour, turning every encounter with the brand into a playful moment.

V&S ABSOLUT SPIRITS
Agency: TBWA\Paris
France – 2006

The playfulness of Absolut's print advertising was extended online with a game that challenged players to find eighty-two Absolut vodka bottles hidden in a crowded illustration in under two minutes. What might seem easy in print was actually quite difficult online, as it required great precision and skill to move the cursor quickly enough across the screen.

YACHT CLUB
SEND ELP
PEACE & HAIR
FASCISM
HOTEL
JOES
BANG
Just Married
POLICE LINE

UNITED STATES ARMY

Agency: n/a
United States – since 2002

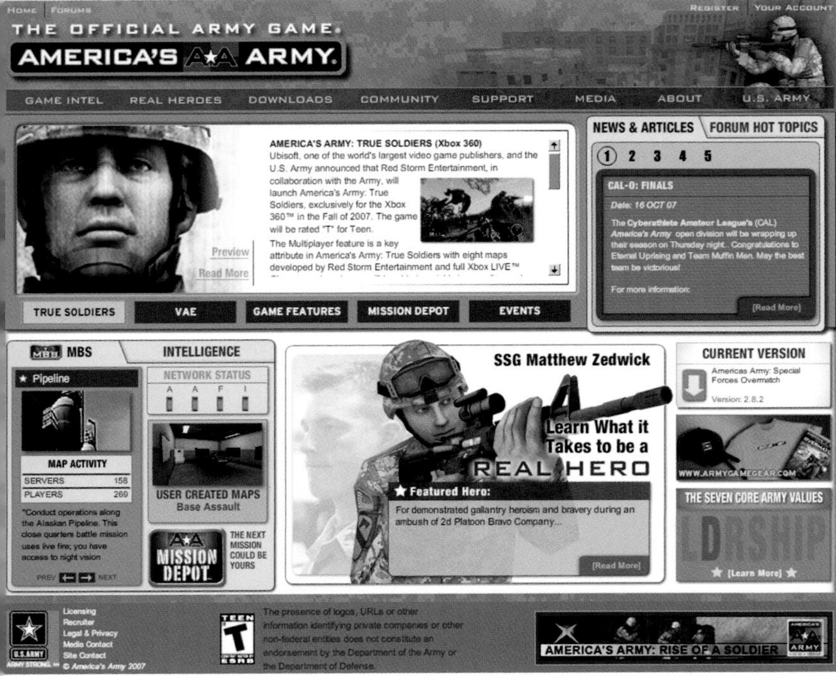

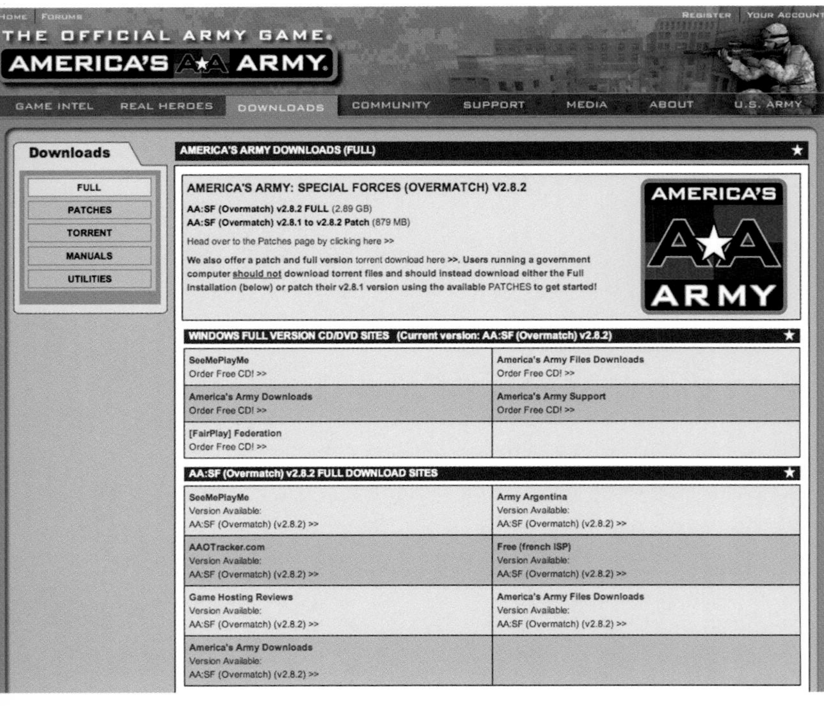

In 1997, a report stated that the US Department of Defense's simulations were lagging behind commercial games, and recommended joint research with the entertainment industry. Recognizing the popularity of computer games, as well as their ability to convey information in an engaging, entertaining and informative manner, the US Army created *America's Army*. The game was designed to give civilians an insight into what it's like to be a soldier and – more importantly – to present a career in the Army as a viable option for young adults in a more cost-effective way.

In 2000, the US Army sent its talented development team to experience training firsthand. They had to crawl through obstacle courses, fire weapons, observe paratrooper instruction and participate in a variety of training exercises with elite combat units. The result was a relatively authentic representation of combat, especially in its depictions of firearm usage and mechanics.

In the game, players gain experience as they navigate challenges in teamwork-based, multiplayer, force-versus-force operations. As in the Army, accomplishing the missions of the game requires team effort and adherence to the Army's values of loyalty, duty, respect, selfless service, honour, integrity and personal courage. Players must also operate under the rules of warfare and the military's Rules of Engagement to advance in the game.

Since its launch in July 2002, *America's Army* (which is rated 'T' for 'Teen') has become one of the most popular computer games in the world, with over 8.6 million registered accounts. Financed with US tax money and distributed for free, the game's popularity has continued to grow with the release of each new version. The Army has also expanded the concept to include mobile phone games, the launch of the Xbox version *America's Army: Rise of a Soldier* and *America's Army: True Soldiers* (exclusively for Xbox 360), as well as the online Virtual Army Experience which offers a virtual 'test drive' of the Army.

At the United States Military Academy, 19 per cent of the new intake in 2003 said they had played the game. Enlistment quotas were met in the two years directly following the game's release.

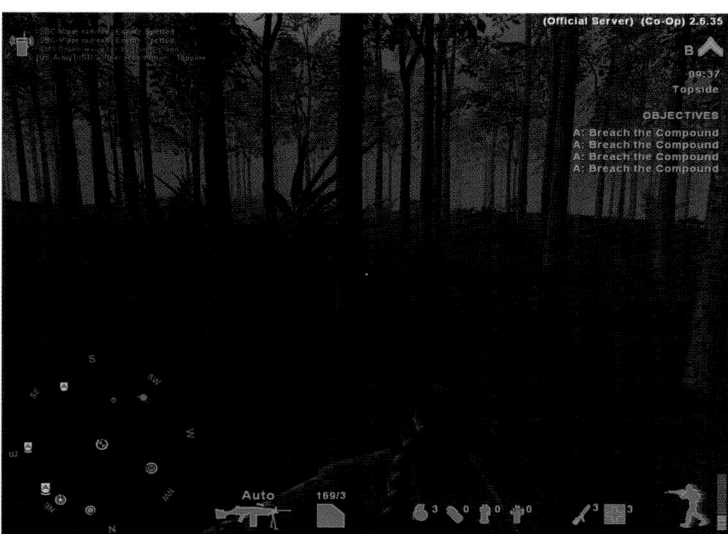

‘*AMERICA’S ARMY* HAS PROVEN TO BE ONE OF THE ARMY’S MOST EFFECTIVE COMMUNICATIONS TOOLS, WITH PLAYERS SPENDING MILLIONS OF HOURS EXPLORING THE U.S. ARMY.’

COLONEL CASEY WARDYNSKI, PROJECT DIRECTOR OF *AMERICA’S ARMY*

BE PLAYFUL
UNILEVER – LYNX
Agency: Dare
United Kingdom – 2005–6

Lynx, which is known as Axe in the United States and elsewhere in Europe, is renowned for its portrayal of young men being pursued by women who are unable to resist the scent of the brand. The internet proved the perfect medium for Lynx guys to explore their success with the opposite sex.

In Lynx Feather, men can use the cursor to move a virtual feather over the body of a gorgeous woman in skimpy red underwear. The feather makes her sneeze, giggle or writhe as it touches her. The content was created from two hours of digital video. Top Slovakian model Silvia Valcikova performed forty moves, eventually edited down to twenty-five, which are triggered when users tickle different parts of her anatomy. To create additional sexiness a professional voice-over artist was commissioned to lip-sync the sound of giggling. The content was initially seeded in an email to Lynx's 30,000-strong customer database in selected European countries. Interest exploded globally, however, and the campaign ended up captivating 15 million unique viewers, with an average tickle time of 8 minutes.

The following year, Lynx returned to the virtual mating game with a new formula, replacing tickling with blowing. A girl is revealed frozen in time and the user has to warm her up by blowing into a microphone or a pair of headphones. As you blow, the girl defrosts and comes to life. Persistent blowing unlocks a variety of reactions until her clothes come off and you see her skydiving. Lynx Blow's innovation lay in the way it harnessed the computer's audio input, turning it into an effective control mechanism. The teaser email to the loyal Lynx UK database was sent out on one of the coldest days of the year with the message 'Baby, it's cold outside'.

BURGER KING

Agencies: Crispin Porter + Bogusky/Equity Marketing
United States – 2006

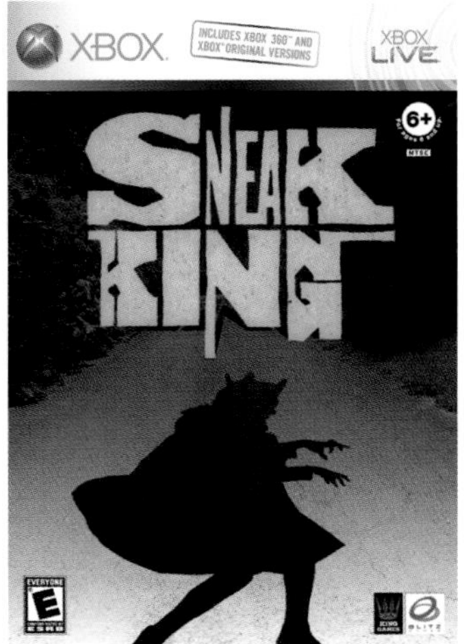

In November 2006, Burger King made gaming history by partnering with Microsoft to develop three Xbox games: *Big Bumpin'*, a bumper-car game; *PocketBike Racer*, a kart racing game; and *Sneak King*, in which players have to sneak up on unsuspecting, hungry pedestrians and surprise them with tasty treats from the menu. The games featured several familiar characters from the Burger King universe, including the King and Subservient Chicken.

The games were priced at $3.99 each and were available with the purchase of a BK Value Meal at branches of Burger King during the holiday season. The five-week promotion kicked off online with trailers. On the day the games went on sale in 6,680 participating restaurants, a variety of television and print executions were launched.

According to Microsoft, the games went 'platinum' with 2.4 million units sold during the five-week promotional period. This put them on a level with the third best-selling Xbox game of all time. The estimated media impressions generated by the Burger King games were equivalent to thirteen Super Bowls and helped Burger King draw in record traffic and sales across the board.

'THE BURGER KING GAMES BECAME THE *MY BIG FAT GREEK WEDDING* OF THE ADVERGAME WORLD.'

DARREN HERMAN, CO-FOUNDER OF IGA WORLDWIDE

‘THE SUCCESS OF THE CAMPAIGN SURPRISED EVERYBODY. NOBODY EXPECTED THE GAMES TO BE AS RICH, AS ENGAGING, AS DIVERSE AS THEY TURNED OUT TO BE.’

PHILIP OLIVER, CEO OF BLITZ GAMES, THE DEVELOPER OF THE GAMES

HONDA

Agency: Naked Communications
United Kingdom – 2005

Honda took the launch of its new Civic as an opportunity to engage with a younger audience. Gaming proved to be the perfect territory for giving people a feel for the car's radical new shape. Working with the most realistic racing game on the market, *TOCA Racing*, the 'Honda Championship' was born. This stand-alone virtual test drive allowed users to experience seven Honda models, with the new Civic positioned at the top level of the game.

Working directly with the programmers, each car was perfectly modelled, from its body and performance to the feel of its gear shift. The total process from inception to execution took nearly two years.

The game was seeded online prior to the launch, with 250,000 people downloading the 100MB file and taking a test drive. In the same week that the cars became available, copies of the virtual test drive were distributed through *Top Gear* magazine as well as Honda dealers.

In one year, Honda normally takes prospective customers on 60,000 test drives through their dealerships. Within six months of the Civic's launch, the virtual test drive reached more than a million people.

ADAC
ADAC
CIVIC TYPE R
HONDA
HONDA
HONDA
13
07
HONDA
HONDA
13

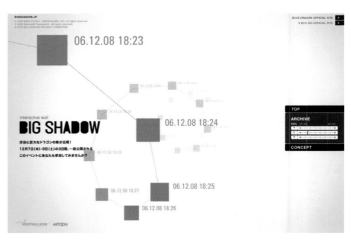

Agency: GT
Japan – 2006

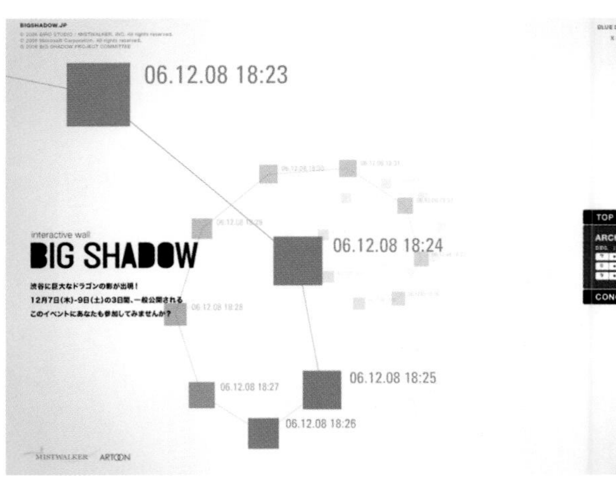

In *Blue Dragon*, a role-playing game for the Xbox 360, the protagonist's shadow grows into a blue dragon when he fights. This visual element was used as a key device in the promotion of the game.

Located in the centre of Shibuya, Tokyo, an interactive wall was devised which involved projecting people's shadows 40 metres (130 feet) high onto a building. When participants performed certain actions, such as raising their arms over their heads, the shadow of a giant dragon emerged from their silhouettes. The dragon could also turn into a minotaur or a phoenix. Other (unrelated) animations created the illusion that participants' silhouettes were being squashed by a large foot, or that water was being poured 'over their shadows' from a cup.

Participants were also able to manipulate virtual shadows online. These were then added to the street projection, which could be followed on the internet through a live video feed. The promotion helped Microsoft to crack the elusive Japanese games market, at a time when Nintendo Wii and Sony PS3 were also being introduced.

'WE COULD CREATE A PRETTY COOL CITYSCAPE BY COMBINING THE DRAGON'S CARTOON-LIKE SILHOUETTE WITH THE NEON SIGNS OF SHIBUYA'S BAWDY NIGHT LIFE.'

KOSHI UCHIYAMA, GT

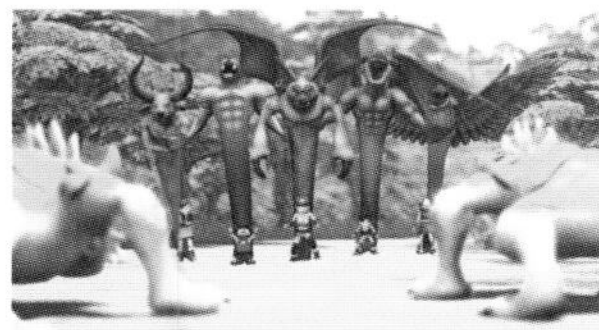

BE PLAYFUL

CALIFORNIA FLUID MILK PROCESSOR ADVISORY BOARD

Agency: Goodby Silverstein & Partners

United States – 2006

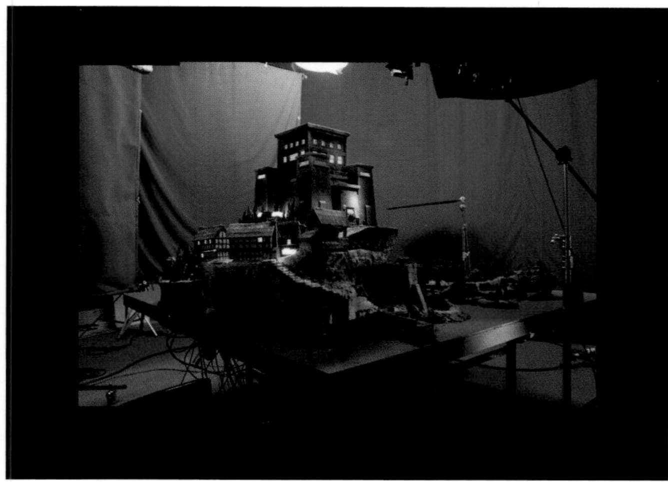

Got Milk? wanted Californians to think about what the world would be like if milk was in short supply. Its answer was an online board game rendered in sophisticated 3D animation at www.gettheglass.com.

Players have to help an ailing family in a van to find a glass of milk. They can move the family forward by rolling a pair of virtual dice and correctly answering a series of trivia-based questions. Every step of the way, players have to overcome debilitating physical conditions associated with calcium deficiency: brittle bones, weak muscles, insomnia, PMS and broken nails. Those that make it all the way to the heavily fortressed 'Fort Fridge' receive a real 'Get the glass' souvenir glass.

The site had 1.4 million visits in the first three months, with an average of 12.5 minutes spent on the site per visitor. The campaign generated a 225 per cent increase in traffic to GotMilk.com. Milk sales increased by 1.5 per cent in California, outperforming US sales as a whole, which were flat.

'THE IDEA WAS TO USE CLASSIC BOARD GAME CUES, THEN JACK IT UP ON DIGITAL STEROIDS.'

MIKE GEIGER, DEPARTMENT HEAD, INTERACTIVE PRODUCTION AT GOODBY SILVERSTEIN & PARTNERS

BMW GROUP

Agency: Naked Communications

Australia – 2006

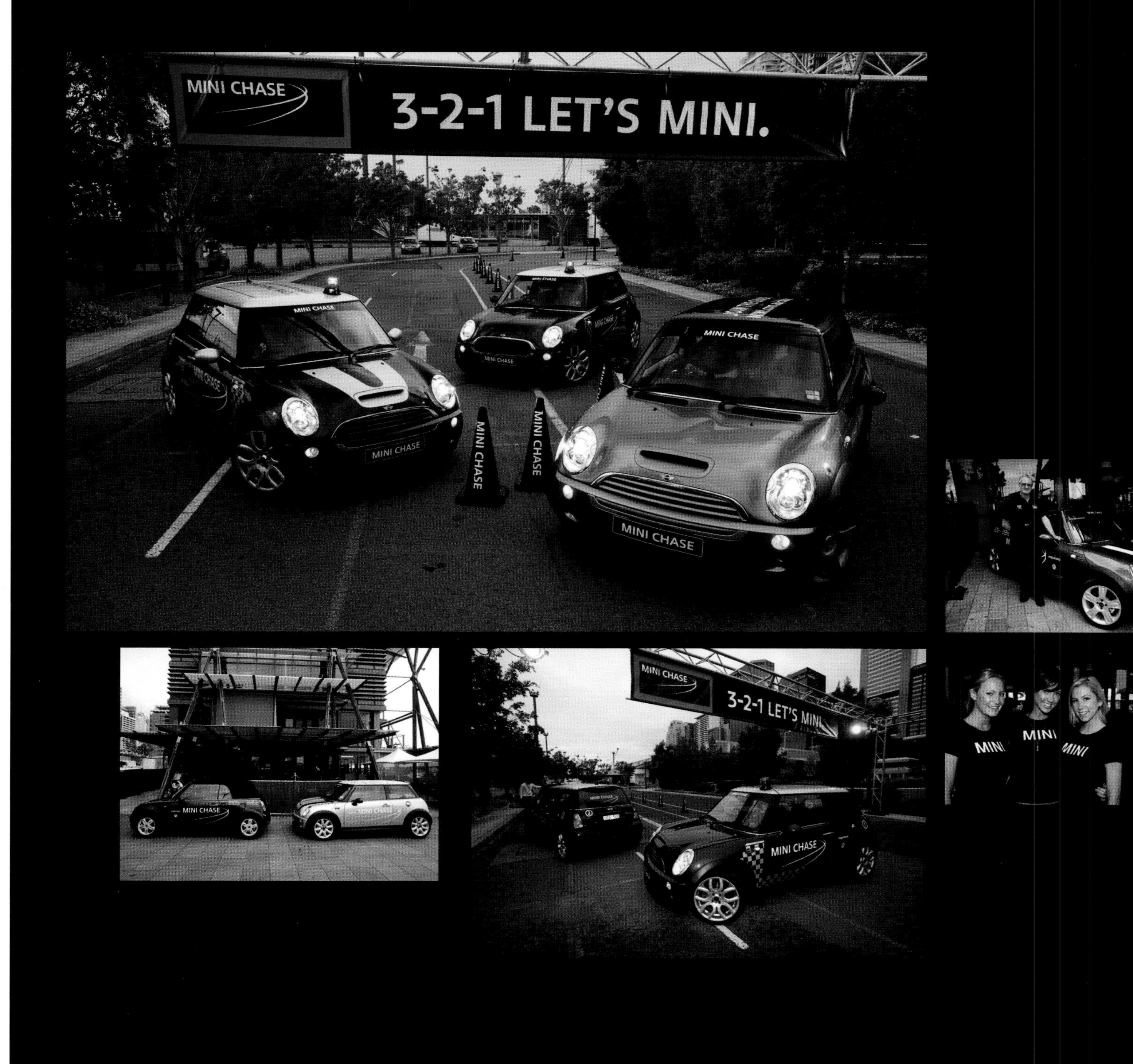

Instead of opting for a classic and static motor show presence, MINI invited visitors to take part in a 'cops and robbers'-themed chase. People queued up to be driven by professional stunt drivers high speed around a track, complete with hay bales, smoke machines and oil slicks. As well as the momentary thrill, the experience gave them a taste of what it would be like to own a MINI. The exercise generated a 177 per cent increase in leads, as well as delivering what previous years had not – five sales on the spot.

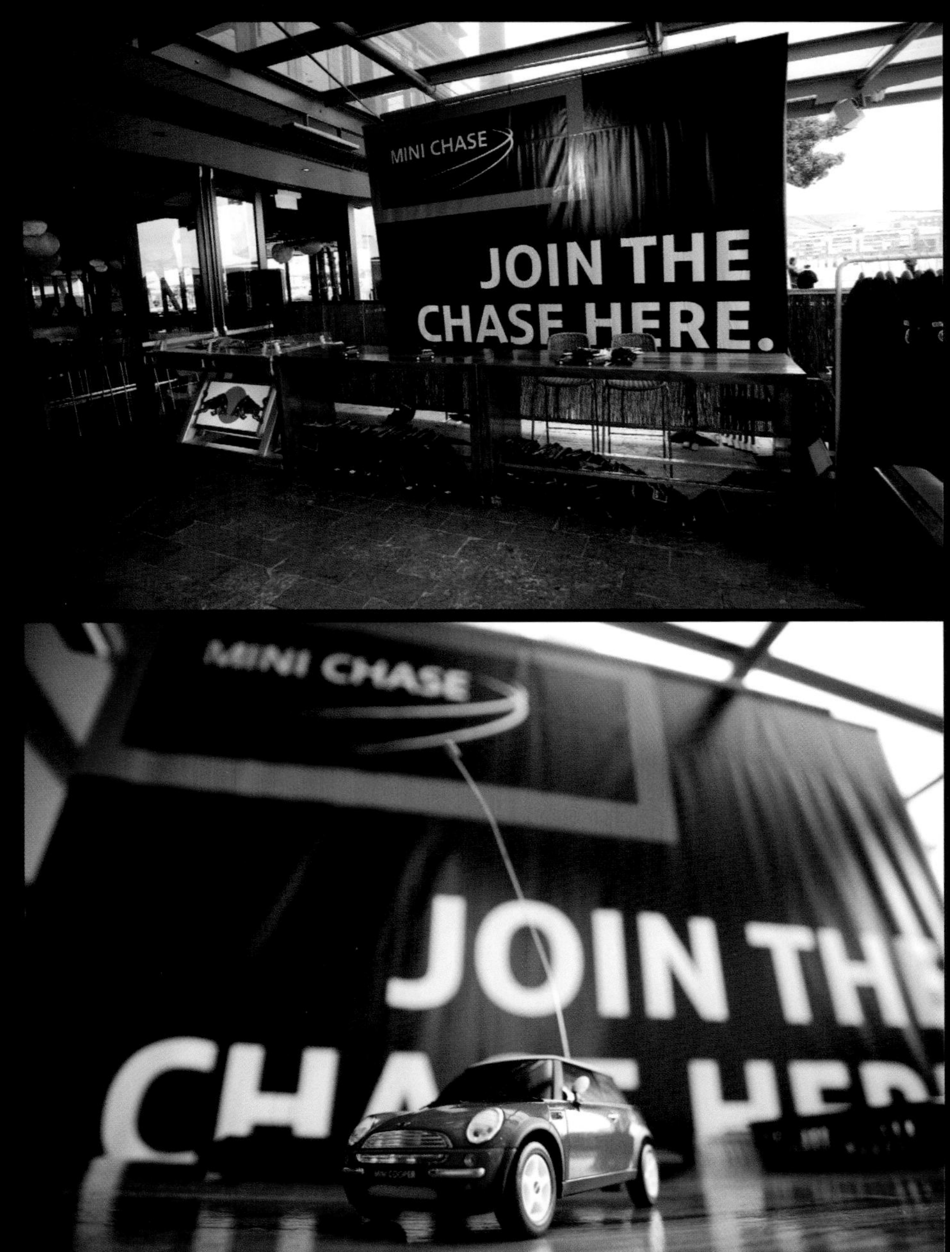

BE PLAYFUL
HASBRO
Agencies: OMD UK/DDB London/Tribal DDB London
United Kingdom – 2005

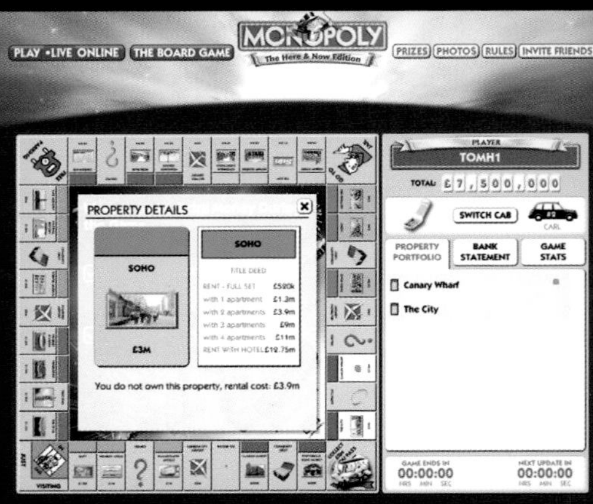

To celebrate the seventieth anniversary of *Monopoly*, an updated limited-edition version of the classic board game was launched featuring London landmarks such as the London Eye and the new Wembley Stadium. Traditional toy marketing was turned on its head for the revamped edition. To bring the new locations on the board to life, an enormous live game of *Monopoly* was created, using the real streets of London as the board and real London taxis as the playing pieces.

To take part in the live game, players had to sign up to an online version of *Monopoly*, choose from a selection of properties, place their houses, choose a taxi and then hit Go! Eighteen London cabs were fitted with GPS devices and represented the playing pieces. As the taxis went about their normal daily business, they passed the locations featured on the board, and this data was fed back to the online game. Players made money when other taxis 'landed on' their property, and lost it if their own taxi passed properties owned by other players. Each player's individual game lasted twenty-four hours, with the whole campaign running for a month. There were daily and weekly prizes to play for, and the winner of the top prize won a year of mortgage-/rent-free living. The integrated campaign included TV commercials, radio spots and online advertising.

More than 190,000 people played the game over the twenty-eight-day period. The PR generated was estimated to be worth over £2 m ($4 m), more than five times the cost of the campaign. Units of *Monopoly* flew off the shelves, with sales reaching Christmas levels. After a flat 2004, total brand sales rose 30 per cent year on year.

'EVER WANT TO PLAY *MONOPOLY* IN REAL LIFE, BUT WITHOUT THE UNFORTUNATE SIDE EFFECTS OF BEING VILIFIED IN SENSATIONAL ANTI-TRUST SUITS?'

ENGADGET.COM

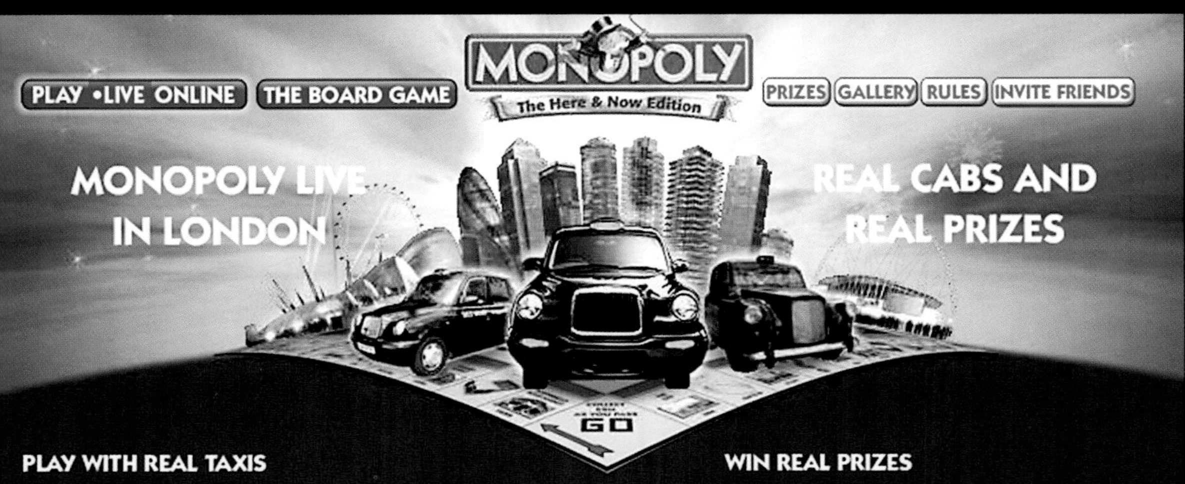

PLAY •LIVE ONLINE
THE BOARD GAME
MONOPOLY
The Here & Now Edition
PRIZES
GALLERY
RULES
INVITE FRIENDS
MONOPOLY LIVE IN LONDON
REAL CABS AND REAL PRIZES
GO

PLAY WITH REAL TAXIS

Monopolylive.com let you play Monopoly in the real London with 18 real cabs fitted with GPS systems as your movers.

MEET THE CABBIES

We pitted your cabbie against 5 others for 24 hours, and you could make millions by buying properties and placing apartments and hotels. There were some amazing prizes up for grabs, including your mortgage or rent paid for a year.

It's FREE

WIN REAL PRIZES

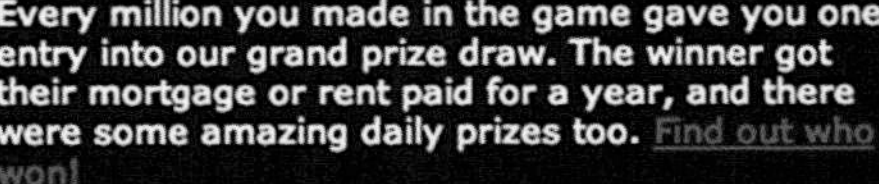

Every million you made in the game gave you one entry into our grand prize draw. The winner got their mortgage or rent paid for a year, and there were some amazing daily prizes too. Find out who won!

FREE MORTGAGE FOR A YEAR

NEW Monopoly Here & Now Ltd Edition

A modern day twist on the classic, Monopoly Here & Now marks the 70th anniversary of the original.

SHOW ME

See the ALL NEW board and playing pieces; find out a few fun facts about the Big Smoke as it is today...

WIN! Snap the Capital

This was your chance to be part of the Monopoly Live experience by sending in photos by MMS.

SNAP HAPPY

Whether it was photos of the new Monopoly locations, the Monopoly Live cabs or even dressing up as Mr. Monopoly, you sure had some fun. Take a look at the results!

Agency: Poke
United Kingdom – 2007

Spot the Bull + Win Glastonbury tickets

‘IT’S A DIGITAL VERSION OF THE OLD CLASSIC “GUESS WHERE THE COW IS GOING TO CRAP IN THE FIELD”.... IT’S AN OLD WORLD COUNTRY LIFE DIGITAL MASHUP.’

OPENHOUSE.TYPEPAD.COM

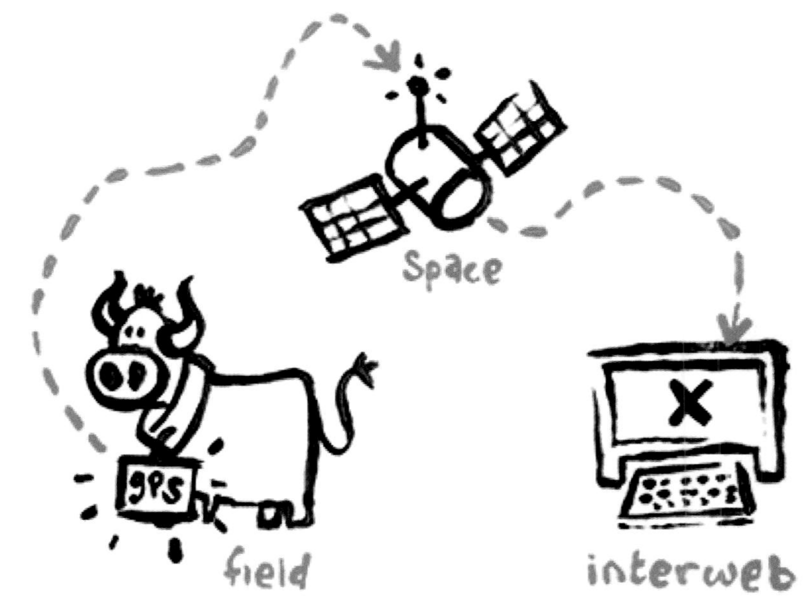

Orange used a real bull called Derek to launch its 'Spot the Bull' competition, which gave revellers the chance to win much sought-after tickets to the Glastonbury music festival. To be in with a chance of winning, participants had to correctly guess Derek's coordinates at 3 pm every day, using bull cams and GPS to select from a grid of eighty possible units that represented sections of the bull's enclosure. In addition there was a live news feed as well as a widget that could be downloaded to track the bull's every move. Hardcore Derek fans could find out more about him online, where they could get the lowdown from the people who knew him best – his farmer, his vet and his psychologist.

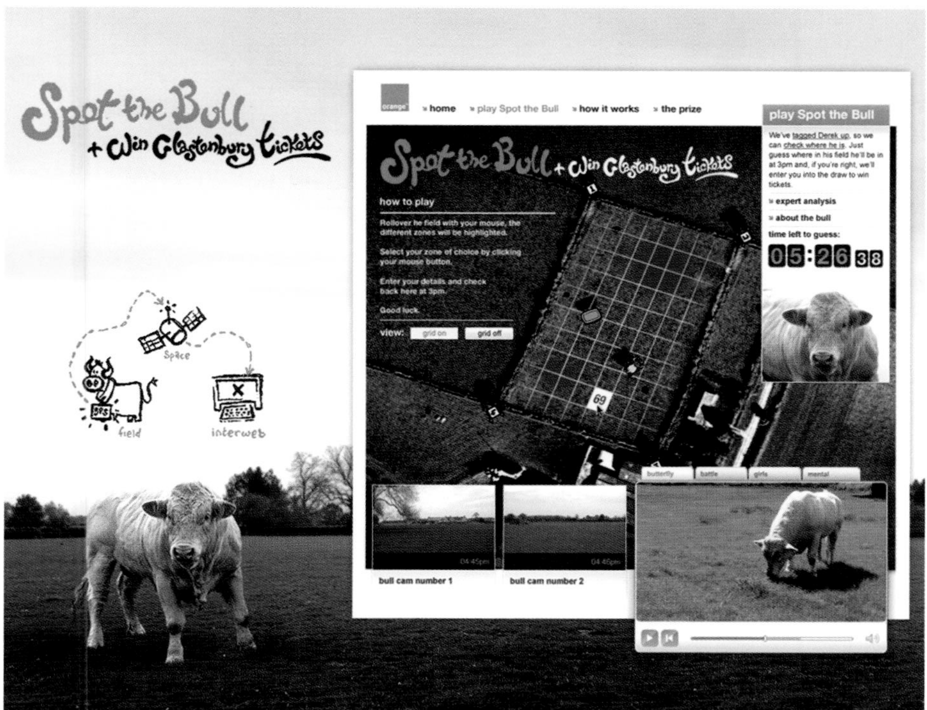

BE PLAYFUL
SONY PLAYSTATION
Agency: McCann Erickson Malaysia
Malaysia – 2006

This bus stop was completely covered with bubble wrap, with one of the iconic PlayStation 2 symbols printed on every single bubble. Rather than talking to people about gaming, PlayStation invited them to play. The panel had to be changed every other day as people couldn't resist 'pushing the buttons'.

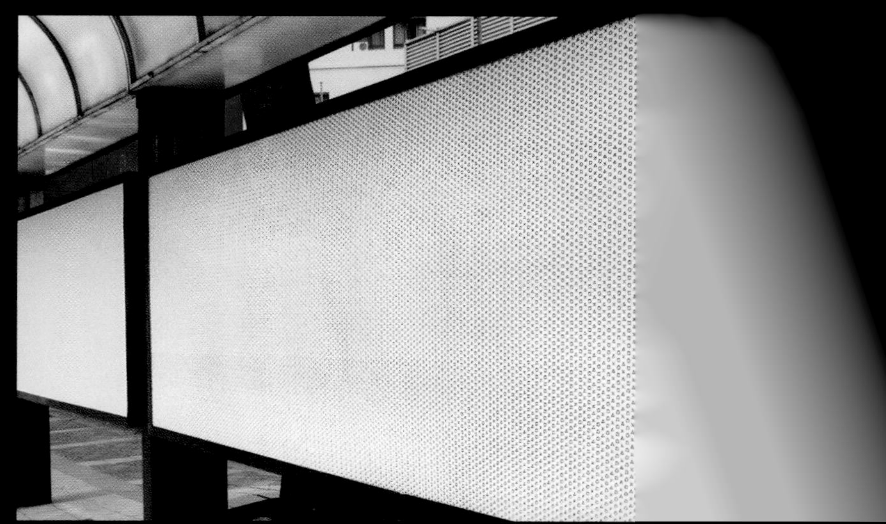

'JUST IMAGINE YOU'RE BORDERLINE OBSESSIVE COMPULSIVE ON YOUR WAY TO WORK. COULD YOU LEAVE THIS BUS STOP BEFORE EVERY LAST BUBBLE IS POPPED?'

JOYSTIQ.COM

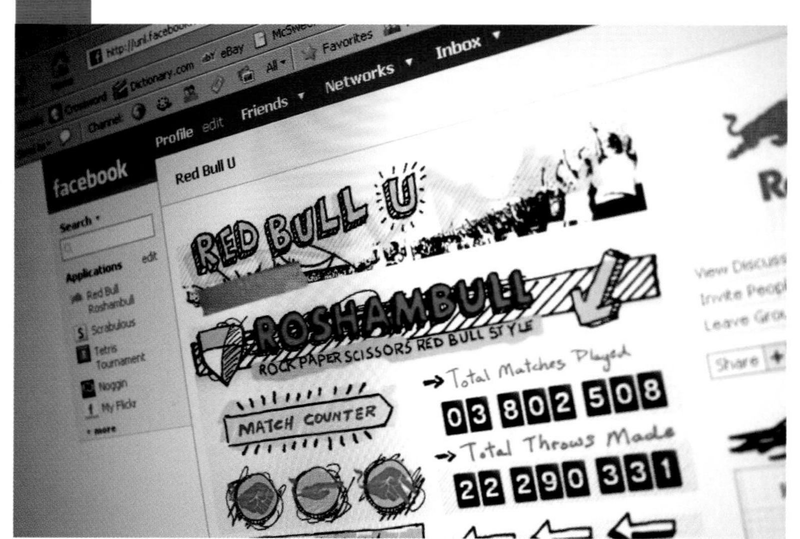
facebook
Profile
edit
Friends
Networks
Inbox
Red Bull U
Search
Applications
Scrabulous
Tetris Tournament
Noggin
My Flickr
RED BULL U
ROSHAMBULL
ROCK PAPER SCISSORS RED BULL STYLE
MATCH COUNTER
Total Matches Played
03 802 508
Total Throws Made
22 290 331
Share

ROCK PAPER SCISSORS RED BULL STYLE
MATCH COUNTER
Total Matches Played
03 802 511
Total Throws Made
22 290 356
PLAY NOW!
Roshambull Strategy Center

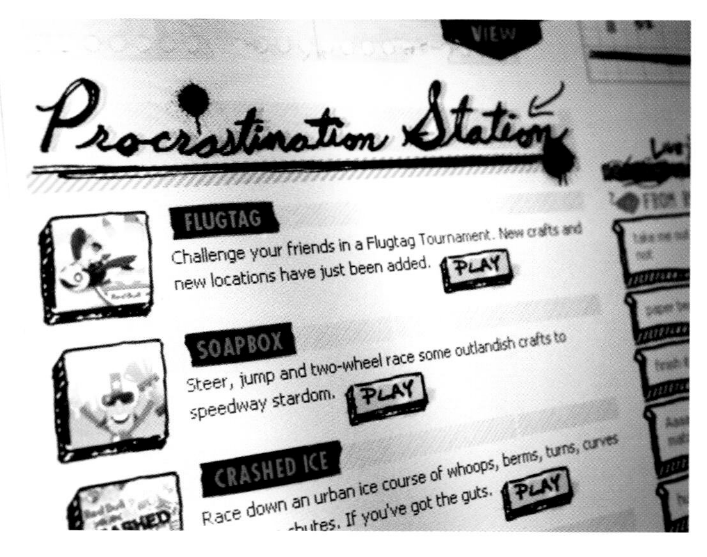
VIEW
Procrastination Station
FLUGTAG
Challenge your friends in a Flugtag Tournament. New crafts and new locations have just been added.
PLAY
SOAPBOX
Steer, jump and two-wheel race some outlandish crafts to speedway stardom.
PLAY
CRASHED ICE
Race down an urban ice course of whoops, berms, turns, curves
PLAY

VIEW
Procrastination Station
Live Smack Talk
ROSHAMBULL
FROM REAL MATCHES
sorry man...
Oh dear you are at zero points!
This should help you get going again lol!!
A little friendly war?
It's been too long..
PLAY

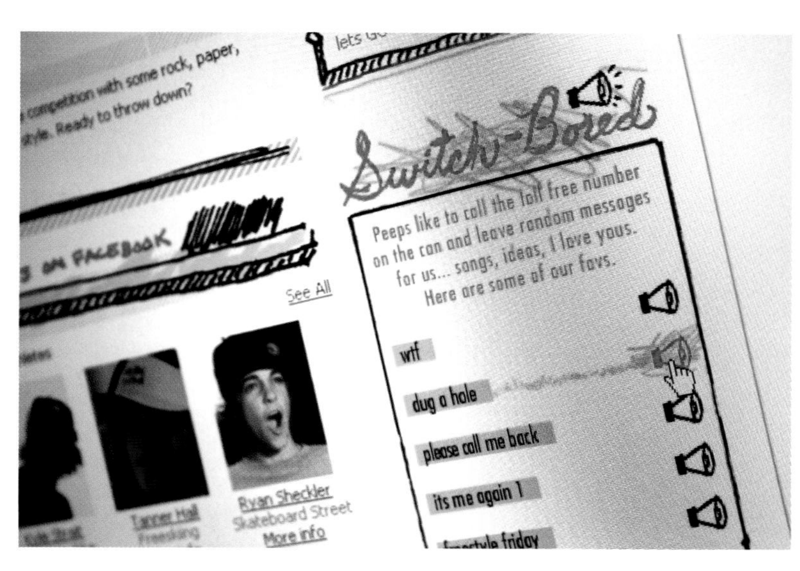
Switch-Bored
Peeps like to call the toll free number on the can and leave random messages for us... songs, ideas, I love yous. Here are some of our favs.
wtf
dug a hole
please call me back
its me again 1
See All
Tanner Hall
Freeskiing
Ryan Sheckler
Skateboard Street
More info

View Discussion Board
Invite People to Join
Leave Group
Share
RED BULL U
ROSHAMBULL
Total Matches Played
03 802 500
Total Throws Made
22 290 289
Roshambull Strategy Center
VIEW
HOW DO YOU DRINK IT?
SIP 36%
SLAM 36%
SHOTGUN 23%
WITH A STRAW 5%

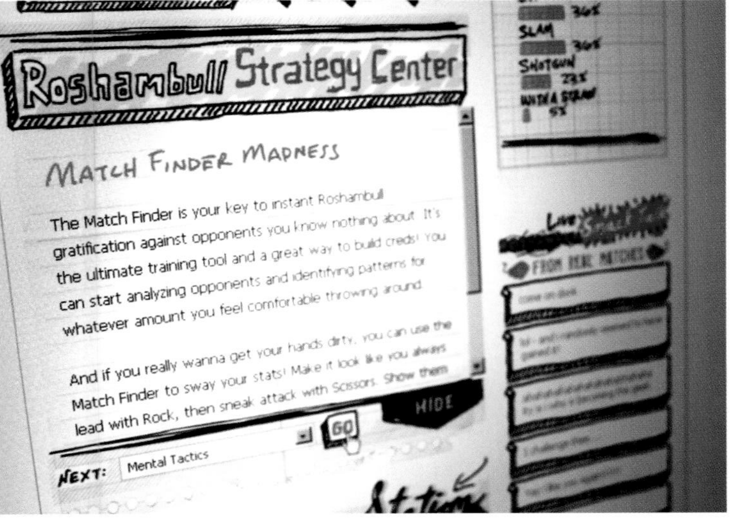

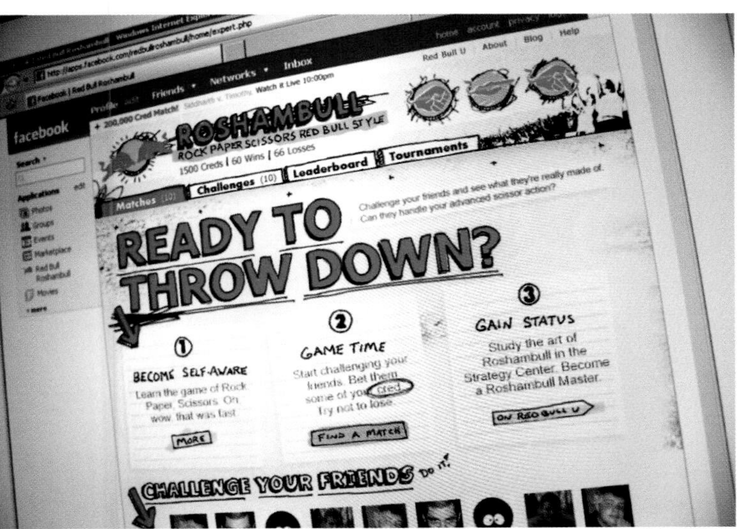

When Facebook decided to allow companies and individuals to build social applications for Facebook users, it took Red Bull only a few days to develop one. It made them the first advertiser to have a branded application on Facebook. 'RoShamBull', as the application is called, is an online version of the old schoolyard game 'rock-paper-scissors' (sometimes referred to as Roshambo). It lets users challenge friends to games of rock-paper-scissors. Red Bull's effort got off to a solid viral start, attracting nearly 60,000 users in its first week, making it the eleventh most popular outside application at that time.

'WE COULD HAVE BUILT IT FOR ANOTHER SOCIAL NETWORK, BUT THE TOOLS FACEBOOK OFFERED REALLY EASED THE DEVELOPMENT. IT WOULD HAVE REQUIRED A LOT OF EXTRA WORK [ELSEWHERE].'

BART JOHNSTON, INTERACTIVE DIRECTOR OF ARCHRIVAL

VOLVO CAR CORPORATION
Agency: Kirt Gunn & Associates/Euro RSCG 4D/Climax Action
United States – 2005

'THE *VOLVO DRIVE FOR LIFE* GAME DETAILS OUR SAFETY IN A WAY NO BROCHURE COULD EVER DESCRIBE OR ANY COMMERCIAL COULD EVER VISUALIZE.'

JOHN NEU, MANAGER FOR CUSTOMER RELATIONSHIP MARKETING AND E-BUSINESS AT VOLVO CARS

Volvo wanted to make younger buyers aware of its leadership in 'active safety' (features that enhance protection on the road). So the brand chose an environment ideally suited to educating and exciting this audience and created *Volvo Drive for Life*, an Xbox game featuring the Volvo S40 and S60R sedans and the XC90 V8 sports car.

Instead of flying around the track at breakneck speeds smashing headlong into every possible obstacle, the Volvo game rewards players for careful driving. Players can explore the different courses with and without Volvo's safety system engaged, highlighting the various safety traits of the particular model. After completing the virtual test track in Gothenburg, Sweden, players are unleashed onto California's Pacific Coast Highway, the Italian Grand Prix circuit at Monza, or even the Ice Hotel at Jukkasjarvi, Sweden.

As well as playing the game, people can watch videos of Volvo's safety centre in Sweden, crash-test footage and safety-related videos for each model.

Players can also build and customize their own virtual Volvo models.

The sophisticated cars, driving environments and challenges attracted veteran gamers and non-gamers alike, who spent an average of 2 hours and 40 minutes playing the game. Players walked away with a better understanding of Volvo's active safety features than Volvo owners, and even some dealers.

A hundred thousand copies of the game were initially handed out at dealerships and car shows, but they were all snatched up within two weeks. The game was so sought-after that it started showing up on eBay. Volvo created a television commercial made from in-game footage, which was the highest-scoring spot in the brand's history. The S40 and XC90 V8 sold out their entire inventory before arriving in the US – another first in Volvo's history.

VOLVO CAR CORPORATION
Agency: EURO RSCG 4D, Amsterdam
Worldwide – 2006–7

'ANYBODY KNOW COORDINATES TO 1ST QUESTION? I'M PULLING MY HAIR OUT HERE!'

DESPERATE PARTICIPANT LOOKING FOR HELP ON YAHOO! ANSWERS

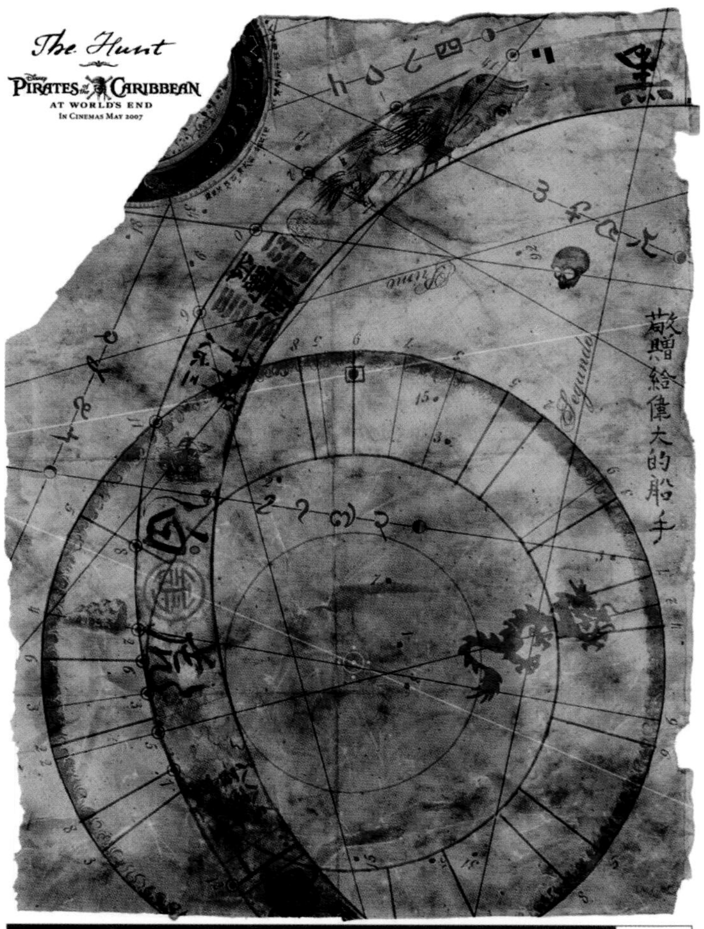

When Volvo teamed up with Disney to mark the release of the second (*Dead Man's Chest*) and third (*At World's End*) instalments of the multi-billion dollar *Pirates of the Caribbean* movie franchise, the Swedish car manufacturer hit upon the idea of a global treasure hunt. For the first hunt, in 2006, the company buried a Volvo XC90 on a sandy beach in the Bahamas. The following year, a treasure chest containing a key to a Volvo XC90 and $50,000 (£25,000) in gold was hidden in the ocean somewhere. Both years running, the promise was the same: find it and it's yours.

The Hunt is a month-long journey across the seven seas. Participants hop from website to website. Each website features a real location on earth and includes a puzzle. The solution to each puzzle is the longitude and latitude of the next location – not only because the numbers look nice, but also to make the game as inclusive as possible. The Hunt can be played in fifteen languages.

One crucial step in The Hunt is a visit to the nearest Volvo dealership to pick up the 'pirate chart'. Participants need the chart several times throughout the game to move on to the next puzzle. The intricate pattern on the pirate chart reveals its secrets when you unlock the clues and fold it in the correct way. One Japanese participant even created a guide to solving the clues, which he shared with his competitors on YouTube.

A raft of new online communities sprung up as a result of The Hunt. The most popular was Prometheus's blog. Fierce hunters from all over the world gathered there daily to learn from each other. The blog received so much traffic that the hosting provider, at one point, forced 'Prometheus' to upgrade his contract. To help keep the blog going Prometheus asked for donations from his visitors and actually raised the few thousand dollars he needed, with some participants donating more than $50 (£25) each.

In the final leg the twenty-two best hunters (one from each participating country) competed with each other in an online final. The demographics of this final were relatively surprising. It wasn't the teenage boys who had made it through but a roughly even mix of men and women aged between twenty and fifty.

The Hunt
Pirates of the Caribbean
At World's End
World's End
36°02' S 175°01' E
WORLD'S END APPEARED ON THE OTHER SIDE
Southern Ocean
53°46' S 99°45' E
Antarctica
64°39' S 96°34' E
Heard Island
53°13' S 73°29' E
Australia
24°36' S 113°31' E
SKIP
The Hunt Terms and Conditions
Build your Volvo
Privacy policy
© 2007 Volvo Car Corporation
© 2007 Disney Enterprises, Inc.
Request a Test Drive
Request a Brochure
VOLVO

UN WORLD FOOD PROGRAMME

Agencies: Playerthree (UK)/Deepend (Italy)
Worldwide – 2005

'NOT ONE SHOT IS FIRED – UNUSUAL IN GAMES THESE DAYS.'

JOHN POWELL, WFP DEPUTY EXECUTIVE DIRECTOR FOR FUND-RAISING AND COMMUNICATIONS

'THIS MAY BE ONLY A GAME, BUT A BIT OF THE CHILL OF REAL LIVES IN JEOPARDY REACHES THROUGH THE PIXELS.'

MARK WALLACE IN HIS ARTICLE 'ALL THE RAGE IN COMPUTER GAMES' IN THE *FINANCIAL TIMES*

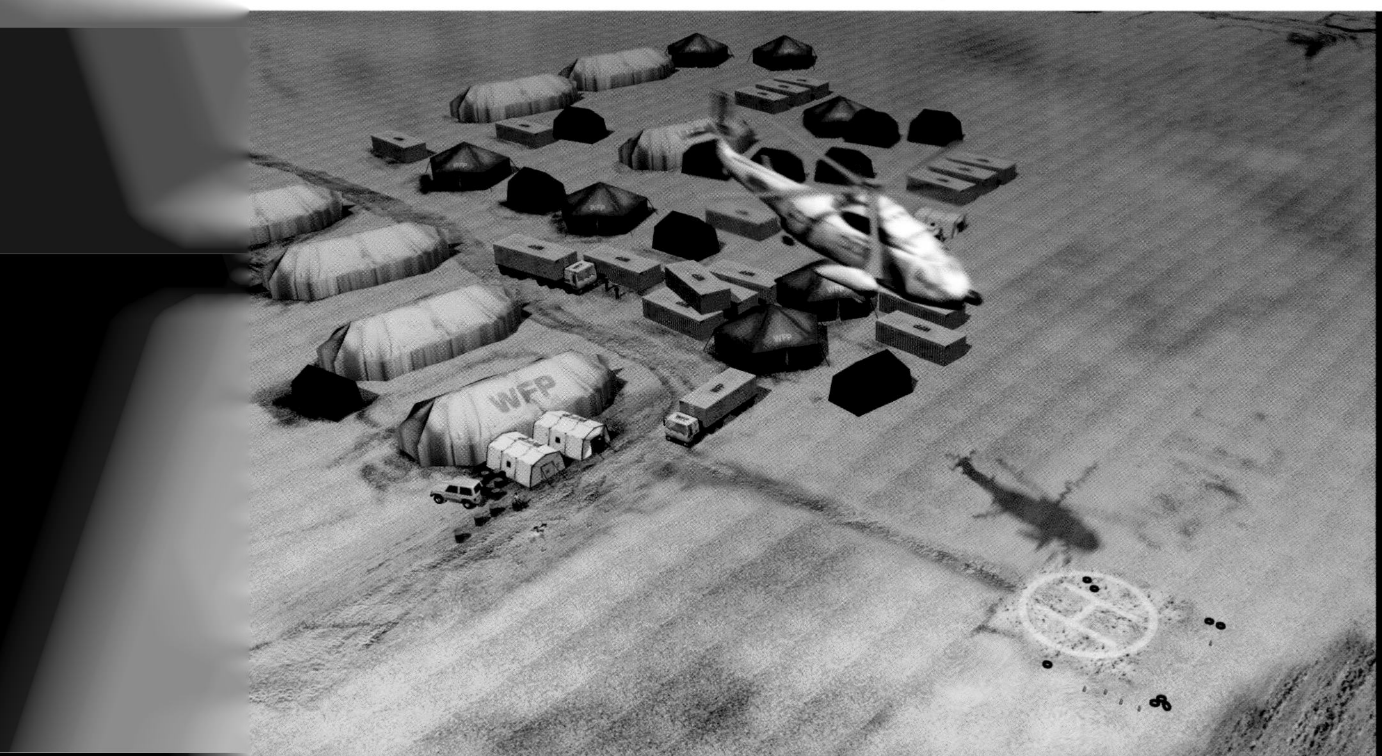

At the end of 2005, the UN World Food Programme (WFP) released an action-packed humanitarian video game called *Food Force*, designed specifically to educate 8- to 13-year-olds about world hunger and the aid agency's work.

Players are put in charge of a hunger relief effort on the fictional Indian Ocean island of Sheylan, which has been ravaged by a civil war, flooding and drought. Players lead a crack multinational team of WFP professionals including a logistics officer, nutritionist and air drop specialist, and must guide the team through six missions to bring food and supplies to the desperate indigenous community of Sheylan – everything from coordinating air surveillance to working out a good balanced diet, airdropping supplies, and helping local people get the most out of their natural resources by planning future farming efforts.

Despite its subdued debut at a children's book fair in Bologna, Italy, the game turned out to be an absolute hit, much to the organization's surprise. It was downloaded more than 1 million times in its first six weeks and more than 4 million times in fifteen months. The WFP also provides teachers with lesson plans if they wish to incorporate *Food Force* into their curriculum.

The idea for the game came from WFP employee Paola Biocca, who died in a plane crash in 1999 in Kosovo. The free game cost about $300,000 (£150,000) and took three years to make.

CENTERS FOR DISEASE CONTROL AND PREVENTION
Agency: Arc Worldwide
United States – 2006

'I LOVE THIS IDEA. WHAT PARENT OR CHILD WOULDN'T?... THE CONCEPT OF PLAY IN ITS PUREST ESSENCE? YES, ABSOLUTELY! GET THOSE KIDS OUTDOORS. THROW 'EM A BALL. HURRAY! BRAVO!'

SHAPINGYOUTH.ORG/BLOG

VERB YELLOWBALL
PASS IT ON.
VERBNOW.COM
VERB
It's what you do.

When kids find a ball, they can't resist picking it up and playing with it. They get active. So to fight obesity among 9- to 13-year-olds and get them active, 500,000 yellow rubber balls were distributed directly to kids. They looked like ordinary balls, except for the unique code that was imprinted on them. Kids were encouraged to enter the code online, blog about what they did with the ball, pass their ball on, and track the ball's journey.

Key to this whole programme was getting the yellow balls to the right kids. Some balls were randomly dropped in selected parks and playgrounds, others were sent through direct mailings, distributed to 6,500 middle schools nationwide, handed out to crowds at street events or during the mobile tour around the United States, reaching kids at summer camps, minor league baseball games and local festivals.

The programme got over 5 million kids active, resulting in 14.9 million hours of physical activity. Twenty-one per cent of the balls were passed on. One ball was passed thirty-one times while another travelled 39,940 miles (64,277 kilometres).

BE CONTEXTUAL

In recent years, there has been a backlash against ambient advertising infiltrating random public spaces. The movement against so-called 'urban spam' (by people within the communications industry as well as city councils and anti-advertising organizations) accuses brands of polluting public environments by randomly dropping commercial messages wherever they see fit. The increasing worries about a visually polluted public domain have led to advertising bans in different forms. Arguably the most famous case occurred in December 2006 in São Paulo, where mayor Gilberto Kassab decided to ban all outdoor billboard advertising, citing advertisers' unwillingness to comply with the city's rules on what sort of billboards can be placed where.

What the São Paulo ban points out, and what brands need to realize, is that outdoor advertising is possibly the most publicly visible and therefore the most sensitive form of advertising. When brands place commercial messages in other traditional media channels, audiences have consciously chosen to watch that specific television channel, listen to that particular radio station, or read a certain newspaper or magazine. In that sense, they have 'opted in' to see the content on those channels, both editorial and commercial. If they want to avoid advertising, they can just as easily 'opt out' by simply deciding to stop reading, watching or listening. It's a different situation when it comes to outdoor advertising. You can't opt in or out as easily. Brands are essentially entering public spaces, forcing passers-by to take notice with or without their say-so. It is much more difficult for people to simply ignore the messages, as ever-larger outdoor formats and intrusive placements push their way into their line of vision.

As a result, brands need to be all the more careful and thoughtful when entering public spaces. Essentially, they have to realize that they don't own the streets. There is increasingly less leeway for brands that randomly stick messages in places without any apparent thought or creative logic. There is, however, still room for clever and relevant messages at the right time and in the right place. The key lies in making the message or format of the advertising contextually relevant. It's about taking into account the specific context in which a message appears, whether it's the external characteristics of a location or object (what something looks like) or the functional characteristics of a location or object (what something does or its purpose). Subtly referring to or incorporating those elements into the communication will make it more surprising and unique. In other words, the more site-specific and contextual the communication, the more likely it is that an outdoor message will stand out and succeed in appealing to passers-by rather than boring or irritating them.

Most outdoor advertising space does not allow brands to be contextual, as it is traditionally bought in large quantities, rather than as a single, specific location. Also, outdoor advertising space is often isolated from the urban context, with no actual function or value within the built environment. The great advantage of leaving the traditional outdoor canvas and opting for more targeted, specific placements is that brands can adapt their message to the environment, with smart, contextual advertising slotting into the surroundings rather than standing out as an eyesore.

The upshot is that you should think twice before entering the public arena and make any outdoor interruption worthwhile. People will continue to embrace clever ambient campaigns only if they are able to upgrade the urban environment and spice up people's daily journeys with a touch of wit and humour.

■ BE CONTEXTUAL
■ **AMNESTY INTERNATIONAL**
■ Agency: Walker
■ Switzerland – 2006

In this site-specific outdoor campaign, Amnesty International brings human rights violations to the streets under the slogan 'It's not happening here. But it is happening now.' Two hundred individual posters were placed throughout Switzerland, each meticulously matched to its specific surroundings, making it seem as if each instance of abuse was taking place directly in front of the spectator. The impact of the campaign led to a twenty-fold increase in the number of visitors to the Amnesty International website.

BECONTEXTUAL
AVON COSMETICS
Agency: Starcom Media, Bucharest
Romania – 2006

Statistics show that one in eight women will get breast cancer. Avon Breast Cancer Crusade, a social programme that has been active in Romania since 2002, brought this alarming statistic into women's daily lives. They went everywhere that women went, and turned one in eight seats bright pink at popular hairdressing salons, at cinemas and on public transport, with the stark message: 'Undetected in time, breast cancer can kill. Go to the doctor now.' The seats were often left empty, as women felt uncomfortable and self-conscious sitting in the branded spots. In some shops, every eighth shelf and hanger were left empty.

The campaign also included testimonials from women who have survived breast cancer in magazines and television slots, and commercials featuring local celebrities were posted online. Donations increased by 43 per cent.

1 din 8
femei

1 din 8
femei*
AVON

1 din 8
femei*
Nedescoperit la timp,
cancerul la sân
poate ucide!

BECONTEXTUAL
CAFÉ COSTUME
Agency: mortierbrigade
Belgium – 2007

Café Costume is a clothes shop in Antwerp, Belgium's fashion capital, offering tailor-made outfits at reasonable prices. To draw attention to the unique shop concept, elements of the street were used in an original way. The typical circular-shaped road barriers near the tram tracks were transformed into giant, custom-made pincushions, the ultimate symbol of haute couture. The campaign generated a lot of free press coverage and there was a 65 per cent increase in the number of visitors to the shop.

This wall poster advertising Organics frequent-use shampoo formed the perfect backdrop to a man-made waterfall at a busy shopping centre.

'UNILEVER LOVED THE IDEA FROM THE START AND EVEN WHEN IT LOOKED LIKE WE MIGHT NEVER BE ABLE TO FIND THE RIGHT WATERFALL IN SINGAPORE, THEY NEVER GAVE UP. LUCKILY WE DID FIND THE RIGHT SPOT.'

ALI SHABAZ, CREATIVE DIRECTOR AT JWT, SINGAPORE

BE CONTEXTUAL
GOOGLE
Agency: Kolle Rebbe
Germany – 2006

Many of the films on Google Video depict everyday life. This outdoor campaign brought Google Video into everyday life by cleverly positioning posters of computer screens at busy locations. The bars at the top and bottom of a Google page were the only visual elements on the posters; the space in between was left see-through, making each street scene look like a film. At the Brandenburg Gate in Berlin, for example, the screen quickly became the second biggest attraction. Images of tourists posing made their way onto blogs and flickr.de, as well as into countless photo albums.

Google
Video
a crowd of tourists
Search
Any Film You Can Imagine.

ISEO Asia

Agency: Naga DDB

Malaysia – 2006

If you spotted a credit card wedged in your door, you would probably take a closer look at it. ISEO played on our natural curiosity by strategically printing a sales pitch on fake credit cards and distributing them at the entrances to office suites. The cards flagged up how easy it would be to break into premises that don't have burglar-proof locks. Enquiries about ISEO products increased by 28 per cent within the first month of the campaign.

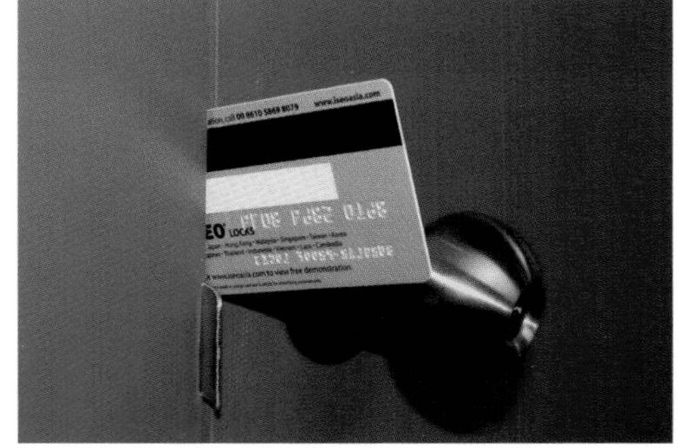

Agency: Dinamo Reklamebyraa
Norway – 2007

Two years after the 2005 Kashmir earthquake, many of the victims remained homeless and exposed to bitterly cold weather conditions. In Norway, Unicef tried to catch the general public off-guard and keep this tragedy at the forefront of their minds. As temperatures in Kashmir can plummet to well below zero in the highland villages where many earthquake victims are living, Unicef placed posters of Kashmiri children in supermarket freezers to confront shoppers with the harsh reality of their lives and to urge them to donate to the relief effort.

MATTEL – MATCHBOX
Agency: Ogilvy & Mather, Mexico
Mexico – 2006

Mattel placed giant (palm-up) hand stickers in parking spaces at toy shops. When a car was parked in a marked spot, it looked like it was being held in the hand like a tiny Matchbox toy.

Agency: Contract Advertising
India – 2006

JK Tyre emphasized the superior grip of its tyres by painting the underside of overpasses to look like roads. As the average waiting time at the crossings under the overpasses was three to four minutes, this proved to be the perfect location.

JOBSINTOWN.DE

Agency: Scholz & Friends Berlin

Germany – 2006

These ads appeared on free-standing vending and cash machines at busy metro stations in Berlin and targeted dissatisfied commuters on their way to work. Life-size images of people working away inside the machines drove home the message that life is too short to be stuck in the wrong job.

Das Leben ist zu kurz
für den falschen Job.
jobsintown.de
Neubau
47
PRESSES
VP
Vorwahl
CAFÉ

BE CONTEXTUAL
WARNER BROS.
Agency: JWT Brasil, São Paulo
Brazil – 2006

Lifts often serve as inspiring locations for contextual advertising ideas, but this campaign for the film *Superman Returns* is by far the most original. The lift doors show a man's hands as he starts to unbutton his shirt; when the doors open, the iconic Superman symbol dominates a poster on the back wall. Through the motion of the lift, the visual plays on Superman's ability to fly.

BESPECTACULAR

One of those terms that regularly pops up in agency briefings and marketing meetings alike is 'stand out'. At the end of the day, that's what every brand is aiming for: a way of distinguishing itself from the competition, leaping out and truly standing out. This is an increasingly difficult task in today's democratic and fragmented marketplace, where everybody – from the local business to the creative entrepreneur – has equal access to online communication tools.

For one, it certainly still helps to be big. A fragmented media landscape rewards anything bigger-than-life and punishes anything small and unremarkable. The events and properties that have truly impacted popular culture in recent years tend to have been big; big in scope, in budget, in length, in everything. They include big-budget films (think *Spiderman*,

Transformers, *The Lord of the Rings*, *Pirates of the Caribbean*), big-budget sport events (the Olympics, World Cup, Tour de France) or big-budget, prime-time television series (*X Factor*, *American Idol*, *Lost*, *Prison Break*). Simply being big and having some scale certainly helps to rise above the pack and grab global attention.

But it's as much about attitude as it is about size. It's as much about being audacious, bold and different as it is merely about scale or budget. *Spectacular*, which is not necessarily about size or scale, would be a more suitable word than *big*. Defined as 'sensational in appearance or thrilling in effect', it's a quality that thrusts itself into our attention. *Spectacular* refers to anything that is hard to ignore and grabs people by the neck, no matter how big or small. It's not about personal preferences either. You might not personally like something spectacular, but because it's spectacular, you will have at least noticed it. It's staring you right in the face, whether you like it or not. And for that very reason, it travels, it's picked up, it's talked about.

It's hard to define what spectacular should look or be like as there's no predefined checklist. You just know it when you see it or hear about it. It has an immediate wow effect. What spectacular things do have in common is that they are out of the ordinary, unlike anything else and downright unbelievable. The famed Trojan Horse, which Virgil likened to 'a steed of monstrous height', wasn't necessarily a great or beautiful construction, but it was certainly spectacular, and to this day the image of a gigantic wooden horse still captures people's imaginations.

This is not the time for modesty or prudence. In order to be heard, brands need to be bold and audacious. The majority of marketing and communication initiatives don't make it through people's filters because the idea or the execution was not audacious or outstanding enough. It may have ticked a lot of boxes, but it didn't tick the spectacular box. In order to become part of the collective consciousness, you need to be, think and act 'spectacular'. Otherwise, it's just another unnoticeable blip on the radar, another footnote in the already lengthy encyclopedia of marketing history.

BESPECTACULAR
ADIDAS
Agency: TBWA\GERMANY (180\TBWA), Berlin
Germany – 2006

To many sports fans, football is their religion, and footballers are gods, especially during the World Cup season. So, to mark the occasion, Adidas commissioned a spectacular 800-square-metre (8,611-square-foot) fresco for the ceiling of the main train station in Cologne, Germany, depicting ten of the world's best football stars. It took Hamburg-based illustrator Felix Reidenbach forty days to complete the fresco, which features portraits of Michael Ballack, David Beckham, Zinédine Zidane, Raúl, Kaka, Nakamura, Lukas Podolski, Lionel Messi, Juan Román Riquelme and Djibril Cissé.

'THE FRESCO PRESENTS 10 FOOTBALL SUPERSTARS EXACTLY HOW MILLIONS OF ENTHUSIASTIC FOOTBALL FANS AROUND THE WORLD SEE THEM ANYWAY — AS REAL FOOTBALL GODS.'

STEFAN SCHMIDT, CO-CHIEF CREATIVE OFFICER OF ADIDAS

adidas

adidas

Very few smokers know that cigarette smoke contains more than 4,000 chemicals. To get this message across and make smokers aware of all the carcinogenic substances they expose themselves to, a cigarette-shaped chemical tanker bearing all the necessary warning signs was driven around the UK and parked in public places. This striking concept was designed to increase the number of visitors to the 'Smoke Is Poison' website and generated £75,000 ($150,000) of free publicity. The number of people informed about hazardous chemicals in cigarettes rose by 178 per cent.

'IT'S REASSURING WHEN A CAMPAIGN THAT SITS OUTSIDE THE DIRECT MARKETING COMFORT ZONE ACHIEVES SUCH HIGH CREATIVE ACCLAIM.'

CAMPAIGN

POLONIUM -210
01234 567890
2RE
AMMONIA
01234 567890
2X
CADMIUM
01234 567890
POISON
6
9
2WE
HYDROGEN CYANIDE
01234 567890
3YE
TOLUENE
01234 567890
BENZENE
1114
01234 567890
2Z
ARSENIC
01234 567890
•2W
FORMALDEHYDE
01234 567890

BESPECTACULAR
THE DISCOVERY CHANNEL
Agency: Mother (Sculptures by Asylum, London)
United Kingdom – 2007

London Ink, a spin-off of the successful US reality show *Miami Ink*, follows the trials and tribulations of daily life in a tattoo parlour, as well as delving into the personal stories of the customers. The series featured artists from a number of UK tattoo parlours, including Dan Gold, Nicole Lowe, Phil Kyle and Louis Molloy, who has already had a taste of fame through his work for David Beckham and Kate Moss.

To promote the show's launch on The Discovery Channel, giant sculptures were unveiled at two of London's busiest locations – a girl looking into a photo booth at Victoria Station and a swimmer half-sunk into the grass next to Tower Bridge. Each sculpture was adorned with an oversize tattoo by Louis Molloy, combining classic tattoo iconography with London imagery: a Japanese Koi carp on a bed of chips in the swimmer's case, and a ratty pigeon in war-eagle pose in the girl's. The theme of the campaign, 'London's Getting Ink', extended to the clean stencilling on the pavements around the sculptures, as if the city too had been tattooed. The campaign also included a dedicated microsite with exclusive footage, interactive games, the history of tattooing and vital information about hygiene.

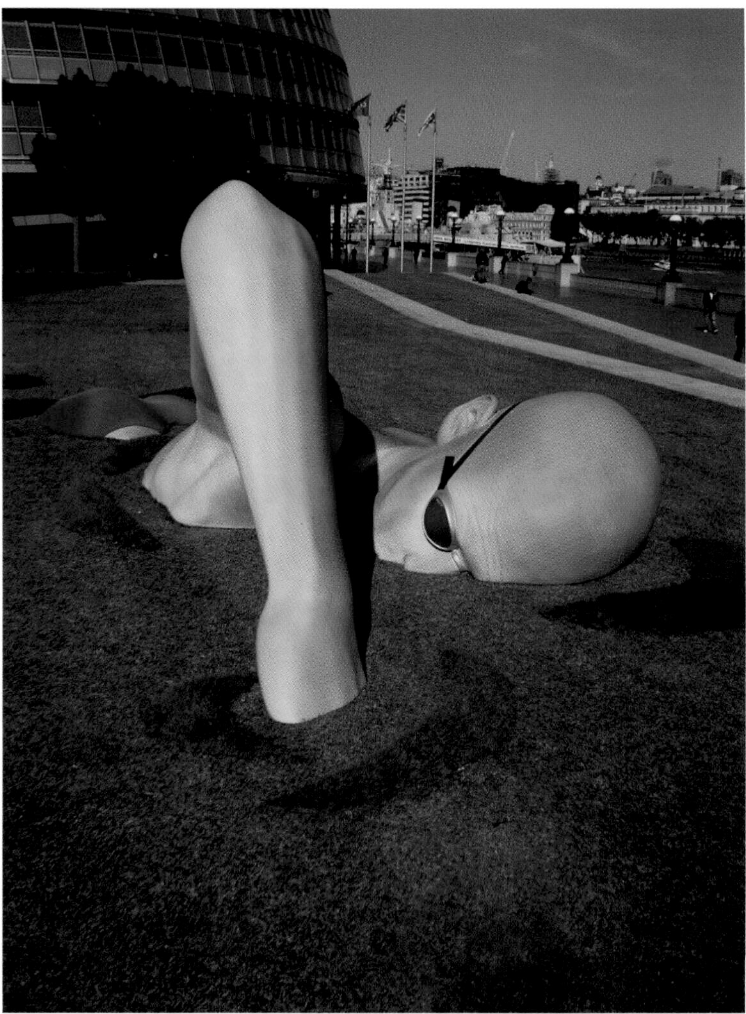

■ **THE DISCOVERY CHANNEL**
■ Agency: Mother (Sculptures by Asylum, London)
■ United Kingdom – 2007

'THIS SHOW IS EXTRAORDINARY, SO WE NEEDED TO APPROACH THE COMMUNICATIONS AROUND IT IN AN UNUSUAL WAY.'

ANDY MEDD, PARTNER AT MOTHER, IN *CONTAGIOUS MAGAZINE*

BE SPECTACULAR
BMW GROUP
Agency: D'Adda, Lorenzini, Vigorelli, BBDO – Italy
Italy – 2007

MINI has developed a tradition of spectacular, three-dimensional billboards, often placing life-size MINIs in breathtaking, vertical situations. This humongous billboard in Italy is one of the most spectacular. It featured a life-size fibreglass MINI that was attached to a ramp and could be moved up and down the billboard like a yo-yo.

RED BULL

Various agencies around the world
Worldwide – since 2003

Dubbed 'the F1 of the skies', the Red Bull Air Race World Series has been held since 2003. Each of the races takes place in a breathtaking location with a spectacular backdrop. The world's best pilots battle for supremacy of the skies by racing through a slalom course in the fastest possible time. The air races are renowned for spectacular low-level flying displays and daredevil manoeuvres. The planes used are light, agile and responsive, enabling pilots to make incredibly tight turns. The spectacle is often broadcast live by major TV channels and attracts huge crowds wherever it lands.

Below: Offices in London's Canary Wharf, along the river Thames, were packed with people trying to get a free view of the aerial action.

Right: Planes fly by the Sagrada Familia in Barcelona. An estimated 1.3 million spectators turned out to watch the race.

Opposite, top left: The scorching desert heat made the race just above the Abu Dhabi harbour even more challenging for the twelve pilots.

Opposite, top right: After performing a large figure eight in front of the Hungarian Parliament in Budapest, the world-class pilots had to fly along the Danube under the Chain Bridge.

Opposite, below: The iconic red mesas and towering buttes of Monument Valley Navajo Tribal Park challenged pilots with uneven terrain and unusual environmental obstacles.

Overleaf: In Rio de Janeiro's Botafogo Bay, dominated by Christ the Redeemer, one million turned up for the race, crowding the coastline and transforming it into the biggest sport event in Brazilian history.

INBEV – STELLA ARTOIS

Agencies: Lowe Worldwide, Lowe Roche and Lowe Tesch/Jack Morton in conjunction with HBSource

Worldwide – 2006

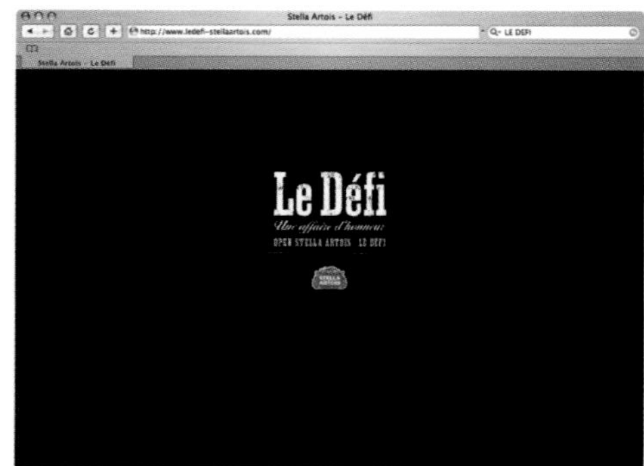

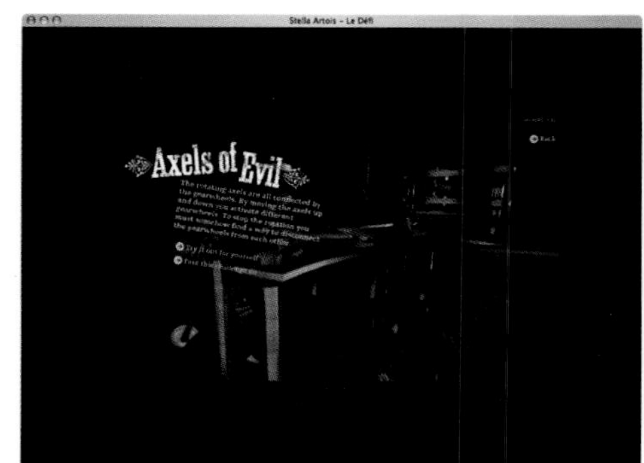

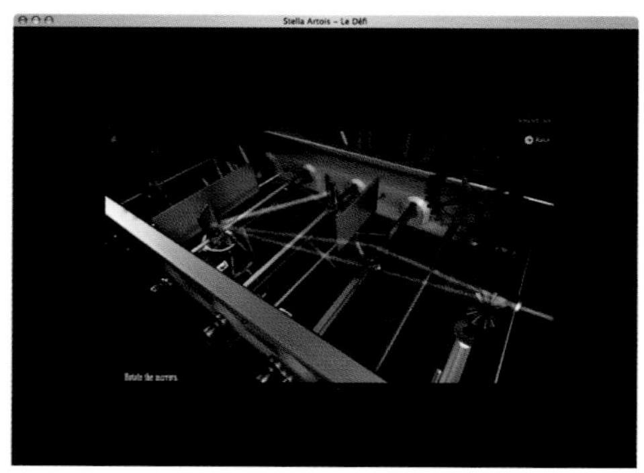

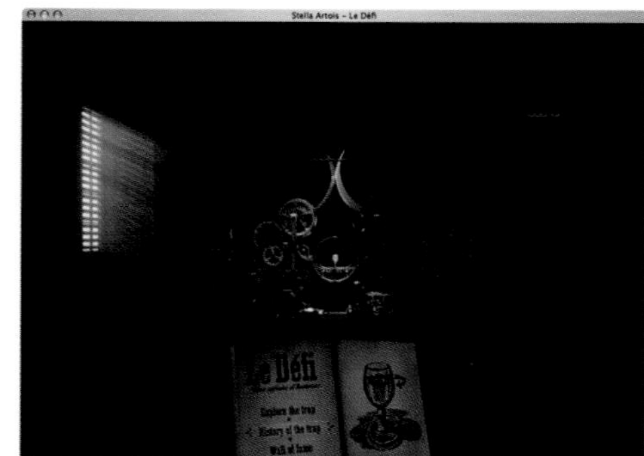

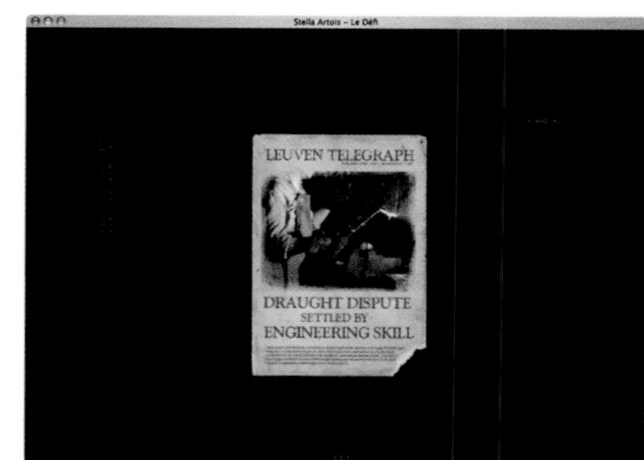

'The trap', as it was called by its makers, was an impressive see-through structure of steel and wood which looked like something out of a Leonardo da Vinci sketchbook. Inside the glass case of the two-tonne, five-metre-high (16-foot-high) construction, which was initially erected at an intersection in Toronto, there was a tempting chalice of Stella Artois on display.

According to Maria Guest, marketing manager for Stella Artois in Canada, the installation demonstrates the lengths someone might go to in order to protect their Stella, in keeping with the theme for Stella's global advertising campaign, 'Perfection has its price'.

The campaign also included newspaper ads featuring da Vinci-like sketches of various traps as well as chalk sketches near the display. Each of the drawings was based on real designs for the installation. The online component, Le Défi ('The Challenge'), is a game of wits with the ultimate goal of unravelling a virtual trap.

After its unannounced debut in Toronto, the installation travelled to other major cities such as New York and São Paulo.

A12 • CANADA

When 'grabby' messages add Grit

Queen's Park

MURRAY CAMPBELL

The issue is if you come out with 29 seconds and at the last microsecond you flash a website, would that be enough? I don't know.

Ontario cuts energy rates amid questions

Critics challenge the figures behind drop

'That's not going to make any difference on people's hydro bills.'

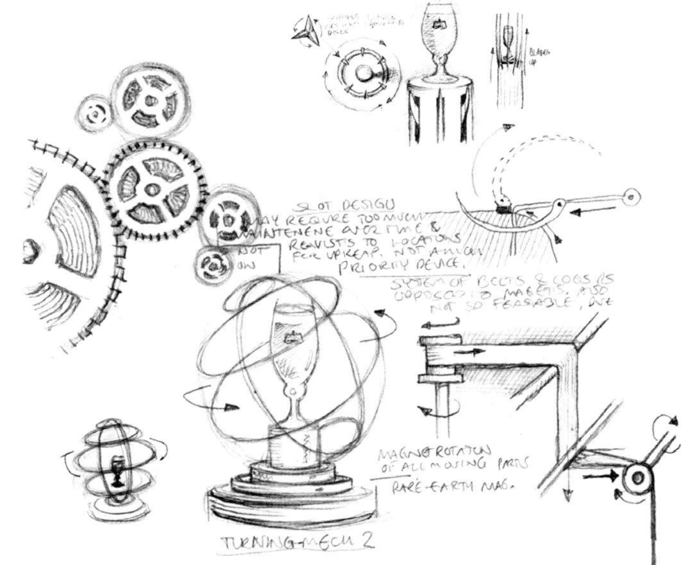

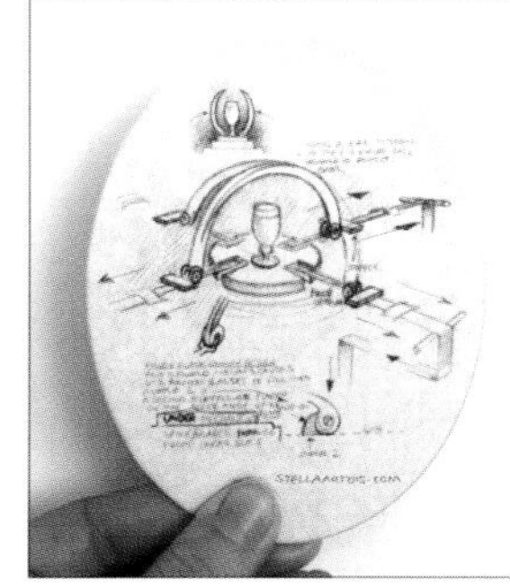

INBEV – STELLA ARTOIS

Agencies: Lowe Worldwide, Lowe Roche and Lowe Tesch/Jack Morton in conjunction with HBSource

Worldwide – 2006

'IT'S REALLY A PIECE FOR PEOPLE TO GO, CHECK IT OUT, THINK ABOUT WHY IT'S THERE AND MAKE THAT CONNECTION.'

MARIA GUEST, MARKETING MANAGER FOR STELLA ARTOIS CANADA, IN *MARKETING MAGAZINE*

THE TRAP

BESPECTACULAR
TELECOM NEW ZEALAND
Agency: Touch/Cast
New Zealand – 2005

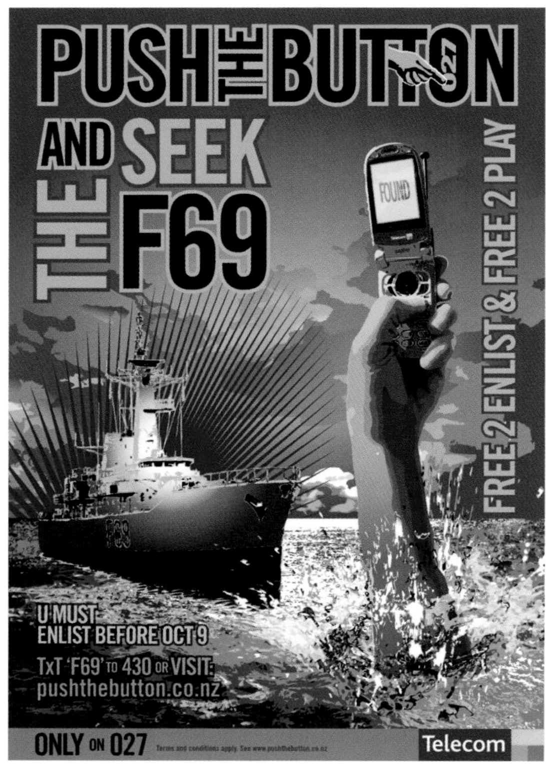

Although there was over £75,000 ($150,000) in prizes to be won in the Telecom New Zealand text competition, there was one star prize that everyone was after. The overall winner got to trigger a detonator and sink a real, decommissioned F69 Leander-class frigate off the coast of Wellington, New Zealand, which was destined for use as a unique recreational dive site.

Inspired by the classic game of Battleships, players had to correctly locate the F69 on a virtual grid of nine squares, corresponding to the 1–9 keys on a mobile phone keypad. Each time a player located the F69 on their handset, they won an entry into that week's prize draw.

A 22-year-old female student won the ultimate prize and got to sink the F69 in front of an estimated audience of over 100,000, watching from land and 220 vessels on the water. More than 90,000 players joined in, and each sent an average of sixty text messages, making it the biggest text event in New Zealand's history.

Keypad buttons 1–9 represented the 'grid' on which F69 was hidden. In each round, players simply texted in which keypad button they thought F69 was on.

Sink the Wellington

Love on board

The explosives expert

Capital City Ford

Farewell, old friend

VISIT LONDON
Agency: Cake
United Kingdom – 2007

In order to promote green spaces and villages in London, 2,000 square metres (21,528 square feet) of grass were laid out for two days on Trafalgar Square, creating a green centre in the middle of London's grey concrete landscape. Visitors could soak up the sunshine in specially laid-out deckchairs or enjoy a picnic. The decision to source organic grass and re-use it after the event limited any negative comment. Media coverage was further fuelled by a computer-generated image of what the square might look like, sent to the national media two weeks before the actual event.

'THIS PROVES THAT AN EXPERIENTIAL EVENT CAN REALLY CREATE A SENSE OF COMMUNITY, EVEN IN A CITY AS BIG AS LONDON.'

JUDE FORBES, PROJECT MANAGER AT CAKE

BE CONTAGIOUS

'Could we make a viral video?' is an overused question in brainstorming sessions and an all too familiar request from clients to agencies. Viral marketing is based on the premise that people themselves become media multipliers, passing messages on to each other. In today's globally connected world, the effects can be instant and utterly overwhelming. Yet asking for a 'viral' piece of content is clearly misleading as videos can only be described as viral in retrospect. Once something has spread successfully and exponentially you can only conclude that it *has gone* viral, but saying that a piece of content *is* viral before it has been unleashed onto an audience is simply wishful thinking. As a result, the number of companies talking about the viral potential far outweighs the actual number of successful cases.

We all know the success stories. Take *The Evolution of Dance*. The most viewed video of all time on YouTube shows motivational speaker and comedian Judson Laipply dancing to a soundtrack that plays through various popular songs from the last decades. In terms of sheer number of views, the six-minute clip sits right up there with the highest-rated programmes in the history of television, such as the final episode of *MASH*, the Super Bowl, the 'Who Shot JR?' episode of *Dallas* and Princess Diana's funeral. Yet for every *Evolution of Dance*, there are millions of mediocre stories and videos that never spread anywhere. In theory, any piece of content has the ability to spread at the speed of light. In reality, only a handful actually do.

Viral success may be impossible to predict, but what content creators can do is strive for an end product that is as contagious as possible. Video-sharing sites have taught us that brands can't just repurpose the same old content that was created for traditional channels, and simply drop it into the digital arena. Clearly, for content to be passed on, it has to be designed to do so. And there are several buttons marketers can press in order to increase the likelihood of something being contagious, both in terms of creation and distribution.

GoViral, a specialist in viral seeding, identified seven key ingredients that determine whether a message will be passed on by people: an outstanding story, stickiness (to what extent something sticks in people's minds), relevance, portability (the idea needs to be free of physical, technical and human barriers), shareability (it has to help people in cementing their networks), timing/actuality and seeding hooks (the one-liner that catches your attention).

Others have found different ways of describing the rules for contagious content. In a popular online video about a so-called 'Viral Video Learning Center', we are told that some of the main tactics for success are filming yourself sitting at your desk, the art of falling, hurting yourself, hurting others, hurting animals, using animals to hurt people, Eastern European dance routines and working with excrement and vomit. The Viral Video Learning Center is not too far off from the truth. Provocation, shock and surprise have proven many times over to be essential ingredients in content being contagious. Market research company Millward Brown summed it up nicely with the acronym LEGS, which stands for: laugh-out-loud humour, edginess, gripping content and sexiness.

The contagious cases in this chapter have some or all of the above ingredients in common. What they also share is a move away from over-polished, commercial-like content towards a more raw, real-life, authentic style and approach. Whether it's Quiksilver's *Dynamite Surfing* (see pages 106–7) or Nike's *Touch of Gold* (pages 104–5), Ray-Ban's *Catch* (pages 108–11) or Marc Ecko's *Still Free* (pages 102–3), it takes a bit of time to figure out who was behind each of them and to what extent they were authentic or not. That small moment of doubt proved crucial in the content being contagious.

BLENDTEC
Agency: n/a
United States – 2007

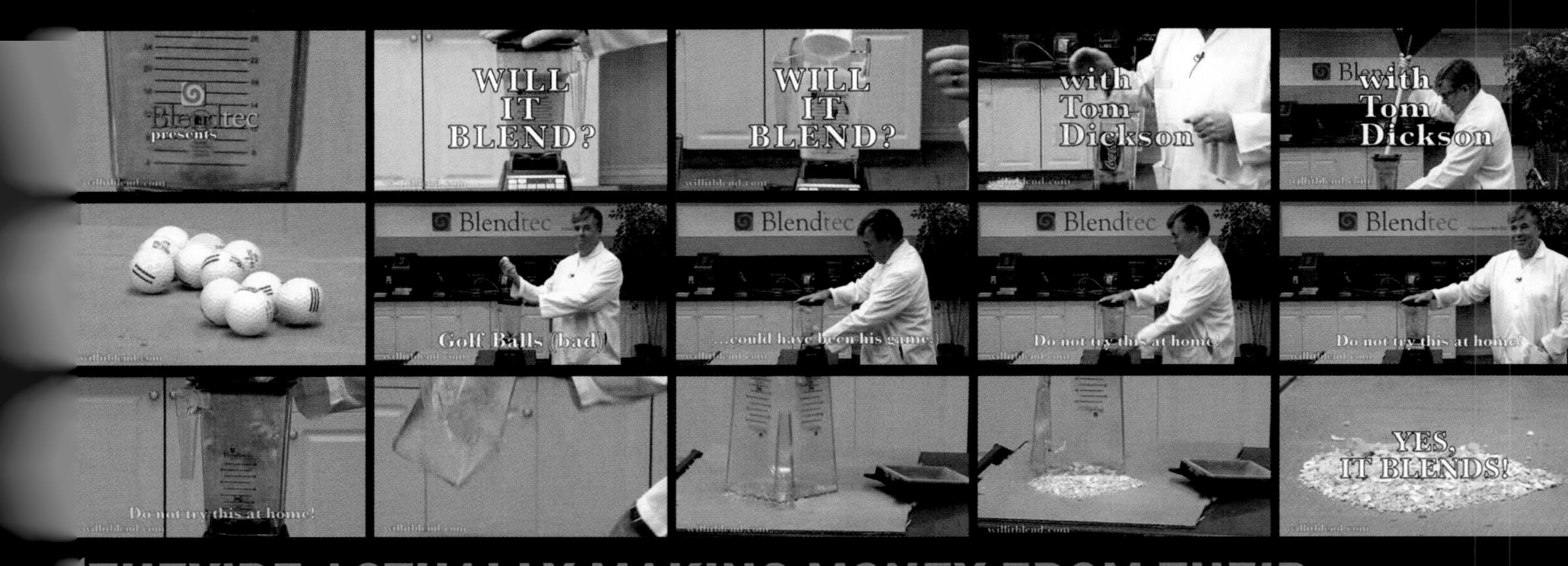

'THEY'RE ACTUALLY MAKING MONEY FROM THEIR MARKETING BY SELLING ADVERTISING AND TAKING COMMISSIONS TO BLEND THINGS, ALL THE WHILE ENJOYING EXPONENTIAL GROWTH IN SALES....'

JOHNNY VULCAN, FOUNDER OF ANOMALY, IN *BUSINESSWEEK*

'Will it blend? That's the question,' asks Tom Dickson, the grandfatherly CEO of Blendtec, before dropping yet another unsuitable object into one of the company's turbocharged blenders. No matter what is added, whether it be rakes, two-by-fours, golf balls, mobile phones, marbles or light bulbs, the blender pulverizes it into fine powder in mere seconds. Only coins and crowbars seem to give the blender trouble.

The clips proved a viral success. Searches for 'Blendtec' or 'Tom Dickson' produced more than 18 million results on Google. The iPod clip was one of the most popular, but even Apple's star product was ground to dust. Tom Dickson also made an appearance on *The Tonight Show*. The brilliance of this viral success, unlike many other viral clips, is that it completely and solely focuses on the strength of the product it promotes. No doubt as a result of this product-centric approach, Blendtec claims to have seen an online sales uplift of 650 per cent.

'THIS IS 21ST-CENTURY MARKETING AT ITS BATTIEST BUT BEST.'

SIMON MARQUIS IN *THE GUARDIAN*

UNILEVER – DOVE
Agency: Ogilvy & Mather, Toronto
Canada – 2006

Dove *Evolution* is a riveting time-lapse film showing a young woman's transformation from a pretty, but ordinary girl into a strikingly beautiful billboard model in just over a minute. It deconstructs the beauty myth by revealing everything in the process, from the impact of lighting and the application of hair and make-up to retouching and the remodelling of the neck and eyes. Using the tagline 'No wonder our perception of beauty is distorted', it was created to promote Dove Self-Esteem workshops in Canada and raise awareness of the Dove Self-Esteem Fund.

Evolution was made exclusively for the web, with no media budget and relatively low production costs. According to Janet Kestin, Co-Chief Creative Officer at Ogilvy & Mather in Toronto, 'This allowed us to tell the story in the time it took to tell it without artificially imposed time constraints. It allowed us to break free of the "rules" of TV (product at beginning/middle/end, reasons to believe, all the traditional ad behaviours), and let us judge the work by whether or not we thought it was fascinating enough for people to want to send on.'

The film fuelled discussions about Dove and real beauty in the blogosphere and, by early 2008, had been viewed more than six million times on YouTube. It has also received plenty of editorial coverage, featuring on TV shows *Ellen*, *The View* and *Entertainment Tonight*.

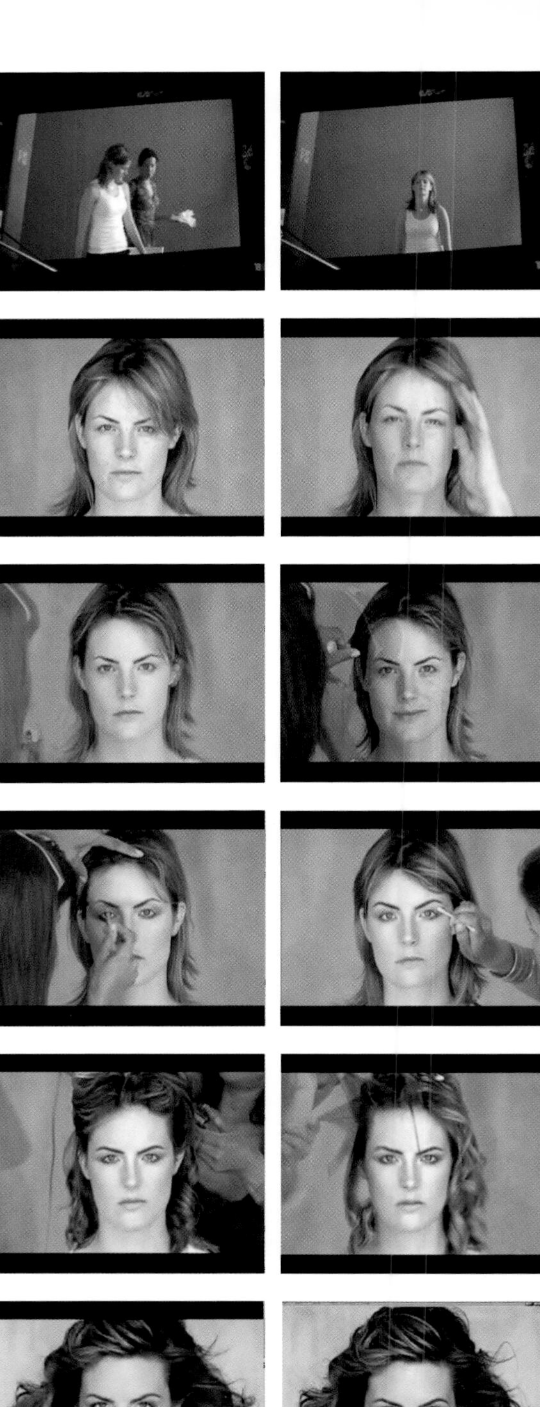

'THE CONTENT NEEDS TO BE STELLAR AND IF IT'S HITTING THE RIGHT CHORD, THE REST BECOMES HISTORY. AS YET, THERE'S NO PLAYBOOK ON HOW TO DO THIS STUFF.'

JANET KESTIN, CO-CHIEF CREATIVE OFFICER AT OGILVY & MATHER, TORONTO

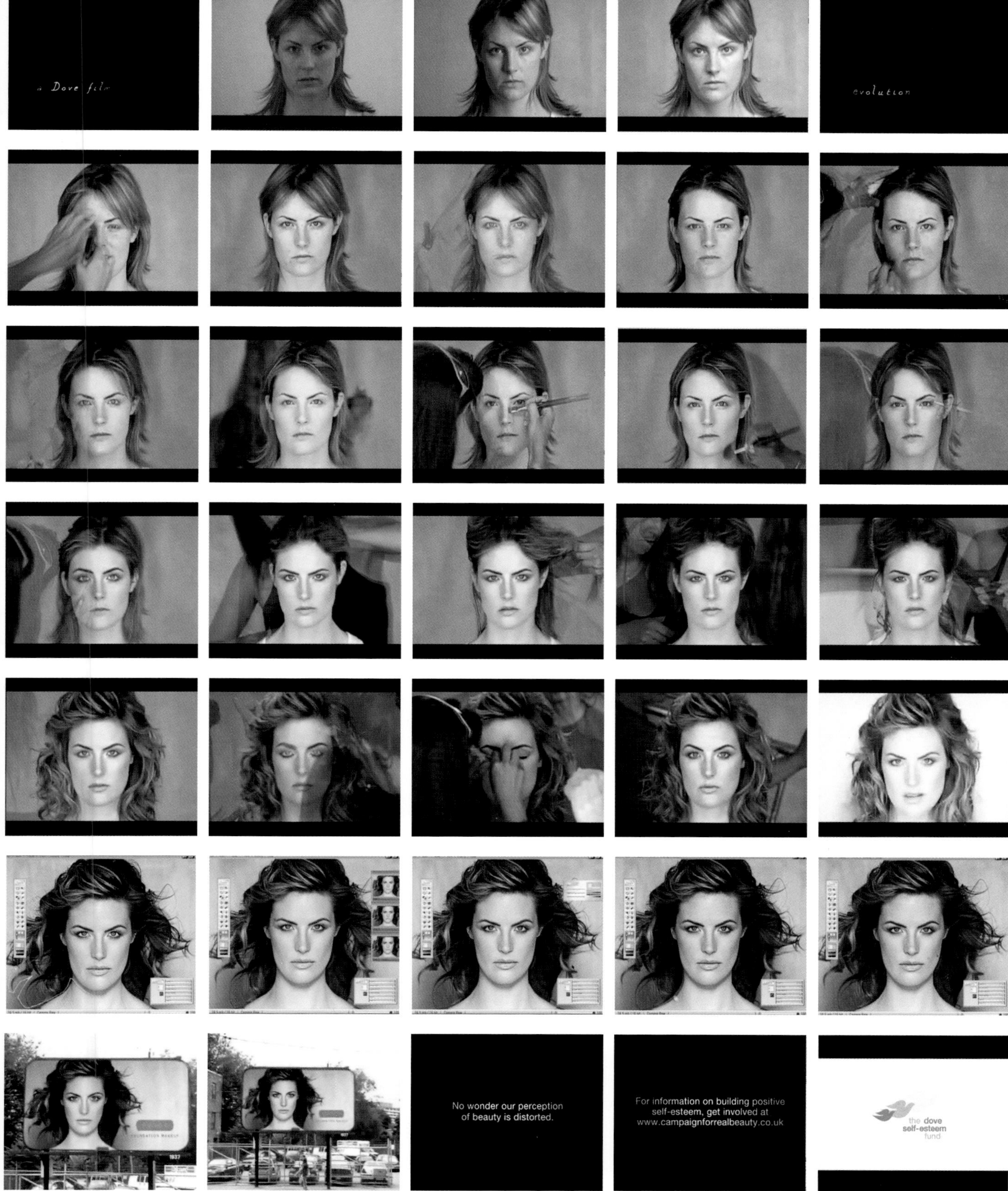
a Dove film
evolution
No wonder our perception
of beauty is distorted.
For information on building positive
self-esteem, get involved at
www.campaignforrealbeauty.co.uk
the dove
self-esteem
fund

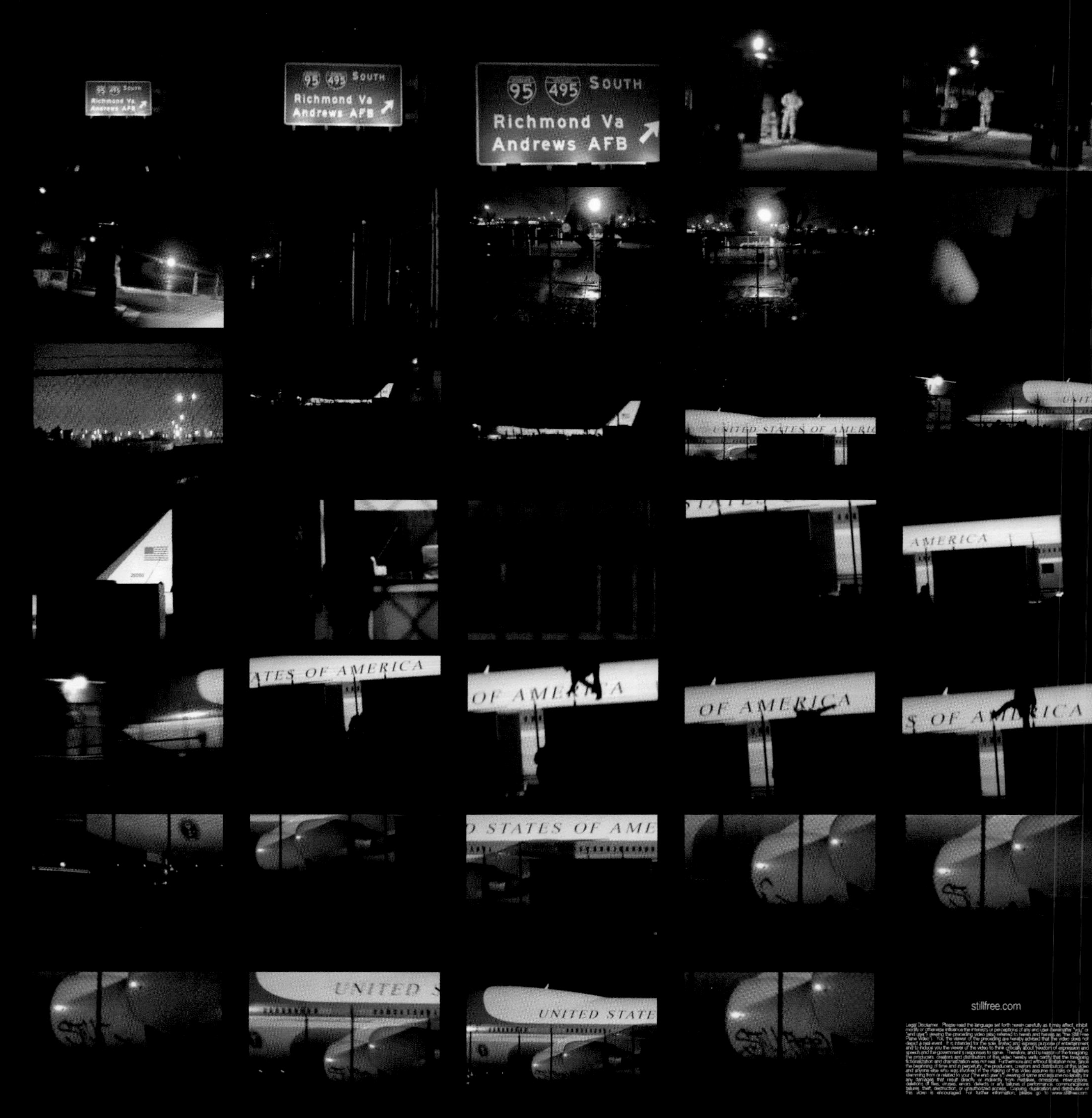
95
495
SOUTH
Richmond Va
Andrews AFB
UNITED STATES OF AMERICA
stillfree.com

'I WANTED TO DO SOMETHING CULTURALLY SIGNIFICANT, I WANTED TO CREATE A REAL POP-CULTURE MOMENT. IT'S THIS COMPLETELY IRREVERENT, OVER-THE-TOP THING THAT COULD REALLY NEVER HAPPEN: THIS FIVE-DOLLAR CAN OF PAINT PUTTING A PIMPLE ON THIS GOLIATH.'

MARC ECKO

Another viral success that plays on the fine line between reality and fiction came from New York fashion designer Marc Ecko. In a video on his site he was shown creeping up to Air Force One and spray-painting it with the words 'Still Free'.

When the film was released, several inconsistencies were found in the footage, and it was later revealed that the real plane was not vandalized. Ecko's company had rented a 747 cargo jet and painted one side of it to look like Air Force One.

In a separate video on the same website, Ecko explained that he had tagged the plane in protest against the strict anti-graffiti laws in many American cities including New York. In some cases it has been made illegal to carry or purchase wide-tipped markers or spray paint. 'No elected official gets to decide what is art and what is trash,' Ecko said. 'Since then I've learned that there are cities all over this country with laws that restrict kids who want to pursue legal art inspired by graffiti.... [The President's] highest responsibility is to protect our freedoms, and the first among those is our right to speech. That's why I tagged the President's plane. The President can't fly around like a rock star, talking about how America is the greatest country in the world, but ignore what makes it great.'

NIKE

Agency: FramFab

Sweden – 2006

Brazilian football sensation Ronaldinho sits on the grass. Someone hands him a gold metal case. He takes out a pair of Nike football boots, laces them up, then shows off his skill by shooting volleys from outside the box onto the crossbar, controlling each rebound to hit the bar four times in a row. A swoosh is subtle but clearly visible in the video which is almost three minutes long.

The Nike video was viewed 1.9 million times on YouTube in a month. For the immediate four-week period, searches for 'Ronaldinho' accounted for 2 per cent of visits to YouTube. Internet chat rooms lit up with conversations about whether the video was staged, computer-generated or edited.

‘MAKING IT TOO PERFECT OR TOO SHAKY WOULD HAVE KILLED IT. IT WAS A MATTER OF FINDING THE RIGHT BALANCE, BEARING IN MIND WE ALSO HAD TO HAVE A PRODUCT PROMINENTLY FEATURED. ONCE WE HAD THE ROUGH CUT DONE, WE WERE PRETTY SURE IT WOULD GO FAR.’

RASMUS FRANDSEN, CREATIVE DIRECTOR AT FRAMFAB

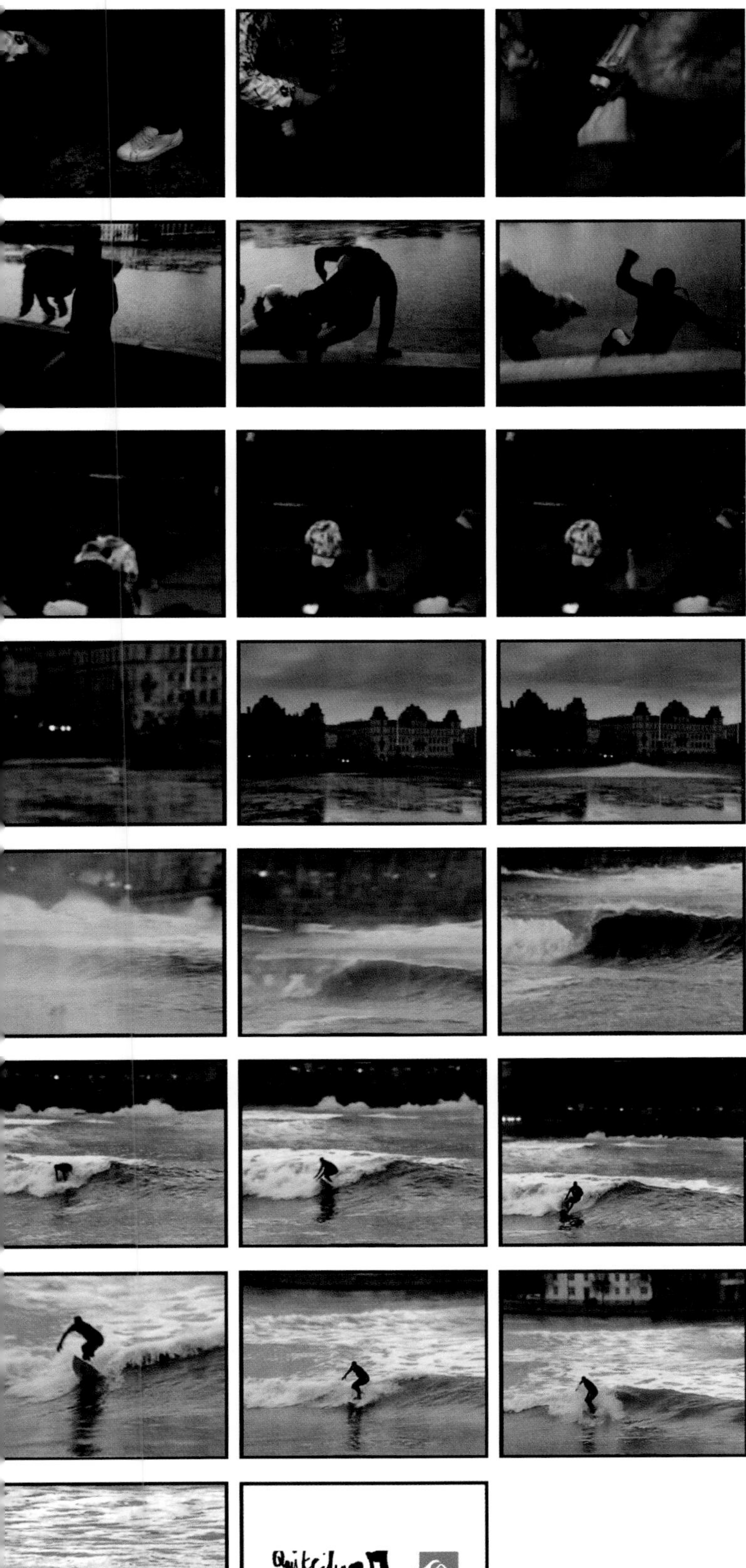

This video features a group of masked teens at a small lake in the centre of Copenhagen. Filmed in the style of a hand-held camera, we see one of them jump into the lake with his surfboard, while his mates run towards the nearby bridge. A self-made explosive device is thrown into the water from the bridge, creating a huge wave that the surfer rides. To get the viral film to look as real as possible, the explosion had to be real. Experts let off a 22-kg plastic device 4 metres (13 feet) under the surface, creating a 50-metre-high (164-foot-high) explosion.

Designed to show Quiksilver as a street-savvy surfing brand for unconventional people, the film turned up on 95 per cent of all surf websites worldwide within four days of its release. In part this was due to coordinated seeding to 1,000 opinion leaders in an initial phase of the campaign. An estimated 25 million people have watched the film online.

'QUIKSILVER IS GIVING US LANDLOCKED SURFERS SOME GOOD IDEAS.'

SURFVIDS.BLOGSPOT.COM

Agency: Cutwater
United States – 2006

Catch shows a man using his face to catch Ray-Ban Wayfarers thrown at him from ridiculous heights. According to the agency, no tricks were used, and the clever effect was down to practice. The amateur-like video registered more than 5 million hits during its first week and inspired a host of imitations, as well as receiving coverage on CNN and the BBC. The theme of the campaign – 'Never Hide' – was subtly included as a finger-written message on the window of a car.

Ray-Ban hoped to repeat the success of the first video with a second release along the same lines. *Bobbing for Glasses* shows the same characters dunking their heads into water buckets and surfacing with pair after pair of Ray-Ban Wayfarers.

NEVER
HIDE
NEVER
HIDE

Millimetres
Matter
2·4mm
www.millimetresmatter.com
Millimetres*Matter

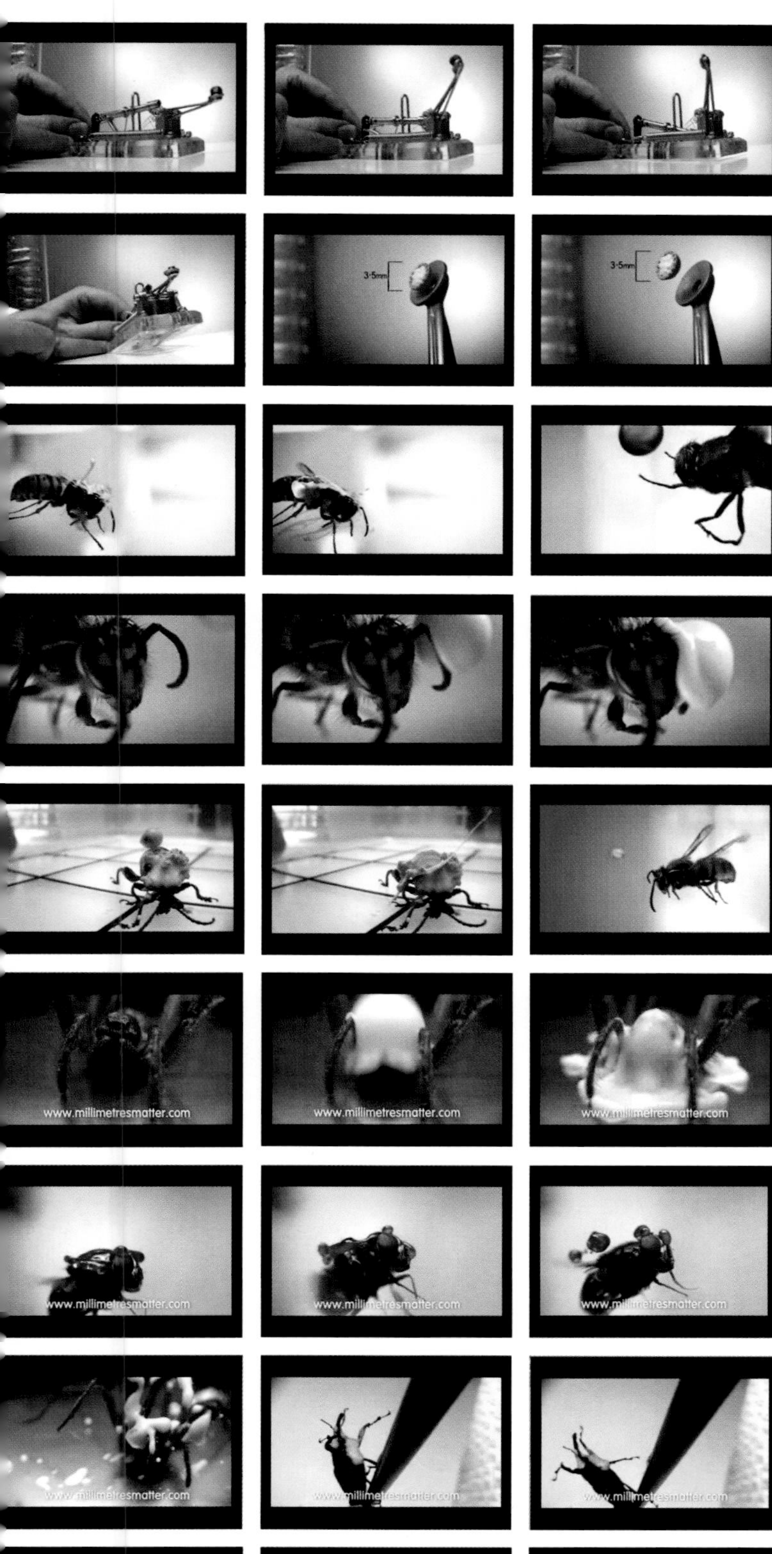

SAMSUNG MOBILE

Agency: The Viral Factory
Worldwide – 2007

In order to promote the slimline handsets of the Samsung Mobile Ultra Edition II, a group of mad scientists set out to prove that millimetres do matter, particularly when firing pies at insects. A video was shot showing insects close-up being hit by miniature pies and desserts.

To recreate this microscopic pie fight, the film made outstanding use of high-speed macro film techniques. With the help of a professional insect handler, no insects were harmed in the making of the film, although some did get a little sticky. The makers used high-speed footage of the insects being hit by droplets of coloured viscous liquid. Maquettes were then created to match the shapes and positions of the insects and painted blue. Real pies were then thrown at the maquettes and shot at high speed.

The film received more than 3 million views. Research showed that 56 per cent of viewers thought the film was impressive, 44 per cent thought the phones were stylish and 21 per cent said they were likely to consider buying the phone.

'IT WAS NO MEAN FEAT TO SHOOT PIES HITTING INSECTS AT FRAME RATES OF UP TO 2,000 PER SECOND.'

ED ROBINSON, CREATIVE DIRECTOR AND CO-FOUNDER OF THE VIRAL FACTORY ON SOURCEWIRE.COM

TRIVIA

The casting for the shoot was an arduous task and resulted in a total of three hundred flies, fifteen beetles, one elephant beetle, six common spiders, one queen wasp and one hundred bees being present on set at all times.

More than two hundred and twenty-five miniature desserts, including lemon meringue pie, coconut custard pie and cranberry jelly pie, were specially crafted by an expert team of miniature props creators.

Source: sourcewire.com

BE INTRIGUING

Anybody who is familiar with the art of seduction and dating will know that you can't just lay all your cards on the table the first time you meet somebody. On the contrary, you need to maintain a bit of intrigue, so that he or she will keep coming back for more. You need to keep the other person guessing, while at the same time revealing yourself little by little. This process of slowly opening yourself up to another person can be equally valid for brand communications.

Brands tend to lack the necessary skills for this seduction ritual. They are used to revealing everything about themselves at the very first encounter, eager to get customers into the sack as soon as possible. But today's savvy audience is reluctant to allow themselves to be seduced so quickly and openly. They prefer brands to seduce them little by little, revealing their messages slowly, intelligently and flirtatiously.

The need for more intrigue in brand communications comes from the simple observation that intrigue generates buzz. Something that raises questions can create more conversation amongst people than something that only gives answers. That makes sense: what is there to say about a campaign that is spelling everything out for us? An intriguing campaign, which is deliberately not telling the whole story, keeps people guessing and gives them something to talk about. By not pouring everything into one single execution and deliberately spreading snippets of information – whether it's across a period of time or across an array of channels – brands make their audience do the work. Henry Jenkins, author of *Convergence Culture* (2006), puts it brilliantly: 'The key is to produce something that both pulls people together and gives them something to do.' Advertising becomes a game of hide and seek, revealing details of the story drip by drip and keeping people on their toes.

The need for more intrigue goes hand in hand with people's altered media behaviour. The multi-tasking audiences of today are able to digest lots of information at the same time, comfortably hopping between different channels. They are used to maintaining multiple identities across different social networks, selecting different facets of their personality for show. As a result, new generations are equally comfortable with dealing with this kind of fragmentation when it comes to brands. They are able to handle an increasing level of complexity in the way campaigns are built and messages are conveyed. The smarter and more experienced people get at decoding complex and multilayered advertising campaigns, the more enigmatic, mysterious and subtle brand communications can afford to become.

The campaigns in this chapter, such as SNCF (see pages 116–17), Court TV (now truTV, pages 118–19), Virgin Mobile (pages 132–3) and Google (pages 120–1), consciously introduce an element of intrigue to keep their audience hungry for more and make them interact with the story while it is being pieced together. By cultivating mystique, these brands leave it up to their audience to compose the picture and tie up the loose ends.

■ BE INTRIGUING
■ VOYAGES-SNCF.COM
■ Agency: DDB Paris
■ France – 2005

CONSTRUCTION DU TUNNEL
TRANSATLANTIQUE.

Bientôt Paris - New York en train en 8 heures.

www.transatlantys.com

TransAtlantys

LE BOUT DU MONDE À PORTÉE DE TRAIN

When the French website transatlantys.com announced the imminent opening of a new transatlantic tunnel – offering an eight-hour undersea direct rail service from Paris to New York – it caused a huge stir. Debate centred on the practical impossibilities of undertaking such a project and the speeds at which the train would have to travel to make the journey in eight hours. Technical details were released, concerning how the tunnel would be built, and how they would protect the flora and the submarine species. The website also claimed that construction would take eleven years to complete and gave visitors the option of registering for tickets. In order to boost its credibility, the ambitious project was promoted on billboards and in the press.

The campaign was later revealed as an elaborate stunt by rail group SNCF to mark the launch of its new online travel agency (voyages-sncf.com). The tagline was 'Because you can't go everywhere by train, voyages-sncf.com also offers trips by plane'.

All the major daily newspapers in France dedicated articles to the campaign, as well as a number of radio and television channels. Nearly two million people visited the transatlantys.com website. Transatlantys.com received more than 4,000 emails and even résumés from engineers and scientists eager to participate in the project. One girl even tried to sell tickets for the first trip on eBay. All this buzz led to a massive 67 per cent increase in sales of plane tickets on voyages-sncf.com, a 62 per cent increase in hotel reservations and a 66 per cent increase in package deals.

Parce qu'on ne peut pas aller partout en train, voyages-sncf.com vous propose aussi de l'avion.
PARIS
NEW YORK
Vol A/R
352€*
voyages-sncf.com
plus loin que vous ne l'imaginez.

COURT TV (TRUTV)
Agency: Deep Focus
United States – 2006

'OKAY, AT THIS POINT WE MAY AS WELL ADMIT THE VIRAL THING WORKED ON US, BECAUSE WE'VE SPENT WAY TOO MUCH TIME ON FIGURING IT OUT.'

GAWKER.COM

To generate a buzz leading up to the season premiere of *Parco PI* on the American network Court TV (now truTV), a show that revolved heavily around the subject of adultery, a campaign was conjured up that – at first glance – looked like every cheating man's worst nightmare. A (fictitious) character called Emily seemed set on exposing her husband's adulterous ways for the whole world to see and having her revenge.

In a blog Emily drew readers into the story of how she came to realize that her husband was cheating on her. Within several days, the blog had received over a million hits and Emily was getting requests for media appearances at a national level. The narrative laid the foundation for a series of billboards on which Emily declared 'Fourteen Days of Wrath' against her cheating husband, Steven. Four of the 'Fourteen Days of Wrath' were actual staged events in New York City. When Emily threw out her cheating husband's belongings, the drama was captured on a hand-held camcorder and uploaded to video-sharing sites.

The campaign as a whole was covered by over 200 news sources on-air, online and in print.

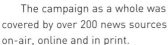

Hi Steven,
Do I have your attention now?
I know all about her, you dirty, sneaky, immoral, unfaithful, poorly-endowed slimeball. Everything's caught on tape.
Your (soon-to-be-ex) Wife,
Emily
p.s. I paid for this billboard from OUR joint bank account.
city outdoor
NO HORN HONKING $350 FINE
ONE WAY
E HOUSTON ST
LUDLOW ST
TURNING VEHICLES
TO
PARKING
Enter on Essex St
SIDEWALK CLOSED USE OTHER SIDE
PEDESTRIAN
WALKWAY
SIDEWALK
1150XH

BE INTRIGUING
GOOGLE
Agency: Crispin Porter + Bogusky
United States – 2004

This billboard, which appeared on Route 101 in the heart of Silicon Valley and in the subway station near Harvard University a few months later, was intriguing in that it carried no branding whatsoever, and gave no apparent indication as to why it was there. The billboard turned out to be the first step in an ingenious Google recruitment campaign, targeted at a very narrow audience: engineers who are geeky enough to feel frustrated by the very existence of a maths problem they haven't solved, and smart enough to work out the solution.

Would-be candidates had to solve the complex mathematical problem on the billboard. That would lead them to a website, www.7427466391.com, which directed them to yet another website with another riddle. If they managed to solve the second problem, they were directed to a web page that invited them to submit their CV to Google.

The genius of this campaign lies in the use of a highly visible medium to communicate to a very narrow audience. The intriguing ad speaks to engineers in their own language, while creating the impression among the rest of the audience that you have to be very smart to work for Google.

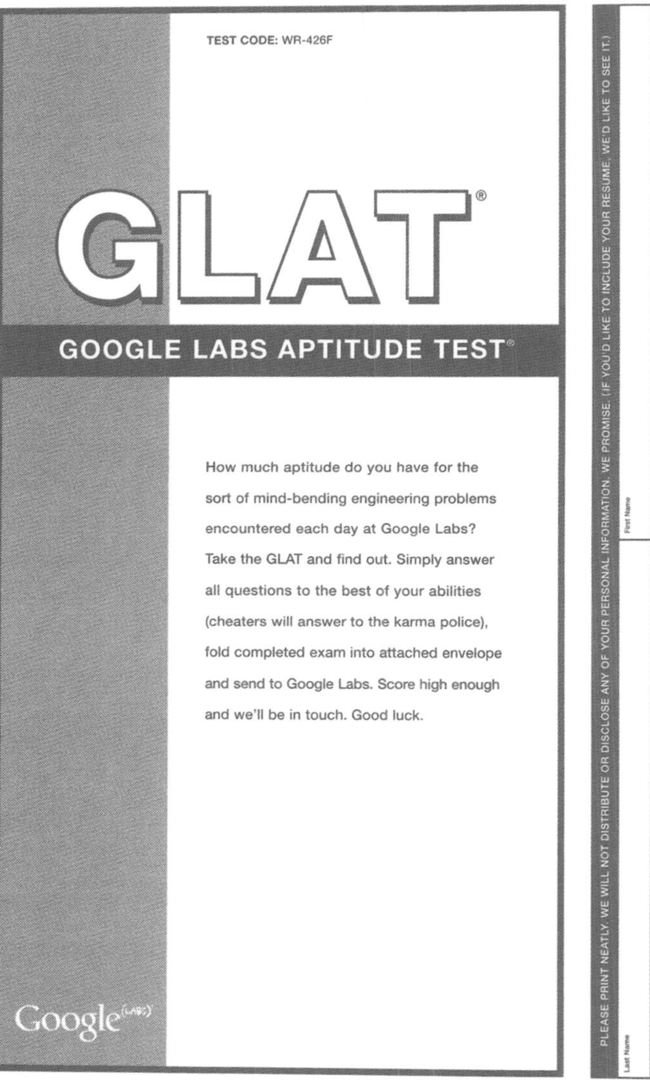

1. Solve this cryptic equation, realizing of course that values for M and E could be interchanged. No leading zeros are allowed.

WWWDOT - GOOGLE = DOTCOM

answer:

2. Write a haiku describing possible methods for predicting search traffic seasonality.

answer:

3.
1
1 1
2 1
1 2 1 1
1 1 1 2 2 1

What is the next line?

answer:

4. You are in a maze of twisty little passages, all alike. There is a dusty laptop here with a weak wireless connection. There are dull, lifeless gnomes strolling about. What dost thou do?

- A) Wander aimlessly, bumping into obstacles until you are eaten by a grue.
- B) Use the laptop as a digging device to tunnel to the next level.
- C) Play MPoRPG until the battery dies along with your hopes.
- D) Use the computer to map the nodes of the maze and discover an exit path.
- E) Email your resume to Google, tell the lead gnome you quit and find yourself in whole different world.

5. What's broken with Unix? How would you fix it?

answer:

6. On your first day at Google, you discover that your cubicle mate wrote the textbook you used as a primary resource in your first year of graduate school. Do you:

- A) Fawn obsequiously and ask if you can have an autograph.
- B) Sit perfectly still and use only soft keystrokes to avoid disturbing her concentration.
- C) Leave her daily offerings of granola and English toffee from the food bins.
- D) Quote your favorite formula from the textbook and explain how it's now your mantra.
- E) Show her how example 17b could have been solved with 34 fewer lines of code.

1

7. Which of the following expresses Google's over-arching philosophy?

- A) "I'm feeling lucky"
- B) "Don't be evil"
- C) "Oh, I already fixed that"
- D) "You should never be more than 50 feet from food"
- E) All of the above

8. How many different ways can you color an icosahedron with one of three colors on each face?

answer:

What colors would you choose?

answer:

9. This space left intentionally blank. Please fill it with something that improves upon emptiness.

answer:

10. On an infinite, two-dimensional, rectangular lattice of 1-ohm resistors, what is the resistance between two nodes that are a knight's move away?

answer:

11. It's 2 PM on a sunny Sunday afternoon in the Bay Area. You're minutes from the Pacific Ocean, redwood forest hiking trails and world class cultural attractions. What do you do?

answer:

12. In your opinion, what is the most beautiful math equation ever derived?

answer:

13. Which of the following is NOT an actual interest group formed by Google employees?

- A. Women's basketball
- B. Buffy fans
- C. Cricketeers
- D. Nobel winners
- E. Wine club

14. What will be the next great improvement in search technology?

answer:

2

'AS YOU CAN IMAGINE, WE GET MANY, MANY RÉSUMÉS EVERY DAY, SO WE DEVELOPED THIS LITTLE PROCESS TO INCREASE THE SIGNAL-TO-NOISE RATIO.' GOOGLE

MICROSOFT
Agency: 42nd Entertainment
United States – 2004

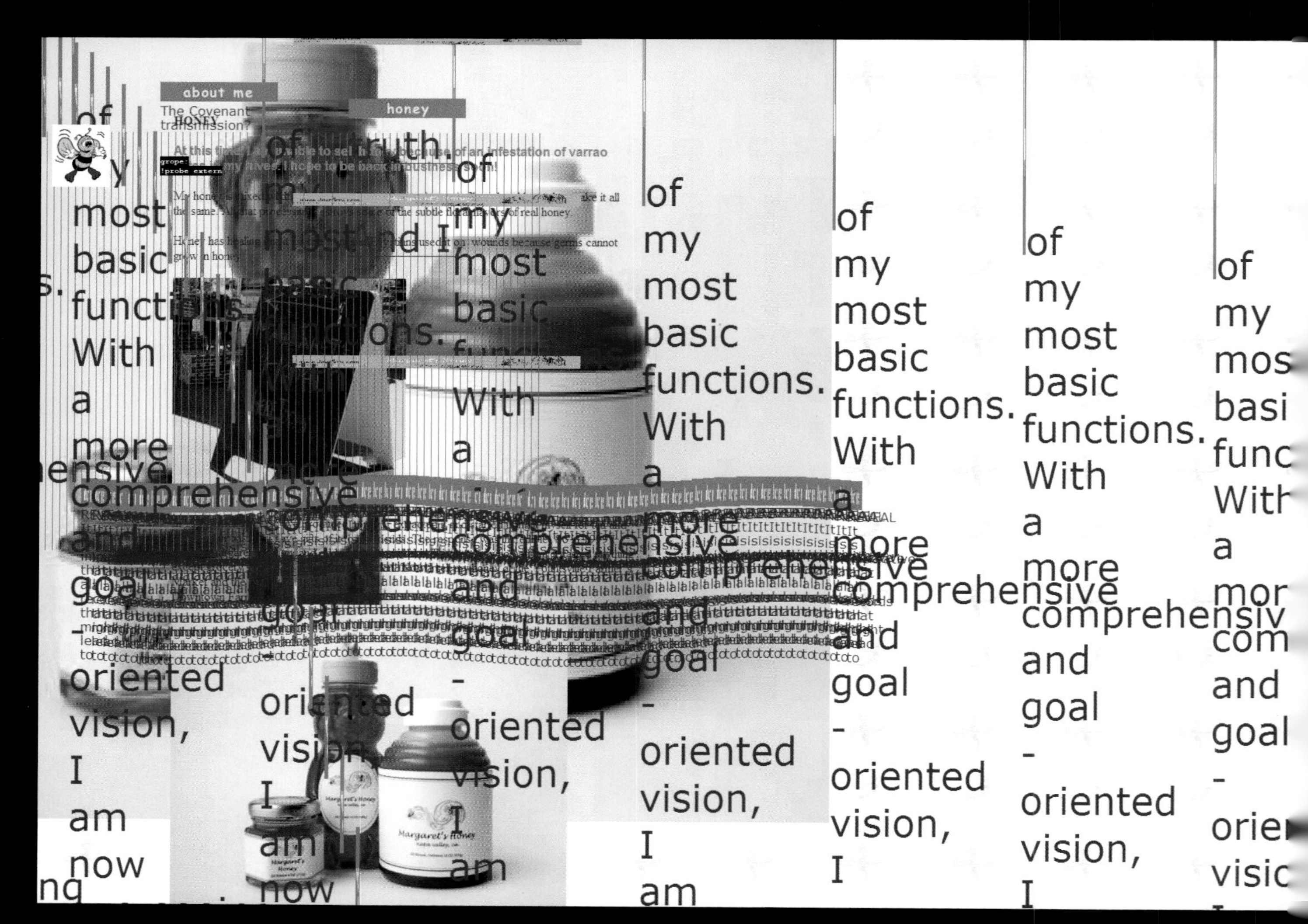

'IT'S LIKE READING A GOOD SERIAL NOVEL – YOU'RE LEFT WITH CLIFFHANGERS.'

EXCITED PLAYER ON WIRED.COM

I Love Bees

www.ilovebees.com
ce whispering in a corridor and a quick clasp of hands; the long elegance of a fine decrypt, it's a spill of
home
honey
I don't know why. More than mostly dead already. Like shooting a broken body on a
SURPRISE!
Look up and smile, honey.
My hobbies include reading, especially mysteries. I especially love Ellis Peters and the Brother Cadfael books and Alexander McCall Smith and the Precious Ramotswe books. As you can see I like my mysteries cozy! And of course, I like reading them with a cup of red tea with my own honey!
But the most important thing in my life is my family. My sister Chloe, and her daughter Dana. My sister and I didn't always get along growing up, but she has always been there for me, and Dana, my niece, is truly the daughter I never had.

Microsoft created *ilovebees* to entertain *Halo* fans in the months leading up to the launch of the sequel, *Halo 2*. Ilovebees.com was flashed at the end of cinema trailers for *Halo 2* and seeded via cryptic messages to keen gamers on the Alternate Reality Gaming Network.

When curious gamers visited ilovebees.com, they found what appeared to be an amateur site run by a Napa Valley–based beekeeper. GPS coordinates pointed to payphones across the United States and several other countries around the world. Players had to hunt down the payphones and wait for them to ring. By answering the phone and giving a secret password, they unlocked the content online for the broader community playing the game. Each week a new episode was released by these means.

More than 10,000 fans mobilized in public places for this pervasive mission, with 600,000 gamers flooding the website to solve the mystery. The *ilovebees* intrigue helped *Halo 2* become a true cultural phenomenon, attracting an audience beyond hardcore gaming.

The campaign generated significant coverage in the mainstream press and almost all of the key gaming publications. *Halo 2* sold $125 m (£62 m) in copies on its first day of release, and surpassed 7 million in units.

BEINTRIGUING
NEW ZEALAND NATURAL
Agency: Contract Advertising
India – 2007

To promote New Zealand Natural's range of ultra-light, 99 per cent fat-free sorbets in New Delhi, India, a spectacle was devised in which a girl eating one of the company's sorbets was made to look like she was floating in mid-air as if by magic. The intriguing live kiosk was set up in select shopping hubs in the city, where health-conscious customers tend to go. Passers-by were handed out pamphlets at the site.

The outdoor activity was covered by the local press and cable channels. Circulation on mobile phones and pictures taken by curious passers-by fuelled the publicity further. Increased awareness of the brand was reflected in a 62 per cent jump in sales at the city outlets.

shopping GUIDE

UNUSUAL WAY TO PROMOTE ULTRA-LIGHT DRINK

उत्पादन के प्रचार का अनोखा तरीका

दिल्ली हॉट में लड़की हवा में उड़ी

TRIGUING
AN
: True Agency
States – 2007

To promote the keyless ignition system in its Altima Sedans, Nissan left 20,000 keyrings in 125 busy public places, including countertops, booths, ATMs and sinks. The anonymous keyrings, holding three real keys and two tags, caused intrigue among visitors to the various facilities.

One tag stated 'If found, please do not return. My next Generation Nissan Altima has Intelligent Key with Push Button Ignition, and I no longer need these' – a reference to the technology that allows an Altima owner to unlock and drive the car without even lifting a key – and invited whoever found it to learn more about the ignition system at AltimaKeys.com. The other tag entitled finders to a $15 (£7.50) petrol card voucher.

■ **SONY PLAYSTATION**
■ Agency: TBWA\GERMANY, Berlin
■ Germany – 2006

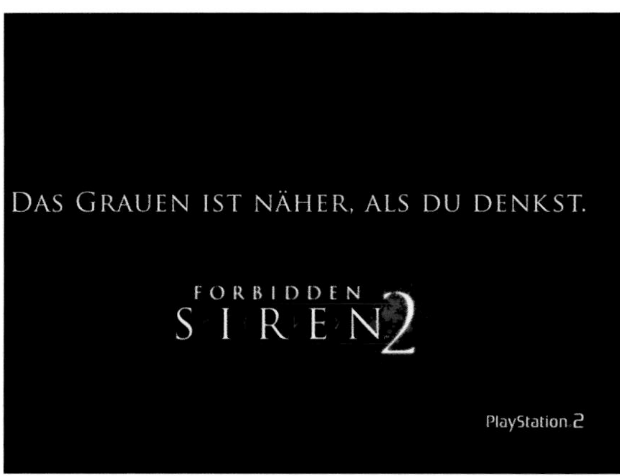

To promote the terrifying PlayStation2 game *Forbidden Siren 2* at the Games Convention 2006 in Leipzig, manipulated snapshot cameras were handed out. Each was branded with the PlayStation logo on the exterior, but the real trick was the pre-exposed film inside the cameras. On every photograph, ghosts and frightening faces appeared, with the mystery only revealed on the last image which bore the line 'The horror is closer than you think. Forbidden Siren 2. Out now for PlayStation2.'

Only a few days after the Games Convention the click rate on the *Forbidden Siren 2* home page tripled. Photos from the cameras started to appear all over the web. Some cameras made it onto eBay as cult items.

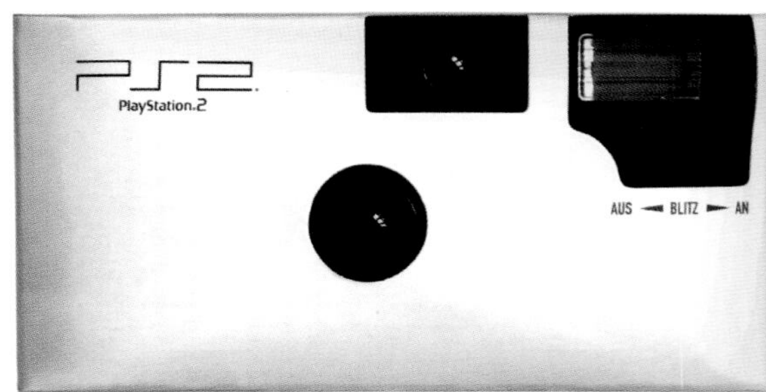

■ BEINTRIGUING
■ **PROCTER & GAMBLE – THERMACARE**
■ Agency: Kirt Gunn & Associates
■ United States – 2006

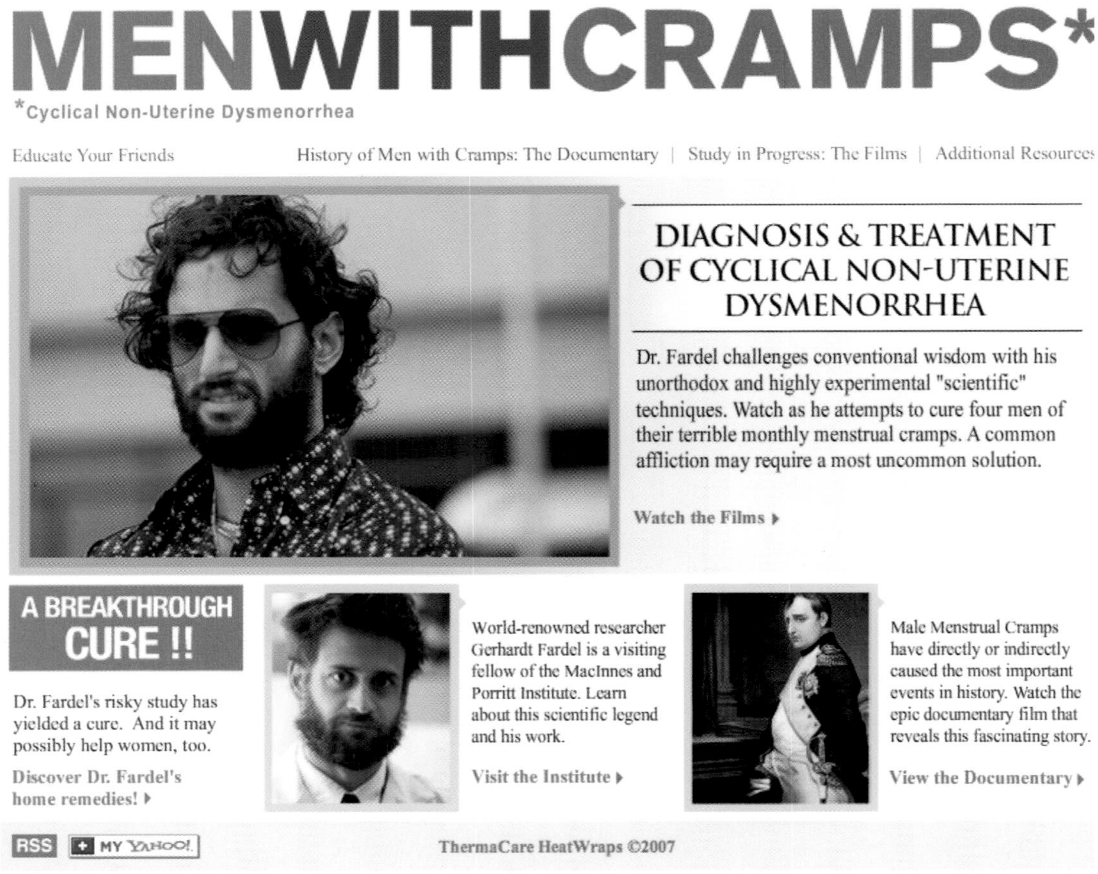

MENWITHCRAMPS*

*Cyclical Non-Uterine Dysmenorrhea

Educate Your Friends | History of Men with Cramps: The Documentary | Study in Progress: The Films | Additional Resources

DIAGNOSIS & TREATMENT OF CYCLICAL NON-UTERINE DYSMENORRHEA

Dr. Fardel challenges conventional wisdom with his unorthodox and highly experimental "scientific" techniques. Watch as he attempts to cure four men of their terrible monthly menstrual cramps. A common affliction may require a most uncommon solution.

Watch the Films ▸

A BREAKTHROUGH CURE !!

Dr. Fardel's risky study has yielded a cure. And it may possibly help women, too.

Discover Dr. Fardel's home remedies! ▸

World-renowned researcher Gerhardt Fardel is a visiting fellow of the MacInnes and Porritt Institute. Learn about this scientific legend and his work.

Visit the Institute ▸

Male Menstrual Cramps have directly or indirectly caused the most important events in history. Watch the epic documentary film that reveals this fascinating story.

View the Documentary ▸

RSS | + MY YAHOO!

ThermaCare HeatWraps ©2007

To get people talking about ThermaCare, Procter & Gamble's line of heat patches to relieve menstrual cramps, women had the chance to give men a taste of their own medicine by making them experience period pains for themselves.

To make this happen, a very legitimate-looking research clinic was created, the MacInnes and Porritt Institute, dedicated to curing 'Cyclical Non-Uterine Dysmenorrhea' or male menstrual cramps. A faux site for the institute was created, complete with board member biographies, company dress codes and the whistleblower policy.

Classified ads started appearing in papers across the United States recruiting male volunteers for an experimental study of male cramps, all carrying the same eye-catching headline: 'Men: Are You Suffering From Menstrual Cramps?'

Another website featured a seven-part documentary called *The History of Men With Cramps*, examining the history of the condition (Achilles's problems are concluded to have been more to do with his stomach than his heel). This was followed by a film series starring the fictional Dr Fardel, who is on a mission to cure four different men with cramps using a unique remedy for each man.

At first, the project was completely unbranded, leading to speculation and debate. Then it looked as if ThermaCare had purchased ad space on the website. Only at a final stage was it revealed that ThermaCare was the full-fledged sponsor.

The films became a hit on YouTube and iFilm, and conversation about *Men With Cramps* leapt from the internet into popular culture. The story was picked up by Jay Leno, *The New York Times*, *BusinessWeek* and CNBC, and ultimately reached over 30 million viewers. Heat patches went from the lowest-performing ThermaCare product to the highest, despite a budget for the *Men With Cramps* campaign of only $1 m (£500,000) – compared with a combined sum of $35 m (£17.5 m) for the rest of the range.

'WE FELT THAT "MAN BITES DOG" ASPECT WOULD ENGAGE THE CONSUMER, BECAUSE WE DO A LOT OF FOCUS GROUPS, AND WOMEN ALWAYS TALK ABOUT MEN'S INABILITY TO DEAL WITH PAIN.'

DAVID CORR, EXECUTIVE CREATIVE DIRECTOR AT PUBLICIS, WHO WORKED ON THE CAMPAIGN, IN *THE NEW YORK TIMES*

This Virgin Mobile campaign was a complex, multilayered, month-long stunt that succeeded in duping the media, consumers and even the company's staff through its clever mixing of fictitious events with spontaneous public response.

The campaign was developed from the simple observation that Virgin Mobile's rates are so low that they are open to abuse. Given half a chance, people will use their mobile phones in an irresponsible manner just because it is cheap.

This is how the intrigue unfolded over time, from a simple picture of Jason Donovan posted online to national hype.

1. Jason Donovan's car is put onto car sale websites and eBay. An eBay history is also created to make the sale seem legitimate.

2. A fabricated 'paparazzi' shot is released onto the internet along with links to Jason's online car ads. The photo is emailed to anyone and everyone.

Anyone calling the number hears a voice mail message from Jason – 'authenticating' the number. Whenever someone texted the number, a response was sent back from a computer posing as Jason, using the subject of their original message to customize the angry response.

The paparazzi shot spreads, making its way onto blog forums and chat sites. The press catch wind of the phenomenon and print the photo in the paper. Calls continue to escalate and Jason's voice mail is updated with a more annoyed message.

3. Seemingly amateur pre-shot videos are placed on internet sites showing people prank calling Jason in compromising situations. The videos spread like wildfire.

4. A story is leaked to the press that Jason has contacted his mobile phone company Virgin Mobile for help. Virgin responds to the leak by placing a small ad in the newspaper encouraging their customers to refrain from calling Mr Donovan. Calls triple instantly.

Statements are sent to the press along with an internal memo to staff alerting them to the problem and urging them not to contact Jason. Virgin staff are not told this is a hoax. Naturally they tell all their friends.

A message from Richard Branson is played on national radio, outlining his disgust at the behaviour and urging customers to use the low Virgin Mobile rates responsibly.

Public ignore the message and calls increase. A website initiative for the responsible use of mobile phones is launched by Virgin Mobile.

5. With calls escalating, a full-scale mainstream campaign is launched, urging people to use Virgin Mobile's low rates responsibly and not to call Jason Donovan on 0403 JASOND. Media included TV, cinema, in-store posters, taxis, websites and retail. The number of calls again escalated astronomically.

6. Public interest in calling Jason gets out of control. The campaign, designed to urge people to stop calling 0403 JASOND, generated over 680,000 calls and texts. Media coverage in press and radio is estimated to have generated over two million exposures.

MPORTANT MESSAGE
ARDING JASON DONOVAN
FROM VIRGIN MOBILE

ENJOY OUR RATES
RESPONSIBLY

DO NOT CALL OR TEXT
0403 JASOND

IMPORTANT ANNOUNCEMENT

It has been brought to the attention of Virgin Mobile that information regarding one of our higher profile customers has leaked on to the internet. We strongly urge people not to call or text TV's Jason Donovan on

0403 JASOND

5c TEXT AND 5c PER MIN* VIRGIN TO VIRGIN 24/7
ENJOY OUR RATES RESPONSIBLY

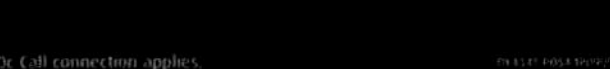

20c Call connection applies.

IMPORTANT ANNOUNCEMENT

It has been brought to our attention that a high profile customer of Virgin Mobile has had his private number leaked on the internet. We strongly advise our customers to refrain from calling Mr Donovan.

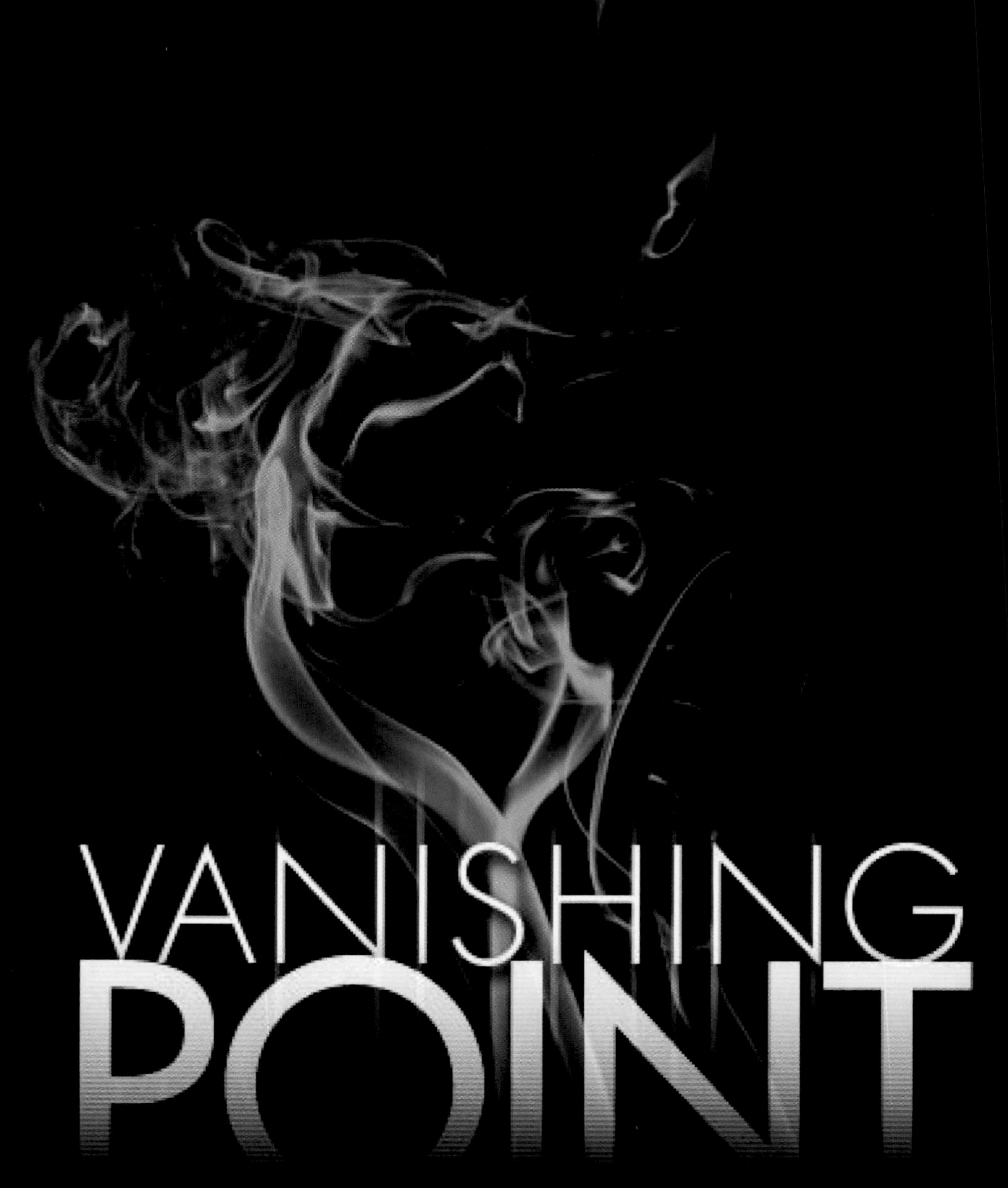
VANISHING
POINT

MICROSOFT

Agency: 42nd Entertainment
United States – 2007

To celebrate the consumer release of Windows Vista, Microsoft launched the first global cross-media puzzle to reward their most enthusiastic, tech-savvy consumers. The game spanned four weeks as players from around the globe worked together to decipher embedded clues in real world events and solve puzzles online to win a trip to the ultimate vista – outer space.

The game launched mysteriously, with a stealth campaign utilizing Japanese puzzle boxes, USB drives, AMD computers and videos on YouTube. Bloggers and players were led to the *Vanishing Point* website and a countdown to the game's launch, pointing to a specific GPS location in Las Vegas, Nevada. Over 200 players arrived at the appointed place to see a fountain show suddenly 'hacked' by a mysterious puzzle-master, Loki. Her image floated on a six-storey-high wall of water as she explained the challenge to the world and presented the first time-based puzzle clues.

In the weeks that followed, more puzzle boxes were unlocked, and players found cryptic clues written in the skies in Sydney, Miami, Los Angeles and Phoenix. They were projected through high-resolution transformations on world landmarks such as the National Gallery in London, Victoria Theater in Singapore, the Brandenburg Gate in Berlin, San Francisco's Palace of Fine Arts and Toronto's Hockey Hall of Fame.

Online communities worked together to solve the puzzles by creating resources such as forums, photo/video archives, online hints and even web-radio stations that broadcast in real-time during the live events. Over a million people visited the website, and nearly 100,000 people registered and actively played. They competed for nearly half a million dollars in prizes and the winner secured a ride into space courtesy of Rocketplane Limited, Inc.

'I'VE SPENT A GOOD FEW DAYS TRYING TO WORK OUT THESE PUZZLES, AND THEN I FIND OUT ONCE I'VE COMPLETED THE FIRST TWO BOXES

MICROSOFT
Agency: 42nd Entertainment
United States – 2007

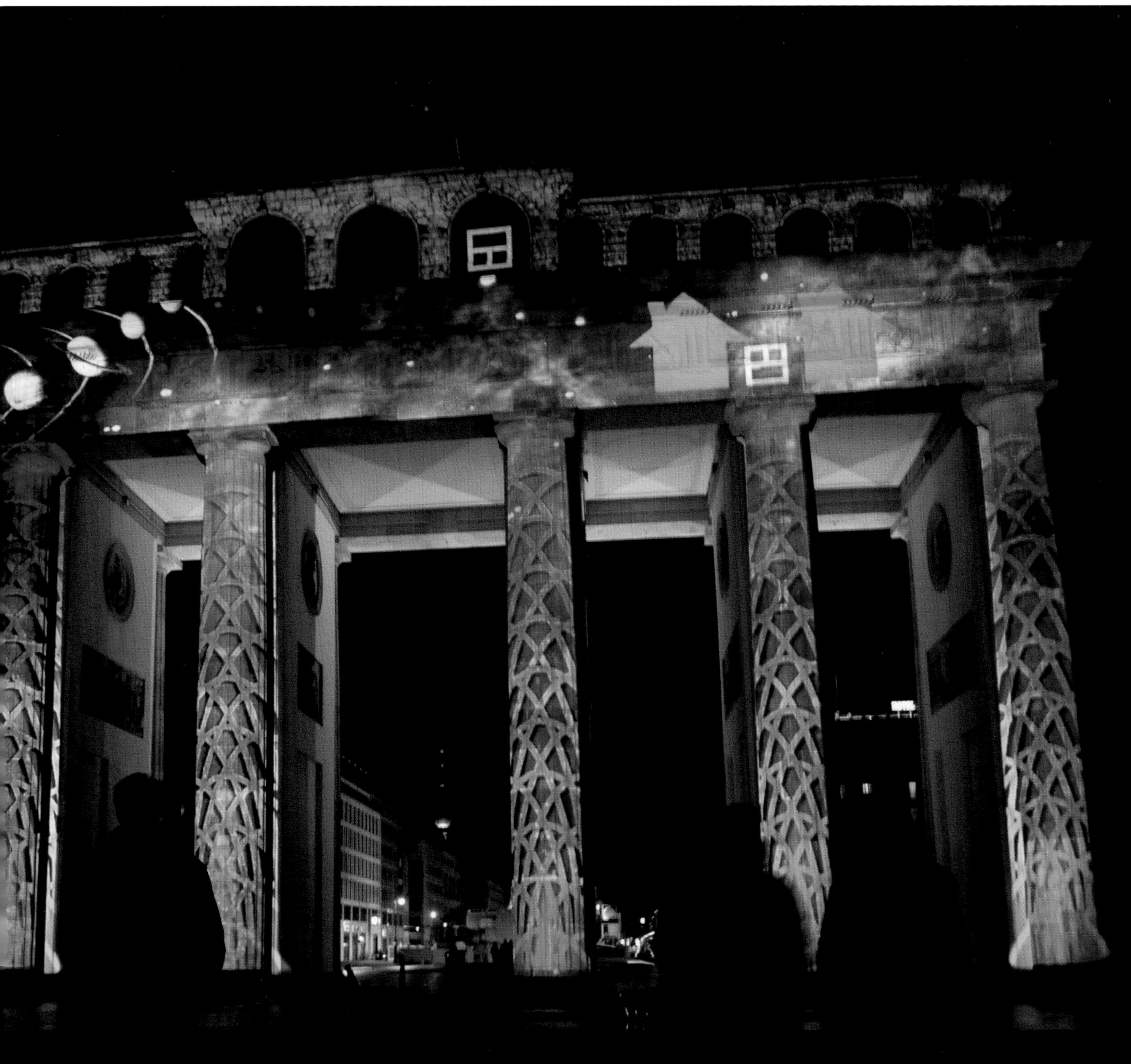

YAYASAN REBANA INDONESIA

Agency: JWT Jakarta

Indonesia – 2007

On Children's Day in Indonesia, 500 life-like children's hands appeared in the pond in Jakarta's busiest traffic roundabout, creating an intriguing, mysterious sight that was hard to ignore. The action reminded people that even two years after the tsunami in Aceh, in which more than 5,000 children were orphaned, there are still children in desperate need of help. A sign near the roundabout said: 'Many tsunami orphans are still in need of a helping hand.'

SENJATA IL

Penyelun
Pistol ke P
Buron

JAKARTA (Media): Polisi hi
masih memburu pemilik
gal yang akan diselundu
pua. Samuel Malo, 34, ters
lundupan tersebut didug
rikan diri ke Jayapura, Pa

Kepala Polres Kesatua
Pengamanan Pelabuhan (
Priok Ajun Komisaris Bes
mawan menegaskan Samu
tangkap dan masih dalam

Pernyataan ini meralat
sejumlah media bahwa
nasional pencak silat, dita
saat hendak menyelund
pucuk pistol dan sejumlah
sangka telah lari ke Jayapur
di Jakarta, kemarin.

Kasus itu bermula dari
tiga senjata api di Pelabuh
Priok, Jakarta, Senin (24/7
buah bungkusan yang aka
KM Sinabung tujuan Jayap

Pungutan liar

arena kondisi jalan yang
dilalui, beban penggu-
jalur tersebut juga se-
tambah akibat masih
ungutan liar.

Aksi Seruan Hak Anak

KOMPAS/PRIYOMBODO

Seni instalasi berupa gambar tangan di kolam Bundaran
Hotel Indonesia, Jakarta, menjadi salah satu media aksi

terjebak pada
penilaian mut

Padahal, ujian
bukanlah satu-sa
mutu pendidikar
tingnya adalah p
rakter manusia
persoalan diriny
syarakat di lingk
persoalan keban

Wacana itu m
diskusi pengem
lum yang diada
Wartawan Pend
sat Informasi d
diknas di Jakart

Diskusi mena
taris Badan St
Pendidikan (BSN

BE A STORYTELLER

Anyone adept in the craft of storytelling, in whatever medium, knows you need time to set up a good story. Characters have to be introduced, the plot gradually unfolds, and little by little the scene is set. This is why the very first episode of a television series is rarely the best, as an audience needs to digest some basic information about characters and context in the first stages of the plot. In screenwriting terms, the revelation of background information about characters is referred to as 'exposition'.

When it comes to traditional advertising formats, there is little time and space for such exposition. Interruptive advertising formats work with seconds rather than minutes. They are driven by first and immediate impressions, rather than long-format storytelling. And increasingly, traditional advertising is designed to deliver hard and fast impact, as people become experts at avoiding, ignoring and filtering out advertising messages, and spiralling media costs require an ever-faster transmission of messages.

Advertising's hunger for impact explains the heavy usage of clichés and jokes throughout its history. The reason is simple: clichés allow immediate recognition and require little exposition; jokes are short and can get a point across very effectively. It is rare for advertisers to construct deeper, more meaningful stories, as time is simply not on their side. Not surprisingly, many creative people working in advertising aspire to work in film, television or publishing, where they have more freedom to express their creativity. The running joke is that copywriters are failed novelists or poets, art directors are failed painters, and account people are just failed human beings.

The good news for some of the more frustrated creative forces working in advertising, as well as for the brands with a more complex and interesting story to tell, is that new tools for storytelling are gaining ground. New, more immersive media are giving brands the opportunity to convey stories with a level of complexity and depth previously unimaginable. Branded or long-form content, whether in traditional broadcast media or an online environment, has opened up the typical constraints associated with the ad format, such as time and narrative structure, and allows brands to convey a philosophy and story that transcend the promotional message of the month.

In an online environment, the possibilities for branded content are somewhat more flexible and limitless. While traditional advertising is essentially about buying time, online exposure is about creating it. It invites people to discover and explore narratives to whatever level they wish. As long as the experience remains worthwhile and interesting, there's no real limit to how long you can stretch the story. Moreover, the internet allows brands to experiment with new, interactive ways of storytelling, in which users can co-decide the turns in a plot or the actions of the characters.

The ever-expanding gaming industry is also embracing the art of storytelling. More specifically, role-playing games are a form of interactive and collaborative storytelling in which gamers can assume the identities of fictional characters and collaboratively create or participate in stories. Gaming legend Chris Crawford even developed specific software, called Storytron, for the creation of more dynamic, character-driven narratives in games.

Retail is another domain in which storytelling can truly flourish. In addition to its obvious sales role, retail has matured and is giving brands the space and time to experiment with their stories. Today, flagship stores are designed to be a unique immersive brand experience, and non-retail brands are reverting to retail partnerships or pop-up retail as a way to create a physical space in which to bring their stories to life.

All these new opportunities, which are not exhaustive, have an impact on the advertising industry's traditional strategic and creative processes. Creative briefings and strategic planning have always been about stripping down rich and detailed stories, most of the time too complex to tell, to a simple, straightforward essence or slogan. But today, advertising needs rich and generous ideas, which stand firm in more immersive media and remain interesting after you've scratched the surface. More than ever, advertising needs people who can craft intricate, interesting and engaging stories.

■ **GENERAL MOTORS – CADILLAC**
■ Agency: Modernista
■ United States – 2007

My Cadillac Story is a web-based community and archive created by the revered American car manufacturer, where Cadillac fans are invited to share their stories about the classic car. The company chose passionate Cadillac drivers to kick off the campaign. Jay Leno, for instance, spoke about his '68 Cadillac, as well as his all-new '08 Cadillac CTS. He was one of several celebrities including Tiki Barber and Joan Jett to feature in the initiative, which encouraged visitors of all ages to create videos, write stories and record audio clips and upload them to a dedicated page on YouTube.

Cadillac successfully tapped into the nostalgia that many Americans feel for the brand by creating the perfect platform for current owners and future buyers to reminisce. Over 2.5 million people participated in My Cadillac Story, with more than 2,500 contributing by video, phone or text.

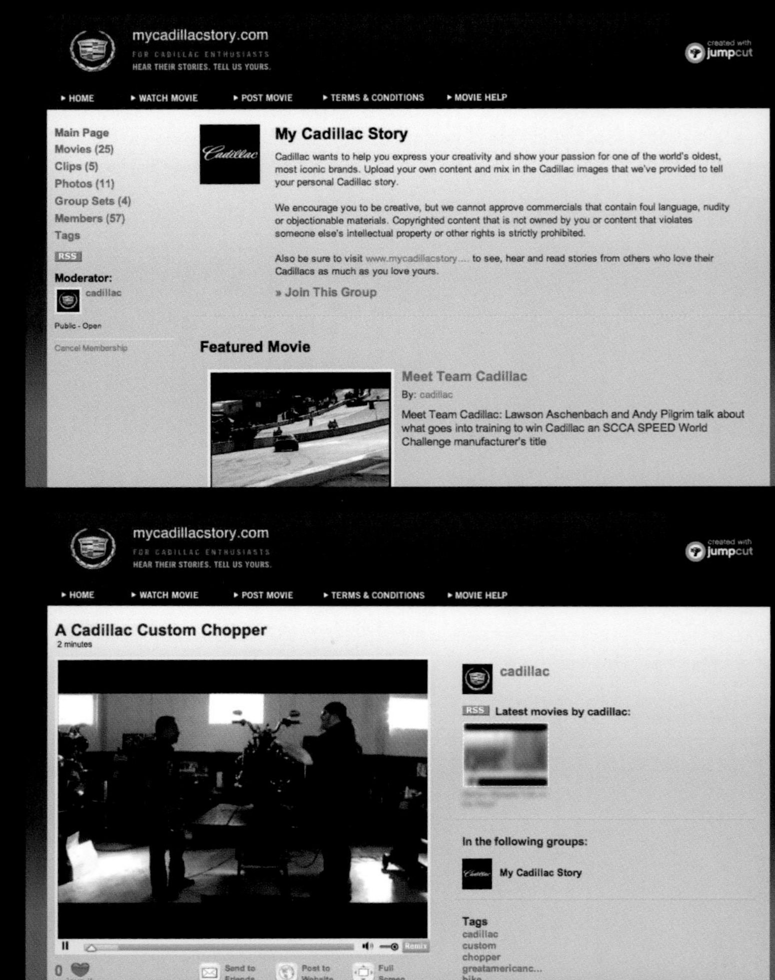

mycadillacstory.com
FOR CADILLAC ENTHUSIASTS
HEAR THEIR STORIES. TELL US YOURS.

▸ HOME ▸ WATCH MOVIE ▸ POST MOVIE ▸ TERMS & CONDITIONS ▸ MOVIE HELP

Jerry Franchi and his 1961 Convertible Coupe
49 seconds

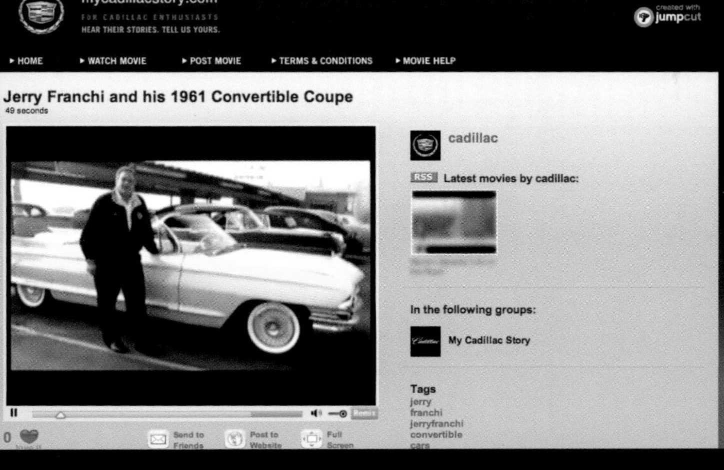

cadillac
RSS Latest movies by cadillac:
In the following groups:
My Cadillac Story
Tags
jerry
franchi
jerryfranchi
convertible

FEATURED STORY : Rajesh & Mohani Chainani

Rajesh & Mohani Chainani

My wife and I have always been big Cadillac enthusiasts, but our love for the brand truly blossomed when the CTS made its debut. Our first purchase was a 2004 model. We loved it so much that when the need came for another car, we happily added another CTS to the family tree. But to be 100% honest, over the last few years we were starting to lose our love for the brand. We read all of the positive reviews (Motor Trend, Car and Driver) about the redesigned CTS but we were not expecting much more than an over-hyped tuner car. We were soon to be pleasantly surprised.

Last Wednesday my wife and I were at the dealership taking care of our 2005 CTS when the delivery truck with the All-New 2008 CTS pulled in the back of the lot. Fortunately, the service representative asked us if we wanted to take a sneak peek. From the moment we laid eyes on the car, which was still on the truck, we knew this was not "Your Daddy's Cadillac." The car was backed in, so the front end of the

▸ Tell Us Your Story ▸ Email This Link

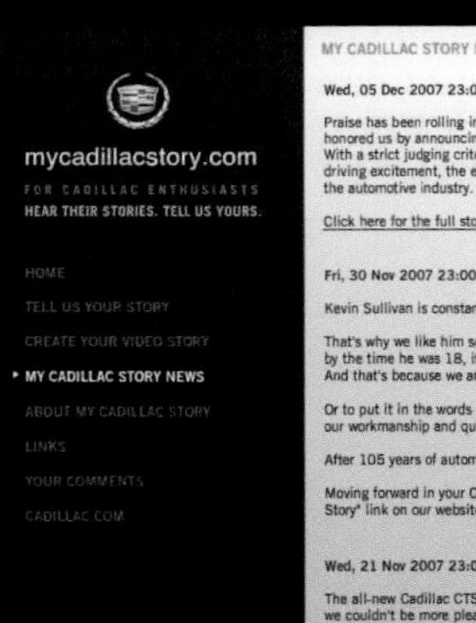

MY CADILLAC STORY NEWS

Wed, 05 Dec 2007 23:00:00 GMT

Praise has been rolling in non-stop for the all-new CTS. And now, Car and Driver has honored us by announcing the 2008 CTS as the Car and Driver's 10Best for 2008! With a strict judging criteria based on everything from performance details to over-all driving excitement, the elite Car and Driver 10Best award is one of the most coveted in the automotive industry. We're proud to say the CTS made the grade with flying colors.

Click here for the full story.

Fri, 30 Nov 2007 23:00:00 GMT

Kevin Sullivan is constantly trying to improve himself.

That's why we like him so much. After reading about the way he earned two Cadillacs by the time he was 18, it's clear why he feels such a strong connection to our vehicles. And that's because we are constantly trying to improve ourselves as well.

Or to put it in the words of Paul Forkus, whose story we received shortly after Kevin's, our workmanship and quality keep getting better from one year to the next.

After 105 years of automotive engineering, well... that's a lot of forward momentum.

Moving forward in your Cadillac? We'd love to hear about it. Click on the "Tell Us Your Story" link on our website. And share your Cadillac story with us.

Wed, 21 Nov 2007 23:00:00 GMT

The all-new Cadillac CTS was just named the 2008 Motor Trend Car of the Year™ and we couldn't be more pleased!

Nearly six decades ago, we were the first to win the golden calipers. They have now returned to their rightful owners. Come meet the car we've been building for the past 100 years at www.cadillac.com/allnewcts.

Fri, 16 Nov 2007 23:00:00 GMT

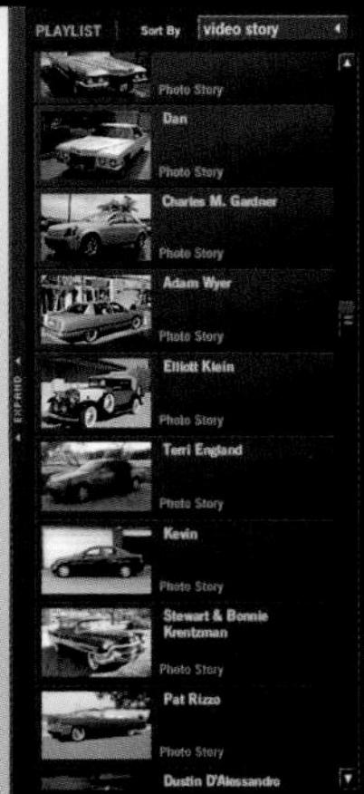

FEATURED STORY : Ryan Gregan

Ryan Gregan

My name is Ryan Gregan and I live in Washington Crossing, Pennsylvania. After many years of driving different automobiles I took a job in sales that required me to travel extensively. Naturally, comfort was a priority as I was going to be spending a great deal of time in the car. Previously I had a regular commute to work and comfort was not as much of an issue. The first car that came to mind was a Cadillac and I purchased a 2004 Seville SLS. The reason I chose Cadillac goes back to my childhood when a friend's father owned one. I remember when he first bought it and how he would talk extensively about how comfortable the car was. I also remember riding in it and being amazed at how comfortable the car was. Years later I had the opportunity to drive a Cadillac that my father had rented when his car was in the repair shop. Being one of the first cars I ever drove, it made a lasting impression. Recently in 2007, still spending a great deal of time in my car, I decided to start shopping around for a new one. I looked at all brands in fairness, knowing I probably would only buy an American car. While I was impressed and

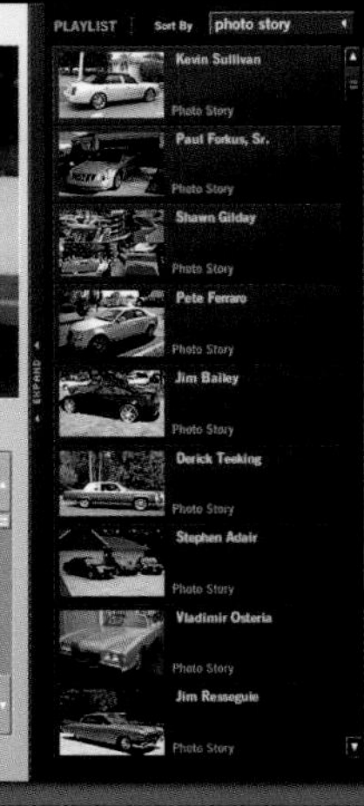

TELL US YOUR STORY

The Cadillac Story is built by storytellers. Be a part of the legacy. Hear their stories. Tell us yours.

We're glad you're interested in submitting your story and photos. We will review all submissions as fast as we can. Because of the sheer volume of stories we receive, we won't be able to publish all. However, we will be sure to feature the best stories that reveal the unique spirit of the people who love Cadillac.

Remember, in order to post your story on this site, we must receive it along with your Caddy pictures, your name, where you're from, plus the model and year of the Cadillac in each photo.

Video Story – YouTube-powered. Google-enhanced.
In co-operation with YouTube and Google, users can submit their stories, check out videos from other users, and maybe see some special surprises you won't find anywhere else. If you've got the story, we've got the audience. We currently do not support direct video uploads. However, videos uploaded to YouTube will also be considered for MyCadillacStory.com

Photo/Text Story
Did Dad borrow his father's Caddy to go on a first date with Mom? We'd like to hear about it. Send us your Cadillac stories and accompanying photos for mycadillacstory.com.

Think your Caddy pictures speak a thousand words? Then forget the story. Just send in the pics. Don't forget to include the model (and model year) of your car.

Keep it simple. JPGs under 1MB only. (No MPEGs or WAVs, please.)

Audio Story
Submit an audio story by phone to our toll-free number. Please try to keep your story to approximately 1 minute. You will ALSO need to PROVIDE us WITH your email address as part of your voice message as we will be contacting you if we choose your Cadillac story.

Remember, this number is for Cadillac stories ONLY. Any inquiries or comments for GM or Cadillac must go through the Cadillac website at http://www.cadillac.com/cadillacjsp/footer/contact_us.jsp

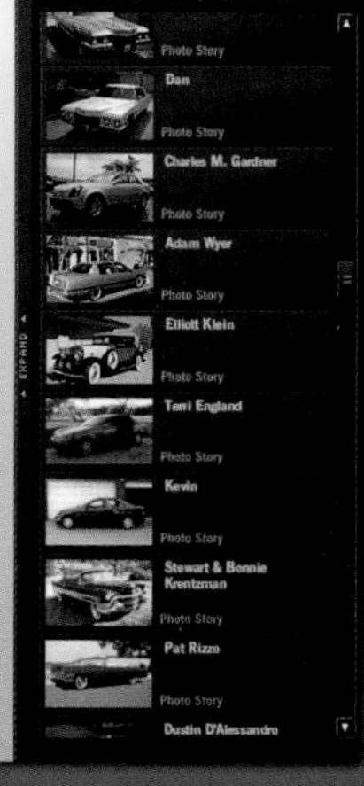

DIESEL
Agency: Vasava
Worldwide – 2005

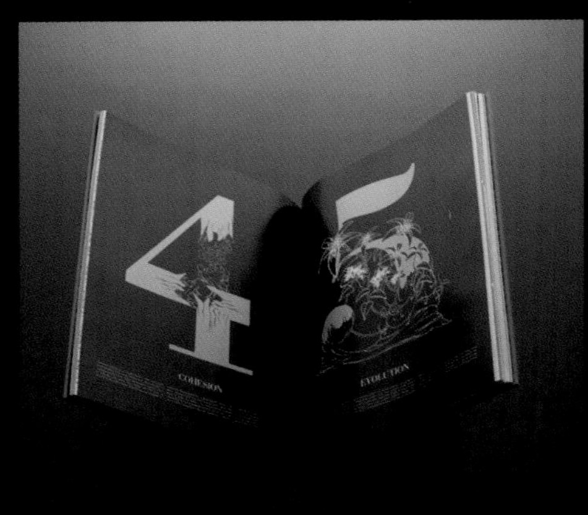

A book is a possession, outliving all traditional forms of advertising. To mark the fiftieth birthday of Diesel founder and president Renzo Rosso, the company decided to draw on the strengths of this format and chart its rich story to date. A combination of biography, history and vision of the future, *FIFTY* explores the ideas and attitude that propelled Diesel from its humble origins in jeans and workwear to its modern-day prestige status. It is the story of a company that thrives on creativity and has built its success on it. Five hefty chapters present a lively portrait of Renzo Rosso, key moments in Diesel's history, its innovative approach to retail and communication, its ongoing support of young creative talent, and Renzo's and Diesel's philosophy for the future.

The book itself is a genuine 'heavyweight', with a large hardcover format, impressive double gatefolds and a DVD of the brand's award-winning advertising, and was sold through traditional retail channels.

People are often surprised when you tell them that Diesel is headquartered in Italy. The name has such global resonance that it has never even occurred to them that Diesel might be an Italian brand. Renzo and his then partner Adriano Goldschmied were thinking internationally from the start, in 1978, when they chose a name that was spelt the same way all over the world. Its designers are a highly international crew, and its advertising agencies have been based in Stockholm, London, Amsterdam and Paris.

With its network of more than 5,000 points of sale around the world, and advertising that effortlessly crosses borders, Diesel is today part of an elite group of global brands. Some people consider "globalisation" a dirty word, but Renzo refers to a concept he calls "new globalisation".

"In many ways the world is made up not of nations, but of tribes," he says. "Everywhere you go there are groups of people who are inspired by the same sorts of music, movies and clothes. No matter what language they speak, they consume the same things. Diesel consumers are very much like that.

"But just as I have a strong sense of who I am and where I came from, I want to encourage that trait in others. I like the fact that people have their own culture and traditions. Years ago, taking the opposite approach to that of our competitors, we decided that we would make each of our stores different, to reflect the tastes of local consumers. We would seek advice from people who would be working in the stores and from local designers. That's why the store in London is totally different from the one in Paris. But also, the store in Covent Garden is different from the one in King's Road or the one in Carnaby Street. We don't treat consumers like some formless mass who blindly follow the same dress code."

Renzo adds that this is also the reason that Diesel's collection is so big. "You have very elaborate and complicated pieces down to relatively simple T-shirts, but all of them intrinsically Diesel. We expect people to adapt our clothes to their own identity. Diesel people can be 15 or 50, elegant or scruffy. They are multi-ethnic and multi-skilled. The one thing they have in common is a sense of liberty."

How they wear their jeans – and what with – may differ, but Diesel fans are a global tribe. Renzo believes in a new type of globalisation, which respects local cultures and values

FOR THOSE WHO DON'T REMEMBER ALL OF DIESEL'S EXPLOITS, THIS CATWALK SHOW COVERS 25 YEARS OF COOL CLOTHING AND CRAZY ADVERTISING

Agency: Imagination
United Kingdom – 2007

'THIS IS AN EXCITING CHALLENGE, EXPLORING NEW WAYS OF DELIVERING AND TARGETING COMEDY IN A TOTALLY ORIGINAL, INTERACTIVE FORMAT.'

HENRY NORMAL, MANAGING DIRECTOR OF BABY COW PRODUCTIONS

'FORD MANAGED TO BRING TOGETHER A DIVERSITY OF PEOPLE FROM AROUND THE WORLD TO SOLVE AN OPEN SOURCE QUESTION: WHERE ARE THE JONESES?'

DAVID BAUSOLA, HEAD OF INSIGHT FOR DIGITAL COMMUNICATIONS AT IMAGINATION, IN *CONTAGIOUS MAGAZINE*

Where are the Joneses? was an interactive online sitcom sponsored by Ford that invited the public to comment on each episode and contribute to the storyline, day by day. The series followed Dawn and Ian Jones, played by comedy actors Emma Fryer and Neil Edmond, as they travelled around Europe in search of numerous siblings by their sperm donor father. Each day, their adventures were filmed and uploaded to the site, and viewers could dictate the following day's events by stipulating who the Joneses came into contact with and the places they explored. Script collaboration happened through a wiki, where viewers could create storylines, write scripts and even submit videos and images. Flickr, Twitter, MySpace and Facebook were all access points to the story and characters. Branding throughout was minimal, with the most visible element being the Ford S-MAX that the Joneses travelled around in.

The online sitcom achieved a high ranking in the blogosphere due to the bloggers who helped to shape and define the project. *Where are the Joneses?* illustrates brands' role as commissioners of media content, distributed with an open media licence across a range of different channels, rather than relying solely on traditional formats such as television. Seven hours of comedy were produced over three months using a team of just five people on the road, smashing the perception that the production of quality entertainment should be controlled by broadcast media.

■ Agency: n/a
■ Italy, Norway, United Kingdom, Germany – since 2003

Illy's marketing approach has always centred on the enhancement of the coffee-drinking experience, among others through its iconic Illy Collection of artist-designed cups. *Illystories* is a series of short books that the company distributes free of charge in cafés serving Illy coffee. The stories, lasting just a few pages, are the ideal length for anyone on a short coffee break. The concept originated from the 'Festivaletteratura' in Mantua, an Italian literary festival that Illy has supported since 1997, which aims to give a voice to young European writers under the age of thirty-two.

In 2005, *illystories* expanded with a new series by established authors. The theme, which is different each year, reflects the Illy world. Travel was the subject of the first series, the café as a meeting place in the second, and art and expression in the third.

Cover art for the *illystories* is created by students at international art schools. Illy also gives people a chance to meet the *illystories* authors by organizing public readings at European literary festivals.

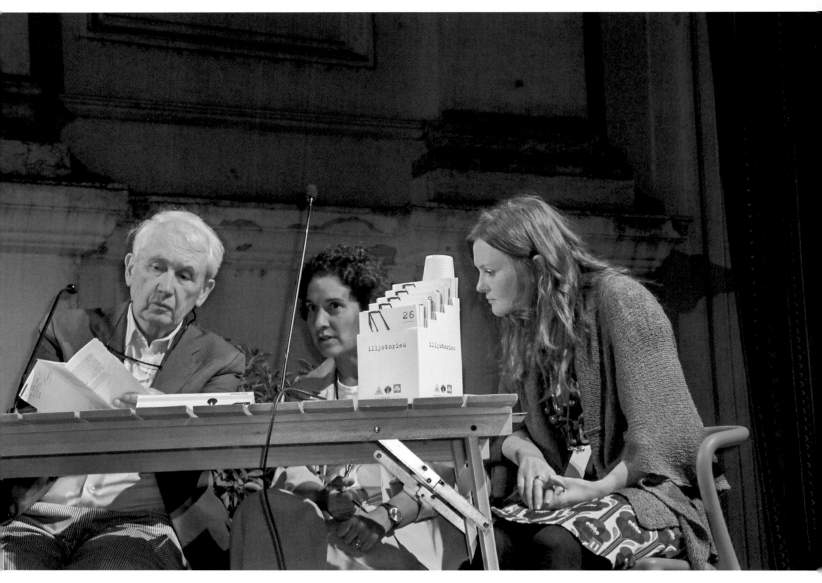

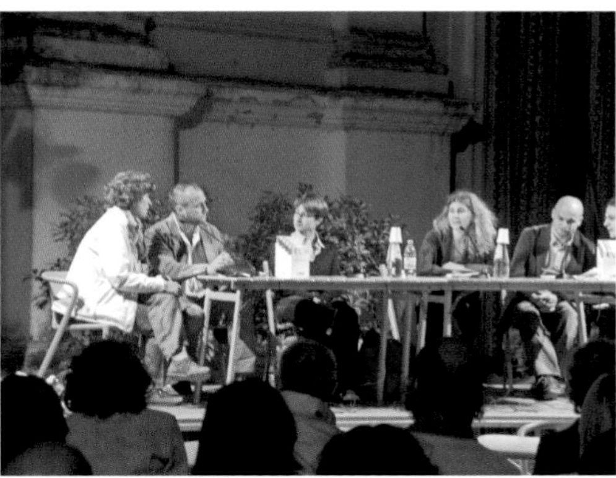

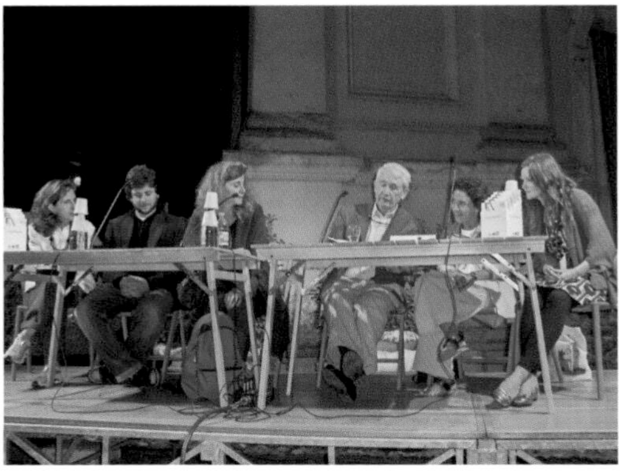

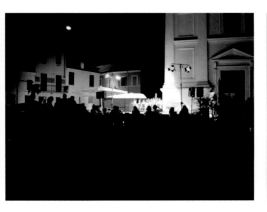

JETBLUE

Agency: JWT New York
United States – 2007

In order to capture the positive word-of-mouth surrounding its brand, JetBlue toured twelve American cities with a 'Story Booth' to record customers' impressions of the company. Passers-by could simply pop in and talk about their experiences with the airline company, guided by a virtual flight attendant inside the booth. One man spoke of his in-flight marriage proposal. A couple described how a JetBlue pilot gave up his hotel room for them at 1 am.

In total, more than a million impressions were recorded. The resulting content was used to create sixteen TV commercials, twelve online viral videos, a half-hour in-flight video and two cinema adverts.

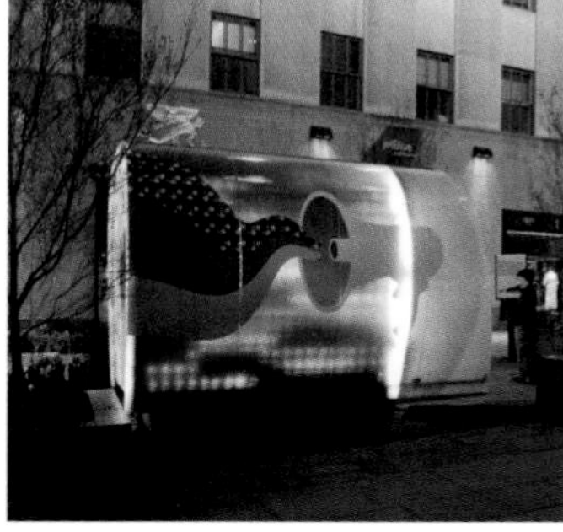

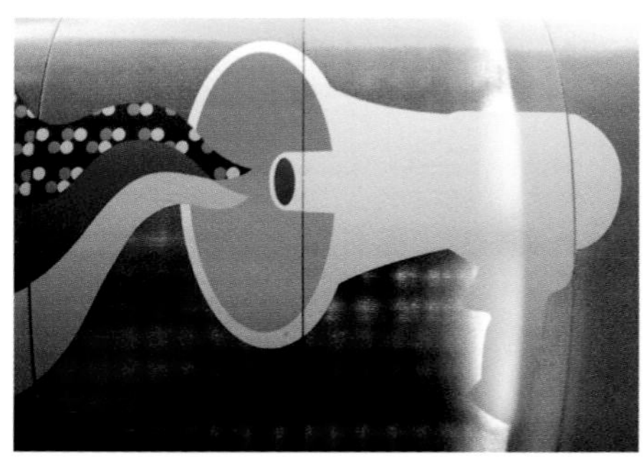

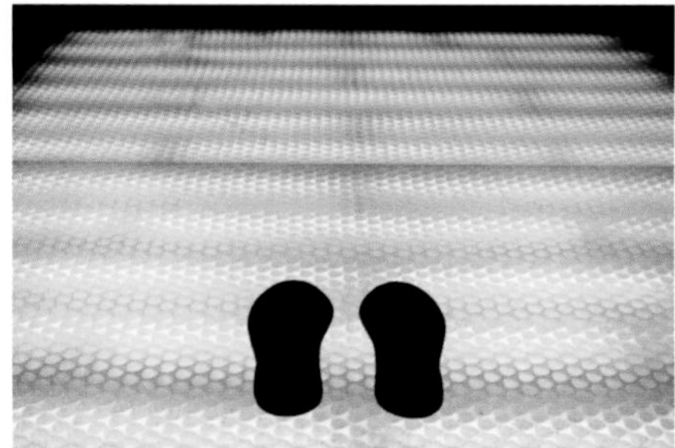

'WHEN PEOPLE FEEL THEY OWN YOUR BRAND, JUST GIVE THEM A MEGAPHONE TO AMPLIFY THEIR VOICES.'

TY MONTAGUE, CO-PRESIDENT AND CHIEF CREATIVE OFFICER OF JWT, NEW YORK

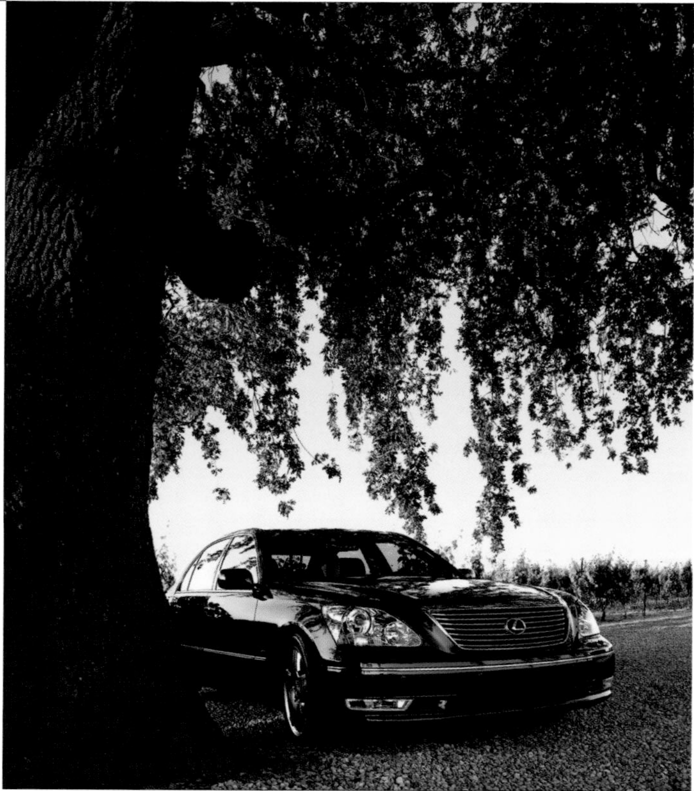

Chapter One:

The Pursuit Begins

The Southern California landscape may be less scenic than that of the Bavarian countryside, but if the autobahn is paradise for speed demons in Euro sedans, the 405 freeway is a fantasyland for rubberneckers.

Cars sashay along this highway like models down the runway—although during rush hour, mannequins in a window may be a better metaphor.

The seemingly unbroken chain of cars between San Diego and Los Angeles reveals just how far Lexus has come since 1989. The LS 400, the flagship sedan that grew to become the LS 430, has been joined by a full complement of vehicles—near-luxury sedans, sport coupes, sport sedans and three different "luxury utility vehicles." And they seem to own Southern California's freeways. Lexus' circle-L may lack the history of the three-pointed star or the blue-and-white quartered disc, but not the popularity.

When does a car truly become part of the American landscape? When it starts appearing in blockbuster movies. In *Three Kings*, the 1999 film about a few American soldiers trying to smuggle gold out of Saddam Hussein's Iraq at the end of the Gulf War, one of the GIs says he's going to use some of his cut to buy a Lexus convertible. The remark prompts a debate that continues through the better part of the movie about whether or not Lexus makes a convertible. (It didn't then; it does now.) When Steven Spielberg went about imagining the future in his 2002 film *Minority Report*, he dreamed up an electric car that climbs the exterior of buildings—and wears a Lexus badge. (See "Lexus 2054: The *Minority Report* Car," pages 194–5.)

Lexus' most enduring impact on

Coming to America

Every Lexus built in Japan comes to America by ship (for North American Lexus SUVs, see pages 182–7). Thousands of cars and SUVs are parked with great precision inside the giant cargo vessels, whose interiors are designed to fit the maximum number.

After Lexus vehicles are driven off the ships—here at the large port in Long Beach, California—they're washed and then parked at a kanban—a staging area for the final Lexus inspection line.

The Lexus Story is the first in-depth account of the rise of the American luxury car brand. Written by a leading journalist who had unprecedented access to all aspects of the company, the book offers a rare glimpse into the private world of Lexus – from its leaders, executives, designers and engineers, to its seldom seen archives.

The book opens in 1989 with the launch of the company's flagship sedan. The idea of a powerful luxury sedan tailored to the American market seemed antithetical for an established car manufacturer that was primarily recognized for economy products. After six years in development, the work of more than 1,400 engineers, hundreds of prototypes, an investment of $1 bn (£510 m), and the support of and close collaboration with the industry's top dealers, Lexus charted new territory. The company reinvented the luxury car market, introducing new levels of service, customer satisfaction and quality that other car manufacturers scrambled to emulate. With it, Lexus moved from being an unlikely outsider to becoming the luxury leader.

Bound in leather, the hardcover book integrates luxury in all aspects, from its sleek protective box and the three-dimensional chrome Lexus badge on the cover, to the slick full-colour images.

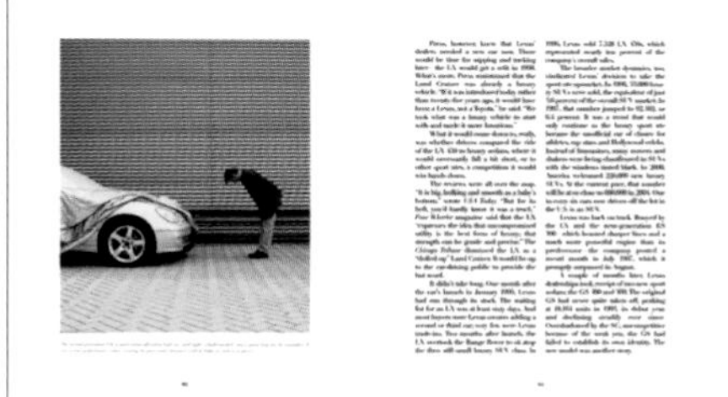

'THIS COMPANY WAS BORN OUT OF A SIMPLE GOAL: TO BUILD THE WORLD'S FINEST LUXURY CAR. HOW THAT HAPPENED MAKES A FASCINATING STORY.'

DENNY CLEMENTS, LEXUS GROUP VICE-PRESIDENT AND GENERAL MANAGER

BEASTORYTELLER
LINCOLN-MERCURY
Agency: Kirt Gunn & Associates
United States – 2006–7

Lovely By Surprise and *The Neverything* are two interconnected series of online short films about an author whose fiction takes over her life. Written and directed by Kirt Gunn and sponsored by the Lincoln-Mercury Division of Ford, they tell the two sides of the same story – one presented by Lincoln, the other by Mercury. *Lovely By Surprise* focuses on the author slowly losing her grip on reality as she becomes absorbed in the story she's weaving, while *The Neverything* is set in the world of her fictional characters, two brothers living on a boat in the middle of the desert and subsisting on a diet of milk and breakfast cereal.

Both storylines later came together in an independent, full-length feature film, titled *Lovely By Surprise*, showing how one of the fictional characters escapes into the real world and comes into contact with his author. The film premiered at the Seattle International Film Festival in June 2007, where it was awarded a Special Jury Prize.

EXIT

NAU

Agency: n/a

United States – 2007–8

Portland-based outdoor-clothing company Nau was set up by a small group of professionals who drew on their impressive industry experience at Patagonia and Nike to reinvent the outdoor category. They set out by committing the company to sustainability and social justice in every aspect of its operations, pledging to donate 5 per cent of sales to environmental and humanitarian charities, but giving shoppers the final say as to where their money should go. Customers in store could go to one of the touch screens to view short documentaries about each partner organization and were asked to pick from a menu of 'Partners for Change' when they paid at the counter.

As a business that explored the implications of sustainability across the board, Nau naturally had to decide on a form of sustainable marketing. They came up with the theme of storytelling because, as co-founder Ian Yolles explains, 'authentic stories that are culturally relevant and convey meaning get passed along from person to person. They also have the ability to transcend time and culture. We're also interested in fostering dialogue and conversation about positive change. Good stories naturally provoke thought, generate inquiry and foster genuine interaction.'

This concept of positive change was central to the company's strategy of building the brand and engaging customers. Nau was launched through a blog called The Thought Kitchen – based on the idea that a party always centres around the kitchen where there are plenty of walls to lean on and people are energized by all the food and drink around them. In another section of the Nau website, The Collective, users could share in thought-provoking video- and image-based stories from a community of artists, athletes and activists as well as submit their own content that reflected Nau's values.

Nau also used its retail environments as venues for storytelling. With the opening of its first four stores, it hosted 'SEE(D) Change' events. In each location a resident 'storyteller' was invited to meet members of the local community. Guests included Alex Steffen, founder and editor of Worldchanging.com, Charles Shaw, editor of *Conscious Choice Magazine*, and Randy Gragg, urban design and architecture critic for *The Oregonian* newspaper.

Unfortunately, Nau was forced to close its books after nineteen months of business due to the risk-averse capital market, despite a strong community of supporters and performing sales.

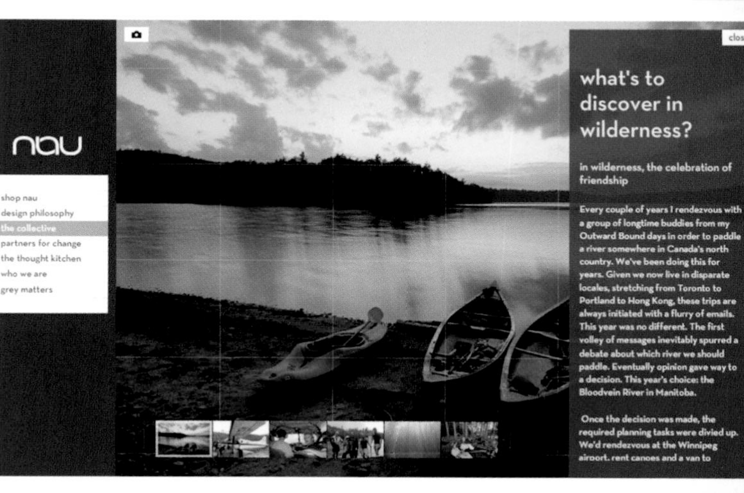

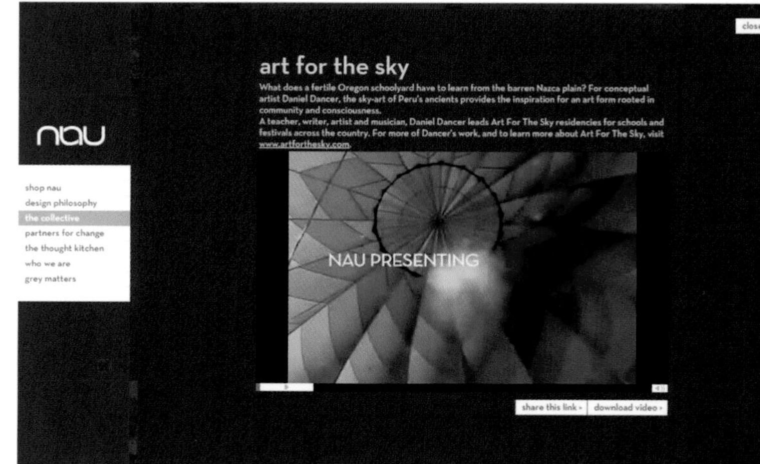

UNILEVER (SUAVE)/SPRINT

Agency: MindShare Entertainment

United States – 2007

'WE PUT A LOT OF UNIQUE ELEMENTS TOGETHER – USER-GENERATED CONTENT WITH TOP-NAME TALENT AND ONLINE, TELEVISION, RETAIL AND MUSIC COMPONENTS – TO CREATE SOMETHING SPECIAL. IT'S ONE OF THE MOST COMPLICATED ENTERTAINMENT PROJECTS WE'VE CREATED.'

DAVID LANG, MANAGING PARTNER OF MINDSHARE ENTERTAINMENT, IN *THE HOLLYWOOD REPORTER*

Toiletry brand Suave and mobile phone company Sprint wanted to appeal to busy mothers. They came up with the idea of creating the first-ever mother-focused web series, *In the Motherhood*, revolving around the hectic lives of three mother friends. The webisodes, written by Hollywood screenwriters, featured TV sitcom star Leah Remini, who also juggles her roles as an actress, wife and mother to her 3-year-old daughter.

Real-life mothers were given the opportunity to contribute their own stories on a dedicated website, inthemotherhood.com. The online mother community voted for and nominated the best entries, which were then polished and incorporated into the webisodes.

The show could be seen on mobile television site Sprint TV and Suave.com, and was publicized on the *Ellen DeGeneres Show* and in *People* magazine. Sprint and Suave also created an online community, hosted by MSN, offering games, blogging and peer-to-peer messaging. The campaign was the best-performing webisode series to date and broke all MSN records for a project of its kind.

'WE WANT TO GIVE MOMS A REAL COMMUNITY WHERE THEY CAN SHARE IN THE TRIALS, TRIBULATIONS AND JOYS OF BEING MOTHERS....'

SARAH JENSEN, DIRECTOR OF UNILEVER HAIR CARE

BEASTORYTELLER
VOLKSWAGEN
Agencies: DDB Germany/DDB Berlin/Tribal DDB
Germany – 2006

SONDERAUSGABE

Grevenbroicher Tagblatt

Zeitung für Grevenbroich und die Region

Horst Schlämmer hat jetzt Führerschein

Deutschlandweit Grevenbroicher Prominenter besteht bravourös Fahrprüfung

To reinforce Volkswagen's image in Germany as 'the people's car', a story of epic proportions was invented starring 'the people's man' Horst Schlämmer, a popular comedy character played by Hape Kerkeling. The collaboration involved creating a completely new chapter in Schlämmer's life – the story of his attempt to get a driving licence in order to improve his chances with the ladies.

Fans were hooked on the story for more than two months. A video-blog was set up featuring documentary-style clips and a diary for people to follow Horst's progress day by day, from his first lesson to his driving test. The blog allowed people to communicate directly with their hero and involved them in the adventure. The story quickly spread through blogs, online magazines, video-sharing websites, podcasts, newspapers, magazines and extensive TV coverage. Once the story was drawn to a close, a website was created to document the adventure. Within a week it had topped the German podcast charts and reached number two in the blog charts.

BE24/7

On 19 March 2007, 23-year-old Californian Justin Kan attached a webcam to his cap and broadcast his day-to-day existence 24/7 on his own channel, Justin.tv. He recorded everything he did live, however mundane or random, from going to the bathroom to going out on a date. As the camera was right at his eye level, viewers could literally see the world from his point of view. Justin promised to 'wear the camera until the day he dies'. A few months later, Justin.tv developed into a proper network of diverse channels, providing a platform for each and every individual to transmit their own lives. Justin.tv wasn't the first to experiment with 24/7 broadcasting; previous ventures include various reality television formats, the 1999 film *EDtv* which tells the story of an ordinary guy whose life is the subject of a 24/7 cable television show, and a host of other online pioneers. While many similar sites and platforms have popped up, Justin.tv was the first to apply the term 'lifecasting' in this context, describing the live broadcasting of events in a person's life through digital media. It allows anyone with a computer, a webcam, a microphone and an internet connection to broadcast to a global audience, twenty-four hours a day, seven days a week.

These experiments and online platforms are merely the most prominent exponents of an increasingly 24/7 society. In the digital era, the internet has given consumers permanent access to companies and brands. The advent of ubiquitous online access through mobile phones has only accelerated the development of this 24/7 mindset. For the new generation, communication is live and ongoing, whether it's lifecasting, live streaming, live chat or instant messaging.

As people grow accustomed to having permanent and instant access to everything, they expect the same from brands. For today's young generation, it's hard to imagine a time when communication with a company was confined to a limited nine-to-five time slot; when companies were not yet able to respond to every customer whim whatever the time of day (or night). In a landscape where anything 'live' seems to do the trick, a brand needs to be equally 'live'. In other words, in a world that never sleeps, people expect brands that never sleep.

This evolution has affected the way brand campaigns are designed and constructed. Rather than being finished items that can no longer be corrected, adjusted or refined once they have been launched into the outside world, digital technology has enabled campaigns to become living organisms that take shape over time as the result of continued interaction with end users. What we're witnessing is the arrival of a new kind of brand communication, one that is no longer about on–off moments or analogue interruptions to people's lives but about continuous, uninterrupted, 24/7 brand experiences. Campaigns are emerging as non-stop live streams rather than blips on people's radars. Audi's 24/7 television channel (see pages 164–5) is one such example.

This shift has an impact on how the communications industry can and should think about campaigns. Rather than letting go of the finished creative material at a specific point in time, from a layout being sent to newspapers or a spot being finalized in post-production, the creative journey only truly begins from the moment the material is sent out into the world. Round-the-clock communication is alive, constantly changing, never-ending, allowing permanent interactivity between a brand and its audience, as companies such as Diesel and Volkswagen have been quick to pick up on. Specifically designed to evolve, their respective Heidies (pages 170–1) and Gypsy Cab Project (pages 172–3) campaigns embraced the live sensation, giving the audience the feeling that they were witnessing something changing as it happened.

'AUDI LOOKS TO BE VORSPRUNG DURCH TECHNIK NOT JUST IN WHAT IT SAYS, BUT IN HOW IT SAYS IT.'

MARK BOYD, CREATIVE DIRECTOR AND HEAD OF CONTENT AT BBH LONDON

In 2005, Audi made broadcasting history with the launch of its own 24/7 digital TV channel. It was the very first car manufacturer in the world to do so, and the first brand-specific entertainment channel in Europe. It took fourteen months of lobbying at both EC and Ofcom levels for Audi to be granted the first self-promotional licence in Europe.

The Audi Channel broadcasts product-related 'infotainment' during the day and more general entertainment-driven programmes in the evenings and at weekends, such as coverage of motor racing, amateur golf tournaments and polo matches. It reaches 8 million homes through Sky Digital satellite TV, and cost Audi around £1.7 m ($3.5 m) to set up, and around the same in running costs each year.

In 2007, Audi extended its non-stop entertainment drive to include two new on-demand platforms: the peer-to-peer network Joost and Nokia N-series mobile phones. Joost, the world's first broadband-quality internet TV service, offers some of the Audi Channel's most popular content, including the latest product ranges, test drives, documentaries, interviews and upcoming events. All Nokia N-series users can download one-minute clips from longer Audi Channel programmes.

The results so far have been impressive. According to Audi, on average 25,000 people watch the Channel on Sky every week. Of those people in the market for a new car, 58 per cent view the Channel during the purchasing process, watching it an estimated eleven times for around 31 minutes per session – that's a total of just over five-and-a-half hours. Ninety-seven per cent of those watching have been positive about their experiences, and 48 per cent of them are more likely to buy an Audi as a result.

COCA-COLA

Agency: Formavision
United States–2007

The dazzling $100 m (£50 m) New World of Coca-Cola in Atlanta is a permanent showcase of the Coca-Cola universe where visitors can immerse themselves in the story behind the brand. It succeeds the World of Coca-Cola, which ran between 1990 and 2007. The museum is expected to draw in 1.5 million visitors a year and is inspired by the brand's themes of optimism and happiness.

Coca-Cola's global reach is highlighted throughout. There is a large-scale mural, an abstract representation of the earth inspired in part by the works of Galileo and Copernicus, with positive words displayed in a range of international languages. In the futuristic 'Taste It!' lab, visitors can sample the 400 soft drinks that the Coca-Cola Company produces and distributes around the world, at a series of tasting stations that have been arranged geographically. The lab features murals and videos that tell the story of the planet's water cycle, the result of a collaboration with multimedia collective Tronic Studio and French illustrators Antoine & Manuel.

‘COCA-COLA ASKED US SEVERAL TIMES TO VISIT THE OLD WORLD OF COKE, BUT WE ALWAYS REFUSED BECAUSE WE WANTED TO START FRESH. TO THIS DAY, I STILL DON’T KNOW WHAT IT LOOKED LIKE.’ **SEBASTIEN AGNEESSENS**, FOUNDER OF FORMAVISION

AMERICA
coke
ASIA

AFRICA

BE 24/7
DIESEL
Agency: FarFar
Sweden – 2007

To launch its new underwear collection, Diesel created an interactive online show that ran for five days non-stop. The campaign starred the Heidies, two gorgeous but slightly unhinged characters set on fame. The premise was simple: having stolen the new, unreleased Diesel Intimate collection and kidnapped a sales assistant, the Heidies locked themselves (and him) in a hotel room; they then hijacked Diesel.com and turned it into their own show.

Visitors to the website could control their own experience of the show to some extent by choosing from five live video feeds from different angles in the room. Users' chat messages and blogs were shown immediately and unmoderated on Diesel's website.

Pictures and videos taken by the Heidies and their hostage were also uploaded in an unedited format to Diesel.com and other popular sites. Viewers could manipulate the story by telling the girls what to do or voting for certain tasks to be carried out (such as choosing between waxing their hostage's legs or putting thirty-seven ice cubes down his pants). Some even became protagonists and earned themselves 'celebrity status' in the online community.

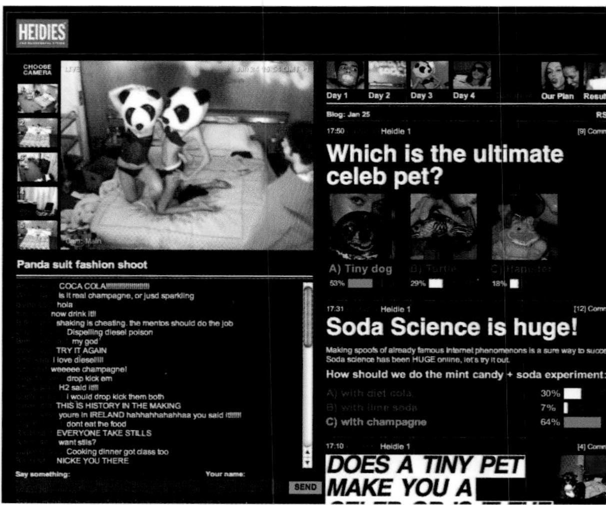

'I WANT 5 YEARS OF HEIDIES!!!'

FAN MESSAGE

In order to position the Rabbit (Golf) as the ultimate city car, Volkswagen launched 'The Gypsy Cab Project'. The fourteen-day event in New York was designed to uncover and record on hidden camera all the things that make urban driving truly unique.

Steve, a filmmaker from Colorado who'd never been to New York, was put behind the wheel of a Rabbit-turned-cab. His mission: to talk a hundred people into swapping their knowledge and experiences of city-driving for a free ride. Passengers ranged from an Asian superstar to an elderly gentleman on his way to a clinic.

All conversations were captured live on four spy cameras and four Mac Minis stored in the wheel well of the car. The footage was then broadcast – initially raw and later edited – on the Gypsy Cab website, for all to view. A blend of documentary film and cultural research, it was like everything else in New York – totally unpredictable.

'ONE OF OUR LOGISTICAL CHALLENGES WITH GYPSY CAB WAS TO FIND A WAY TO MOUNT FOUR CAMERAS IN THE VEHICLE AND RECORD EVERYTHING SO WE COULD EDIT IT LATER.'

MARCELINO ALVAREZ, INTERACTIVE PRODUCER AT CRISPIN PORTER + BOGUSKY

- Asphalteroid
- Back Porching
- Blinker Slinger
- Block Buzzard
- Bumper Broadcasting
- Carmakazi
- **Curb Rash**
- Dial Hunting
- Eye Contract
- False Alignment
- Freeway Pick
- Hand Hooking
- Hatch Hiker

Curb Rash: (kerb ra sh)
To scrape your rims on the curb when parking. These scars mark you as an urban driver.

"I got a little curb rash pulling into that space. No biggie. It's not like it rolls any slower."

GypsyCabProject
100 fares in 14 days to uncover what it takes to be the ultimate city driver.

Back to the map ›

042

Are you kidding me? These guys TOOK ME to a concert. Sure, I gave them a ride...but they offered me a ticket to a band that I love just to take them to New Jersey to see a heavy metal concert. I knew we would get along fine because we had the metal in common, but the truth is that we clicked on lots of levels...music was just the catalyst. I hope these guys realize that they met the real "me" and that I might be promoting a car but only because I like the car and I get to meet people in the process. These are affluent kick-ass Colombian "dudes" who just happen to love the metal. Thanks guys!!

hop on board **favorite fares** about the project city driving dictionary

Back to the map ›

075

These gals were from Switzerland. They came back to "the City" because they said they missed it. They gushed about how beautiful and cool Switzerland is and how I should check it out. "But" they said, "it's not New York" and then they giggled like little girls.

hop on board **favorite fares** about the project city driving dictionary

BE TRANSPARENT

When English bobbies noticed that a crime had been committed, they would blow their whistle and thereby alert both law enforcement officers and the general public of danger. The later use of the term 'whistleblower', whereby current or former employees report on the misconduct of an organization, is derived from this practice. Whistleblowers, although small in number, have always played an important role in revealing a company's malpractices to the outside world.

You could argue that today's internet culture is breeding a nation of whistleblowers. While the English bobbies had their whistles, the internet has given today's employees unparalleled access to publishing, making it increasingly easy for them to speak out about anything happening within the company walls. The more competing sources of information exist on any given company, the more transparent that company is likely to be. Microsoft alone has more than 4,500 employee bloggers, who are free to speak their mind about whatever is going on. Together, these voices constitute an enormous flow of information, creating great transparency throughout the company's daily business operations.

The internet has not just altered the quantity of conversations but also their quality. People tend to speak more openly, informally and directly online, embracing dialogue and criticism. Robert Scoble, a reputed ex-Microsoft blogger and co-author of *Naked Conversations: How Blogs are Changing the Way Companies Talk with Customers* (2006), advises any corporate blogger to tell the truth, the whole truth and nothing but the truth: 'If your competitor has a product that's better than yours, link to it. You might as well. We'll find it anyway.'

More importantly, the digital revolution is creating transparency outside the four walls of a company, breeding an army of vigilante reporters, reviewers, critics and citizen-journalists, eager to report on every encounter they have had with a brand or company. Together, they are transforming organizations from closed entities into lumps of Swiss cheese, enabling anybody to look right through them. For every business or product category imaginable, no matter how niche or obscure, there is a vast array of specialized forums, blogs and review sites that mercilessly judge the genuine qualities of a product or the company's true colours. This level of transparency has made some companies increasingly vulnerable to small mistakes, blatant errors, inconsistent behaviour or empty promises. It has rewarded other companies for actually walking the talk.

The result is what *Wired* has baptized 'radical transparency': 'It is a strange and abrupt reversal of corporate values. Not long ago, the only public statements a company ever made were professionally written press releases and the rare, stage-managed speech by the CEO. Now firms spill information in torrents, posting internal memos and strategy goals, letting everyone from the top dog to shop-floor workers blog publicly about what their firm is doing right – and wrong.'

For brands, being transparent is about responding openly to the conversations that take place about their products and services, proactively creating the platform where these conversations can take place and giving people more direct and unfiltered access to whatever is going on inside the company. The only thing brands can no longer do in this see-through age is hide behind a curtain of marketing fluff. They need to show their true colours, whether it's by inviting consumers to have a look behind the scenes, letting insiders spread the word or simply revealing their processes more openly.

BE TRANSPARENT
DELL
Agency: n/a
Worldwide – since 2006

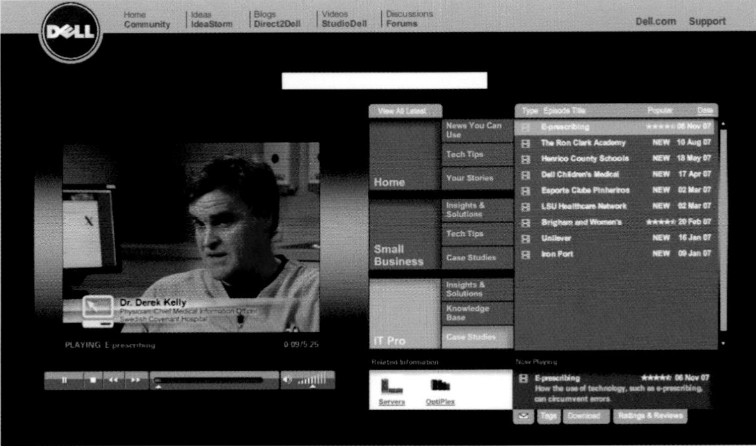

'IF YOU OPEN THE LINES OF COMMUNICATION, CUSTOMERS WILL TELL YOU WHAT IS WRONG WITH YOUR BUSINESS. PROBABLY THE BEST TIME TO LAUNCH A BLOG IS WHEN THINGS AREN'T GOING SO WELL.'

LIONEL MENCHACA, DIGITAL MEDIA MANAGER AT DELL

Dell learned its lesson in transparency the hard way through the Dell Hell PR disaster. When one blogger, Jeff Jarvis, started complaining about Dell's apparent reluctance to listen to customers, it was quickly picked up by other bloggers and eventually by national news media. The incident painfully laid bare how little Dell was listening and responding to customer complaints and influenced public perceptions of the company to such an extent that, according to market researchers, the firm had 'sustained long-term damage to its brand image'.

Having learned from the experience, Dell set up a series of digital media initiatives, with one thing in common: to give customers a way of interacting and sending feedback to the company, leading to a more transparent communication process. The first initiative was an internal blog, called Direct2Dell. The blog attracts thousands of readers and has well over a million page views each month. The blog was also launched in Chinese, Norwegian and Spanish, making Dell the first computer systems company to open a corporate blog in Spanish.

'At our worst point, almost 50 per cent of the commentary was negative,' says Lionel Menchaca, Digital Media Manager at Dell. 'That made it easy for us to decide to jump in. These negative conversations were happening with or without us, and it was pretty clear we had a better chance if we entered those negative discussions. Today, we're seeing about 23 per cent negative. While that's moving in the right direction, there's plenty of progress to be made.'

A second initiative is StudioDell, which is designed to help people get the most from their Dell experience. Through videos and podcasts, Dell shares expertise on emerging technologies through simple video and audio tutorials. There are three channels, based on the type of user (Home, Small Business or IT Pro).

Dell IdeaStorm, a third initiative, allows customers to participate in the development and enhancement of Dell's products and services by sharing their ideas online. Products based on customers' ideas have already been developed.

SUPPORT FORUMS

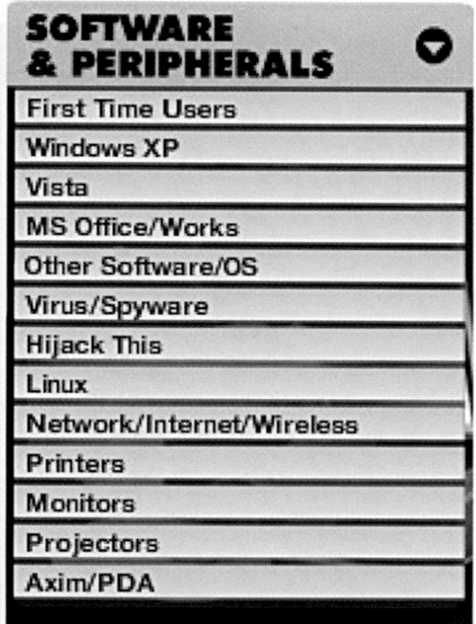

DISCUSSION FORUMS

BE TRANSPARENT
INNOCENT DRINKS
Agency: n/a
United Kingdom – since 1998

Founded in 1998 by three college friends, Innocent has become the UK's fastest-growing food and drink business in less than a decade. Not only does Innocent make pure and natural smoothie drinks, but it is a brand known and praised for its honest and transparent approach to business and marketing.

Top left: When Innocent decided to trial smoothies for children in seventy McDonald's restaurants in the UK, a meeting was held at which the entire Innocent team were able to air their concerns. Expecting the inevitable consumer backlash, the founders explained on their blog the reasons for climbing into bed with a company whose values so starkly differed from their own, declaring that the deal would mean that 'more kids would get the opportunity to eat more fruit'.

Response from hardcore fans was far from positive. Hundreds of comments appeared on Innocent's website, with many people vowing to stop drinking Innocent smoothies unless the company pulled out. Yet Innocent tried to track and contact every negative blogger on the website to personally explain why Innocent did the trial with McDonald's. The company didn't necessarily succeed in changing people's minds but they did convince the majority to respect Innocent's decision.

Centre: From very early on, Innocent declared in all transparency how much of its packaging was made of recycled plastic, always admitting it was 'working on the rest'. In September 2007, Innocent bottles were at last made from 100 per cent recycled plastic, a world first.

Bottom: Visiting the London HQ is also encouraged on the packaging of most Innocent products, and interested parties are given a tour and a bag of free smoothies. People can also contact the people at Innocent by ringing the quirkily named 'banana phone'.

innocent
pure fruit smoothie

MCDONALD'S
Agency: TBWA\London
United Kingdom – 2007

As a response to the negative publicity generated by Morgan Spurlock's film *Super Size Me* (2004) and Eric Schlosser's book *Fast Food Nation* (2001), McDonald's decided to opt for a more transparent communications approach. Shunning its traditional response of 'no comment', the company decided to enter into the debates going on around it. In both Australia and the United Kingdom, McDonald's opened its doors and revealed what went on behind the scenes.

In the United Kingdom, the fast-food giant invited ordinary people with a sceptical and yet open-minded approach to become 'quality scouts'. More than 1,000 people responded to a radio and press recruitment campaign. The selected few – chosen for their cynicism and curiosity – visited cattle farms, processing plants and restaurants. They interviewed nutritionists and animal welfare experts, and brought their kids along to ask the difficult questions. They filmed and wrote reports, which they put their names to online (makeupyourownmind.co.uk). The scouts' findings were published in magazines and restaurants. Recruits could create their own advertising, with minimal agency input so their stories did not feel stage-managed.

The website also gave everybody the chance to ask any questions. Because there was no censorship from McDonald's, even the toughest and harshest questions were published and answered, including 'Is there really cow sperm in the burgers?'

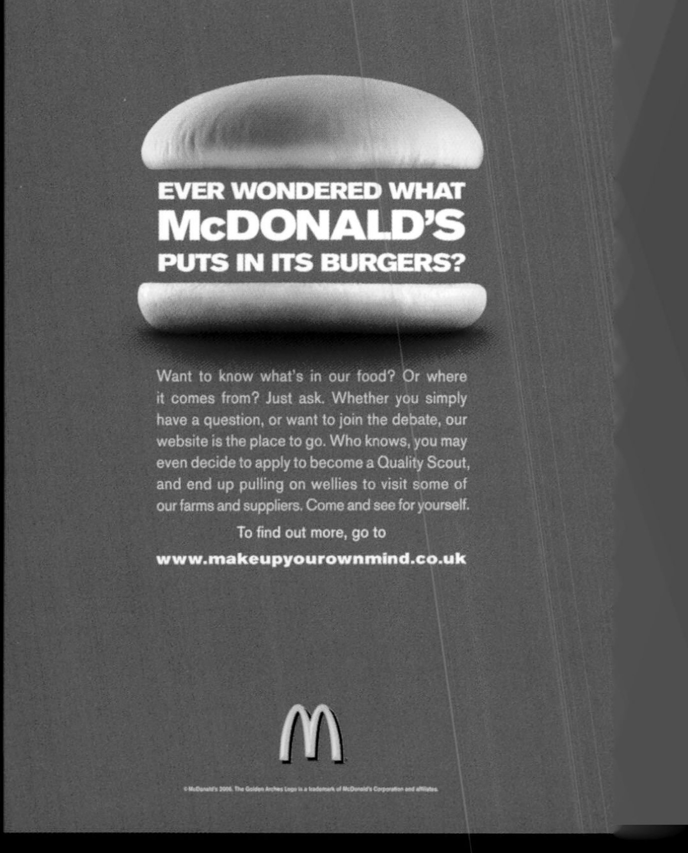

EVER WONDERED WHAT
McDONALD'S
PUTS IN ITS BURGERS?
Want to know what's in our food? Or where it comes from? Just ask. Whether you simply have a question, or want to join the debate, our website is the place to go. Who knows, you may even decide to apply to become a Quality Scout, and end up pulling on wellies to visit some of our farms and suppliers. Come and see for yourself.
To find out more, go to
www.makeupyourownmind.co.uk

'ALL THE PEOPLE PICKED TO BE QUALITY SCOUTS WERE INITIALLY SCEPTICS. WE WANT TO SHOW A JOURNEY WITH OPEN-MINDED PEOPLE.'

STEVE HENRY, EXECUTIVE CREATIVE DIRECTOR AT TBWA\LONDON

EVERYTHING McDONALD'S DOES IS QUESTIONABLE...

If you have a concern, just ask us. We'll give you a straight answer. You see, we're happy to have a healthy debate about our food and our business practices. And if what you've read today has proved a little tough to swallow, here are some facts you should know:

Our hamburgers are made from 100% whole cuts of beef, no additives, no fillers, no word of a lie. All we add is a pinch of salt and pepper after cooking. Over 16,000 British and Irish farms are proud to supply us with their beef, every one of them accredited by Farm Assurance schemes. We've even been recognised by the RSPCA for our commitment to improving animal welfare.

Our 'McJobs' offer excellent benefits, like flexible working hours and an award-winning training scheme. Plus there's a genuine opportunity for career advancement; 80% of our restaurant managers started out behind the tills. And we've been an Investor in People, and a Times Top 100 Graduate Employer for over seven years now.

Of course, one ad won't change your mind. So keep asking questions. Demand answers. After all, debates should be balanced, and for that you need all the facts.

So go on, ask us anything you want. Give us a proper grilling.

Post your questions online at **www.makeupyourownmind.co.uk**

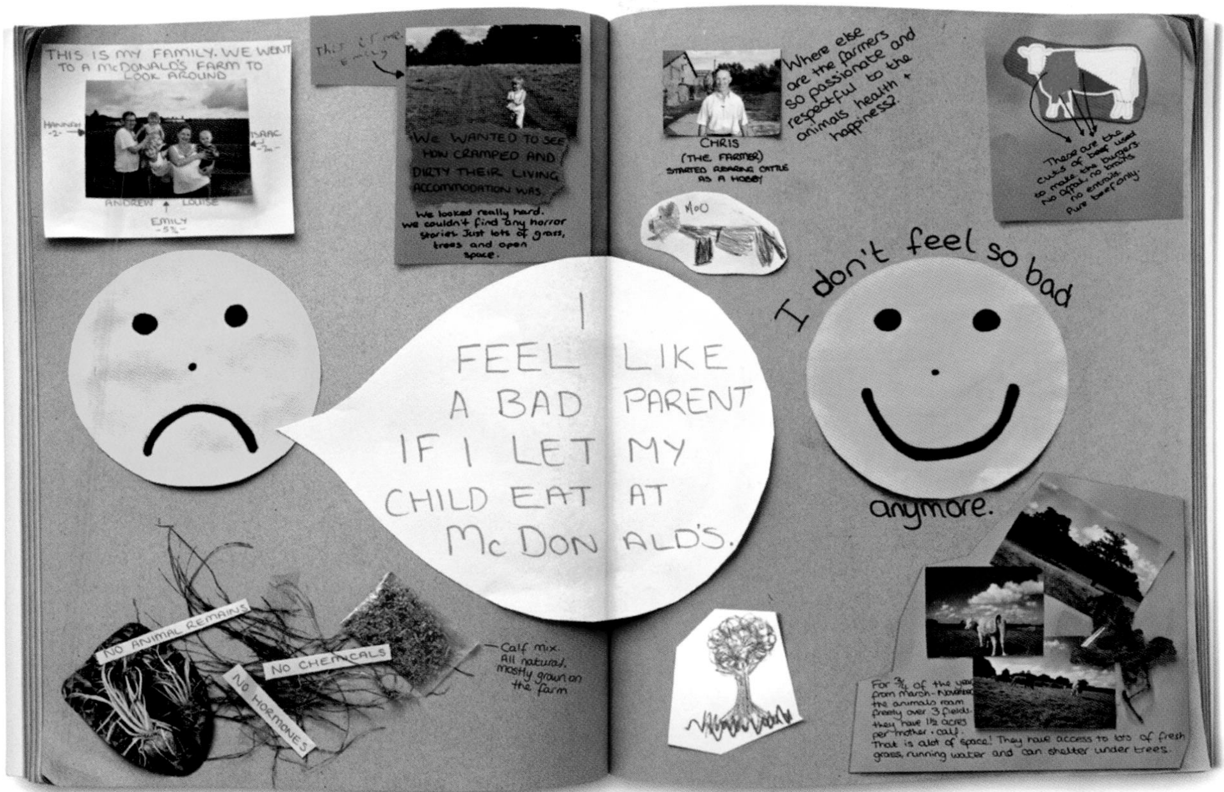
THIS IS MY FAMILY. WE WENT TO A McDONALD'S FARM TO LOOK AROUND
ANDREW
LOUISE
EMILY
ISAAC
We WANTED TO SEE HOW CRAMPED AND DIRTY THEIR LIVING ACCOMMODATION WAS.
We looked really hard. We couldn't find any horror stories. Just lots of grass, trees and open space.
CHRIS (THE FARMER) STARTED REARING CATTLE AS A HOBBY
Where else are the farmers so passionate and respectful to the animals health + happiness?
MOO
I FEEL LIKE A BAD PARENT IF I LET MY CHILD EAT AT McDONALD'S.
I don't feel so bad anymore.
NO ANIMAL REMAINS
NO CHEMICALS
NO HORMONES
Calf mix. All natural, mostly grown on the farm
That is alot of space! They have access to lots of fresh grass, running water and can shelter under trees.
Visit www.makeupyourownmind.co.uk to watch the Burton Family's video of their behind the scenes look at McDonald's.

ind
website has been set up for you to find out anything you would 's food, business, people and practices.
2 of your questions and we're answering more all the time. You'll terviews from the Quality Scouts - independent members of the the scenes at McDonald's and its suppliers. Plus, details of , how to subscribe to the Make Up Your Own Mind newsletter, and
maybe
yes
no
Tell us what you think of this site
Quality Scout Reports
Charlotte, a teacher and mother of one, enjoys Chicken McNuggets with her daughter. But she wasn't sure about the overall standard of chicken used, or the recipe for the batter. So see what she decided when she actually visited the supplier that makes McDonald's Chicken McNuggets.
Charlotte Haile wanted to see exactly what goes into a McDonald's Chicken McNugget...
Read Charlotte Haile's report
Your latest questions
1. Please can you tell me why mayonnaise is not available in your restaurants?...
2. Do all of the restaurant management staff work six days per week 12 hours p...
3. do your Staff Have training in health and safety? if so, how are they trained
More questions
ws
nald's restaurants is gs. The initiative will in Sheffield, ipate in a pilot se sites will be turned al buildings.
annel 4 News
Watch the webchat on the definition of a "McJob"

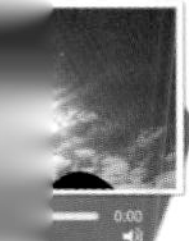

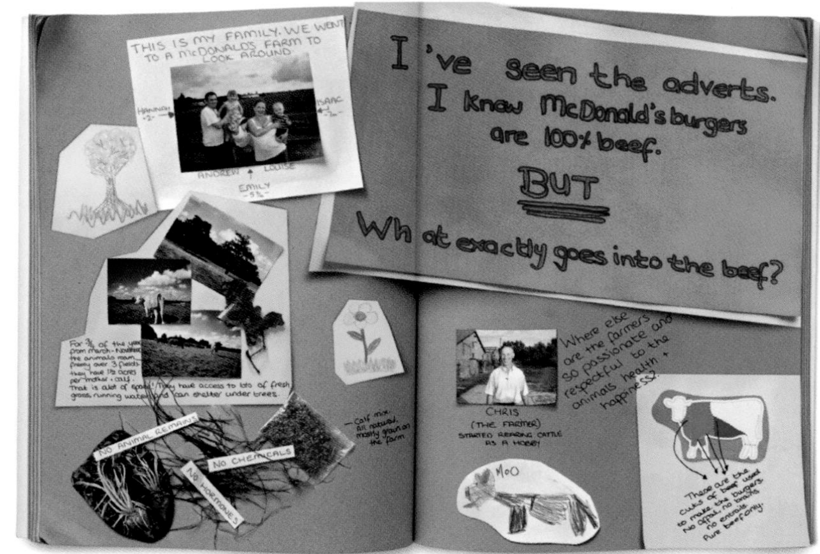
THIS IS MY FAMILY. WE WENT TO A McDONALD'S FARM TO LOOK AROUND
I've seen the adverts. I know McDonald's burgers are 100% beef.
BUT
What exactly goes into the beef?
CHRIS (THE FARMER) STARTED REARING CATTLE AS A HOBBY
Where else are the farmers so passionate and respectful to the animals health + happiness?
NO ANIMAL REMAINS
NO CHEMICALS
NO HORMONES
MOO
Visit www.makeupyourownmind.co.uk to watch the Burton Family's video of their behind the scenes look at McDonald's.

In Australia, the campaign featured television commercials and print ads of McDonald's scouts going out and discovering the facts behind the myths for themselves, all highlighting the Make Up Your Own Mind website. The site allowed people behind the scenes of the company and its products and invited them to ask questions about anything they were unsure about. Online media also got people thinking by posing myths and facts that could be further investigated on the site. The campaign spawned multiple blogs as well as debate in the advertising and cinema industries.

i'm lovin' it
THE MYTHS ABOUT OUR BEEF TURNED OUT TO BE BULL.
We've all heard them. But the facts about McDonald's delicious Big Mac beef patties are much easier to swallow than those crazy myths. Why do they taste so good? The answer is the beef, naturally. We simply take 100% Aussie beef (no, not 99.9%... 100%) and mince it up. And no, there's no company called '100% Aussie Beef', our beef patties are supplied by the Australian Food Corporation and OSI Foods. We then stamp the mince into a patty and snap freeze it, so we don't have to use any preservatives at all. The frozen patties are then boxed up and sent to your local restaurant. Hang on a sec. Is that it? Yep... that's the whole process - no bull. Want to find out more? Check out our website: MAKEUPYOUROWNMIND.COM.AU
MCD0524/NI/B

PIG FAT IN OUR SHAKES? JUST ANOTHER CURLY TALE.

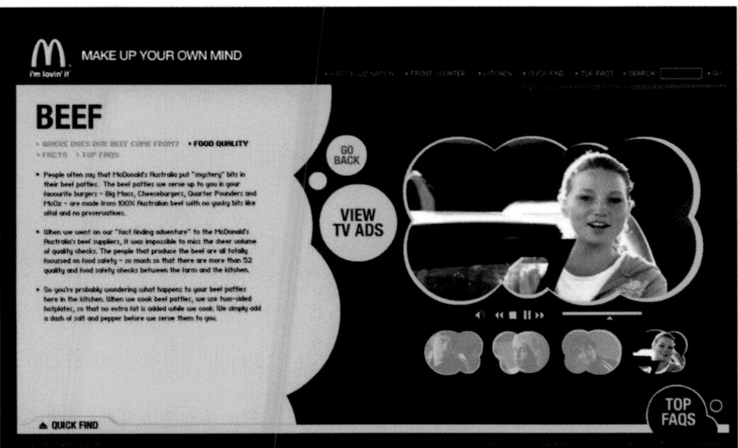

MAKE UP YOUR OWN MIND
i'm lovin' it
BEEF
WHERE DOES OUR BEEF COME FROM? • FOOD QUALITY
• FACTS • TOP FAQS
• People often say that McDonald's Australia put "mystery" bits in their beef patties. The beef patties we serve up to you in your favourite burgers – Big Macs, Cheeseburgers, Quarter Pounders and McOz – are made from 100% Australian beef with no yucky bits like offal and no preservatives.
• When we went on our "fact finding adventure" to the McDonald's Australia's beef suppliers, it was impossible to miss the sheer volume of quality checks. The people that produce the beef are all totally focussed on food safety – so much so that there are more than 52 quality and food safety checks between the farm and the kitchen.
• So you're probably wondering what happens to your beef patties here in the kitchen. When we cook beef patties, we use two-sided hotplates, so that no extra fat is added while we cook. We simply add a dash of salt and pepper before we serve them to you.
GO BACK
VIEW TV ADS
QUICK FIND
TOP FAQS

MAKE UP YOUR OWN MIND
i'm lovin' it
ENTER FRONT COUNTER
OIL POTATOES
LETTUCE TOMATOES EGGS
FISH CHICKEN BUNS
ABOUT US
BEEF
QUICK FIND
TOP FAQS

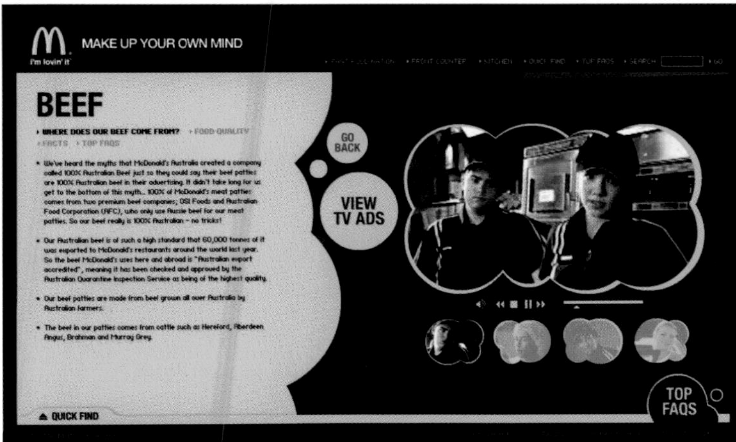

MAKE UP YOUR OWN MIND
i'm lovin' it
BEEF
• WHERE DOES OUR BEEF COME FROM? • FOOD QUALITY
• FACTS • TOP FAQS
• We've heard the myths that McDonald's Australia created a company called 100% Australian Beef just so they could say their beef patties are 100% Australian beef in their advertising. It didn't take long for us get to the bottom of this myth... 100% of McDonald's meat patties comes from two premium beef companies; OSI Foods and Australian Food Corporation (AFC), who only use Aussie beef for our meat patties. So our beef really is 100% Australian – no tricks!
• Our Australian beef is of such a high standard that 60,000 tonnes of it was exported to McDonald's restaurants around the world last year. So the beef McDonald's uses here and abroad is "Australian export accredited", meaning it has been checked and approved by the Australian Quarantine Inspection Service as being of the highest quality.
• Our beef patties are made from beef grown all over Australia by Australian farmers.
• The beef in our patties comes from cattle such as Hereford, Aberdeen Angus, Brahman and Murray Grey.
GO BACK
VIEW TV ADS
QUICK FIND
TOP FAQS

MAKE UP YOUR OWN MIND
i'm lovin' it
ENTER KITCHEN
HAPPY MEALS
WORKING @ MACCAS
DAIRY
APPLE
QUICK FIND
TOP FAQS

MAKE UP YOUR OWN MIND
i'm lovin' it
GO BACK
POTATOES
OIL
QUICK FIND
TOP FAQS

MAKE UP YOUR OWN MIND
i'm lovin' it
HAPPY MEALS
APPLE
DAIRY
LIGHTER CHOICES
WORKING @ MACCAS
ENTER FRONT COUNTER
BEEF
CHICKEN
OIL
FISH
BUNS
POTATOES
LETTUCE
TOMATOES
EGGS
ABOUT US
ENTER KITCHEN
QUICK FIND
TOP FAQS

In a bid to prove to customers that its luxury Phaeton is indeed different from other cars, Volkswagen decided to give people full access to the production process, which is traditionally kept behind closed doors. The brand set up a so-called 'Transparent Factory' in the heart of Dresden, Germany, at a cost of some €186 m (£142 m/$287 m). The factory's walls are made almost entirely of glass – over 27,000 square metres (290,000 square feet) of it. Its floors are covered entirely in Canadian maple. And its layout is visitor-friendly, set up to receive 250 tourists (by advance reservation at €5 each), customers or prospects per day. There are no smokestacks, no loud noises and no toxic byproducts. Parts arrive, and luxury cars depart.

27
DEMAG

BE EXPERIMENTAL

'Safe advertising is the riskiest advertising of all,' the legendary American advertiser Bill Bernbach (1911–82) once proclaimed. If that was true in his time, it is even more pertinent today. The value of (calculated) risks and (smart) experimentation cannot be underestimated in an industry in full transformation, where the rules are being completely rewritten, and where the latest and newest technology is setting the agenda. In such a context, experimentation is the only way forward.

The experimental approach can unfold in two ways: it's either about embracing the newest and latest, requiring brands to act speedily and instantly, or embracing the different and unknown, requiring brands to be audacious and bold. The first kind of experimentation focuses on responding quicker than the competition to the constant avalanche of new opportunities.

In today's fast-paced world, energy is often around whatever is most recent – the latest update, the latest cool website, the latest application, the latest gadget. Trends are reported almost in real time. New online platforms and tools can gain mainstream appeal within the course of a few months. But because technology is changing almost constantly, things also have an expiry date of days or weeks, rather than months or years.

Brands have to adopt this accelerated pace if they want to take full advantage of new opportunities. They need to hone their response time and develop quicker reflexes. For bigger organizations in particular, encumbered by more complex and lengthy decision processes, the race is on to speed things up. Rather than being continually stuck in the development of the ultimate plan that never gets executed, there's much more to be learned from actually trying something out very early on. Branding speaker Martin Lindstrom talks about instant branding in this regard: 'Things no longer happen according to a 24-month deadline. You might be lucky and have a deadline stretch to 24 hours. Brands must prepare themselves to be able to react within hours to trends. Consumers will love you for it.'

Of course, any brand needs a framework that sets out major decisions and choices – what the brand wants to convey, which audiences it wants to engage, how and where to spend its budgets. But any plan needs enough leeway to allow for experimentation, so brands can try out whatever happens along the way. Otherwise, they risk missing out on the best bits. In today's world, where nothing is ever finished and everything is in constant development, there is no such thing as the perfect, foolproof, risk-free plan.

The second dimension of experimentation is the willingness to try out completely different things, stretching the brand to the extremes, going where you haven't gone before. In an increasingly noisy as well as transparent conversation ecosystem, the extreme, different, random things rise to the top, leaving the average, mediocre, clichéd alternatives at the bottom of the chain.

Whether it's about the latest and newest, or the different and unknown, in both cases experimentation means exploring new ground. It implies doing things without necessarily knowing all the pitfalls and solutions beforehand. That makes it all the more exciting, but also all the more risky. You can't be 100 per cent sure where you'll end up, and a degree of unpredictability is part of the game. It's a reality marketers need to embrace. That is not to say that an experiment is ever carried out merely for the sake of it – quite the contrary. Its aim is to learn something new, to acquire insight and knowledge about that new and uncharted territory. An experiment is by definition a series of actions carried out to test a theory or find out what happens in certain scenarios. By trying something out, brands learn how to do it better, more effectively and more successfully the next time around.

The encouraging news is that people reward experimentation. They seek out the brands that push the boundaries, boldly reinvent the rules of their category, embrace experimentation and go with the flow of the moment. Experimental brands are perceived as more open-minded and more self-assured than those that stick to the rulebook and yet always seem to miss the boat.

ADOBE

Agency: Goodby Silverstein & Partners
United States – 2007

This interactive mural was designed to showcase the potential of Adobe CS3 software. Experimenting with sophisticated programming and tracking hardware, people's movements were recorded and translated into a mixed-media graphic display. People walking past the mural from left to right triggered increasingly detailed animations that continually evolved as more and more elements filled the screen.

Designers from the Brand New School created all the graphic elements for the mural, which debuted at a CS3 launch party in Manhattan. The display was also installed at a Virgin Megastore in New York and in London's Piccadilly Circus.

'EACH LAYER IS INSPIRED BY THE ACTUAL SOFTWARE. SOMETHING MIGHT LOOK LIKE IT WAS MADE IN ILLUSTRATOR, AND SOMETHING ELSE WAS A PRODUCT OF SOMETHING YOU CAN DO IN PHOTOSHOP. THIS WAS AN EXPLORATION IN THE AESTHETICS OF WHAT YOU CAN DO IN CS3.'

JONATHAN NOTARO, CREATIVE DIRECTOR/FOUNDER OF BRAND NEW SCHOOL

THIS WAS
THIS WAS
CREATIVE LICEN
Take as much as you w

CADBURY

Agency: Fallon

United Kingdom – 2007

'THERE'S CLEARLY NO PRODUCT BENEFIT, NO USP, NO REASONS TO BELIEVE. DOES THAT MATTER ANYMORE? ESPECIALLY WITH A BRAND AS WELL ESTABLISHED AS DAIRY MILK?'

TALENT IMITATES, GENIUS STEALS (FARISYAKOB.TYPEPAD.COM)

'THE GENIUS ABOUT THE CADBURY "GORILLA" AD IS THAT IT'S INCREDIBLY SIMPLE TO DESCRIBE BUT ALMOST IMPOSSIBLE TO UNDERSTAND.'

THE GUARDIAN

Cadbury experimented with the boundaries of conventional advertising with a 90-second commercial that does not even mention the word chocolate once. The film opens with the words 'A Glass And A Half Full Productions presents' and the opening bars of the Phil Collins hit 'In the Air Tonight'. The camera shows a close-up of a seemingly real gorilla before pulling back slowly to reveal a man in a monkey suit sitting behind a drum set. As the song reaches its epic climax, the gorilla starts drumming.

The idea behind the commercial was to show viewers a moment of pure joy, rather than talking about happiness while giving the hard sell. As Laurence Green, planning director at Fallon, explains: 'Chocolate is about joy and pleasure. For years Cadbury has told us that it was generous, through the glass and a half strapline. We thought, don't tell us how generous you are; show us. Don't tell us about joy; show us joy.'

It didn't take long for the ad to be spoofed with a toy gorilla as well as remixed with music from 50 Cent, Bon Jovi, Guns and Roses, Deep Purple and Bonnie Tyler.

'FOR A BRAND THAT IS SO WELL KNOWN, IT'S ARGUABLE WHETHER THE OLD STYLE INTERRUPTION ADVERTISING MODEL IS THE BEST MODEL FOR THE FUTURE. SO WE ARE TRYING TO ENGAGE MORE GENUINELY WITH OUR AUDIENCE.'

LAURENCE GREEN, PLANNING DIRECTOR AT FALLON

ABC
Agency: Glue Society
Australia – 2007

In order to promote the second series of *The Chaser's War on Everything*, which is known for its irreverent humour, billboards were set up in deliberately bizarre locations that couldn't be further removed from the target audience: in Iceland, in front of the biggest iceberg in the northern hemisphere; in India, where a hand-painted version of the promotion was mounted; in Estonia, where English writing on a billboard has to be accompanied by an Estonian translation by law; and in the beleaguered city of Baghdad. The show attracted few viewers from the four countries in question, but all the more publicity around the rest of the world.

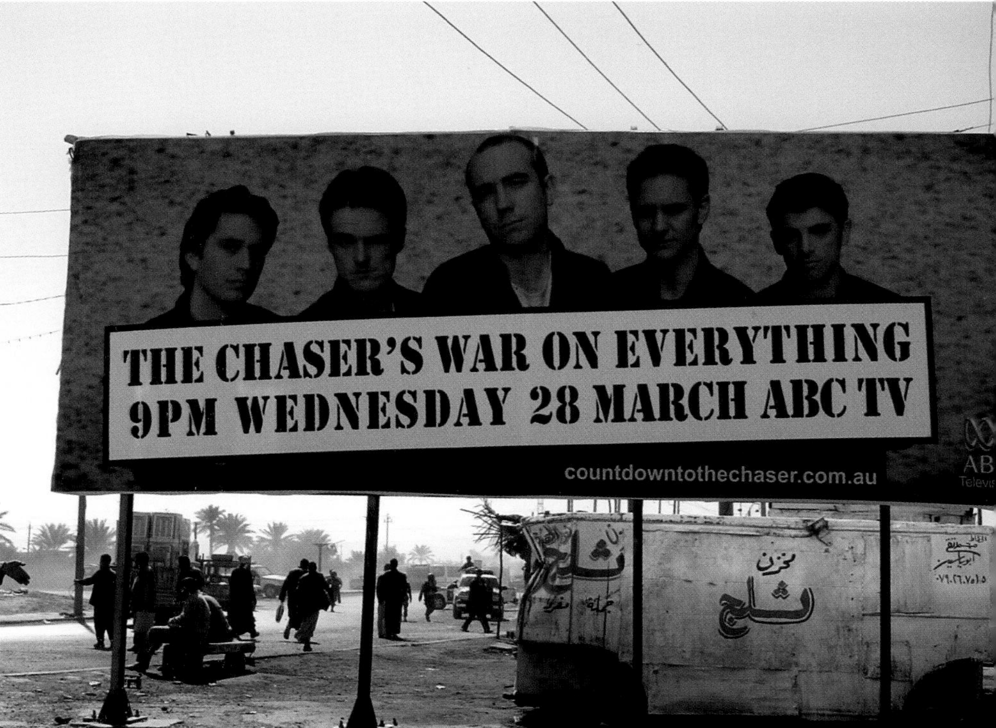

DIESEL

Visual Effects by Dvein/Technology by Vizoo

Italy – 2007

When giant aquatic creatures from the deep and futuristic machines appeared alongside models at a Diesel fashion show in Florence, Italy, the audience was left stunned. It was the first time that multiple holograms had been projected along a traditional catwalk with real models, transforming the fashion spectacle into a technologically advanced and surreal visual feast. The 'Liquid Space' holographic show previewed the brand's Spring/Summer 2008 collection.

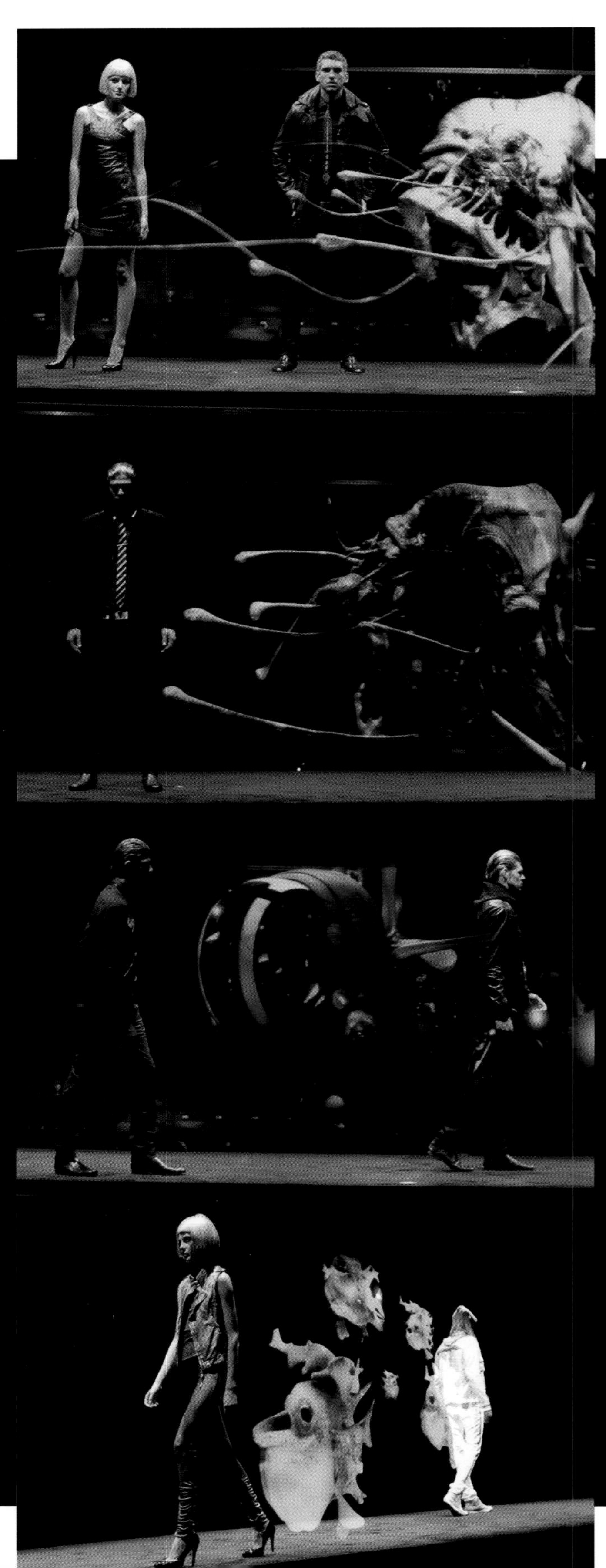

'THIS WAS NO PAUL DANIELS MAGIC SHOW TRICKERY – MORE A PERFECT BLEND OF CUTTING EDGE DIGITAL ART AND PERFORMANCE.'

CREATIVEREVIEW.CO.UK

SONY ERICSSON

Agency: Iris

United Kingdom – 2007

'NO ONE HAS EVER DONE A GIG LIKE THIS BEFORE! ROCK AND ROLL IS ALL ABOUT PUSHING BACK THE BOUNDARIES AND GIG IN THE SKY CERTAINLY DOES THAT.' JAMIROQUAI

To promote its new Walkman W950i music phone and break a few world records, Sony Ericsson took live music to a whole new level with 'Gig in the sky'. A specially chartered plane with a built-in stage and no seats became the venue for a live concert by the British band Jamiroquai. The plane flew at 30,000 feet as the band played, breaking several records including 'highest concert ever performed', and there was a Guinness World Records adjudicator present during the flight to officiate.

Two hundred special guests were at the gig. After the concert, the plane landed in Athens where a luxury after-party and another live Jamiroquai performance was held. The event was also made available as an exclusive download later in the year.

'Gig in the sky' was at the heart of an integrated campaign across the internet, PR, press and radio.

EXIT
YAMAHA

I first class music
YOUR
PASSPORT
TO THE EVENT EVERYONE WILL BE TALKING ABOUT
Win tickets to see Jamiroquai peform live at 30,000 feet, with Sony Ericsson's Gig in the sky.

OUR EXCLUSIVE MILE HIGH CLUB.
IT'S LUXURY THAT OTHER
AIRLINES CAN ONLY DREAM OF.
LYNX jet
GET ON · GET OFF
lynxjet.com

INTRODUCING A LEVEL OF
COMFORT NEVER EXPERIENCED
BEFORE IN AIR TRAVEL
lynxjet.com

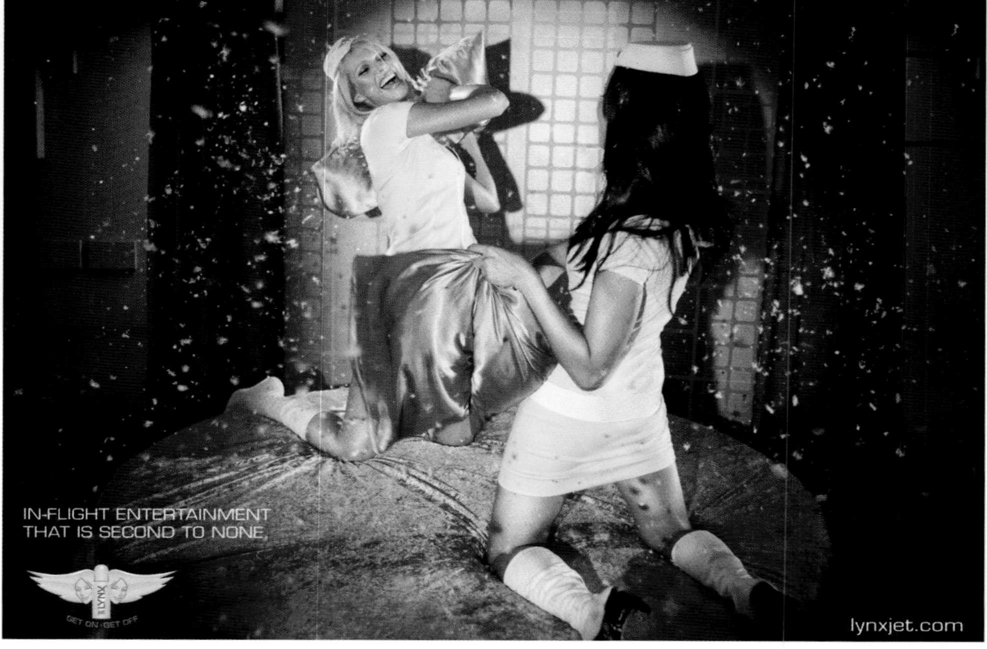
IN-FLIGHT ENTERTAINMENT
THAT IS SECOND TO NONE.
LYNX jet
GET ON · GET OFF
lynxjet.com

An essential ingredient of experimentation is not always knowing where things will lead you. In 2005 Lynx came up with a new marketing story to up the ante on its 'sex appeal' image. In Australia, the launch of the fictitious airline LynxJet combined familiar features of air travel with elements of male fantasy including racy in-flight entertainment such as pillow fighting, spanking and mud wrestling. When Lynx tried to get the airline off the ground for real, with sexy Lynx air stewardesses, the high-flying fantasy of a private luxury jet came crashing to earth when it was grounded by the Australian Aviation Authority.

In 2007, a new attempt was made to turn the male fantasy campaign into an ambitious reality, this time in South Africa. Celebrities, competition winners and journalists were promised the trip of a lifetime on a specially prepared 'AxeJet' to party hotspot Ibiza, Spain. The South African Aviation Authority had given permission for the take-off, but the exclusive crowd was left stranded at the airport when the private jet didn't show up. The party-goers ended up flying to Ibiza on 'ordinary' flights. It's clearly easier to devise and create a male fantasy airline within the safe confines of advertising than it is in the real world.

SONY ERICSSON

Agency: Iris

Spain & United States – 2007

'I'M VERY INTRIGUED BY THE WHOLE NIGHT TENNIS CONCEPT – WHO WOULD HAVE EXPECTED SPORT AND ELECTRONIC CULTURE TO COMBINE IN THIS WAY?'

PAUL OAKENFOLD

Sony Ericsson brought together sports and music for its 'Night Tennis' event. Imagine a pitch black tennis court lit only by UV light, eight players wearing neon clothes, a bright ball and live background music from the likes of Groove Armada and DJs Darren Emerson and Paul Oakenfold. Each tennis game was punctuated by explosive beats and an incredible light show, broadcast to the audience on a 25-metre (82-foot) projection screen.

In between games, a UV fashion extravaganza showcased the latest styles. As the matches were played, the tennis court naturally transformed into a dance floor. 'Night Tennis' took place during the Sony Ericsson Championships in Madrid and the Sony Ericsson Open in Miami.

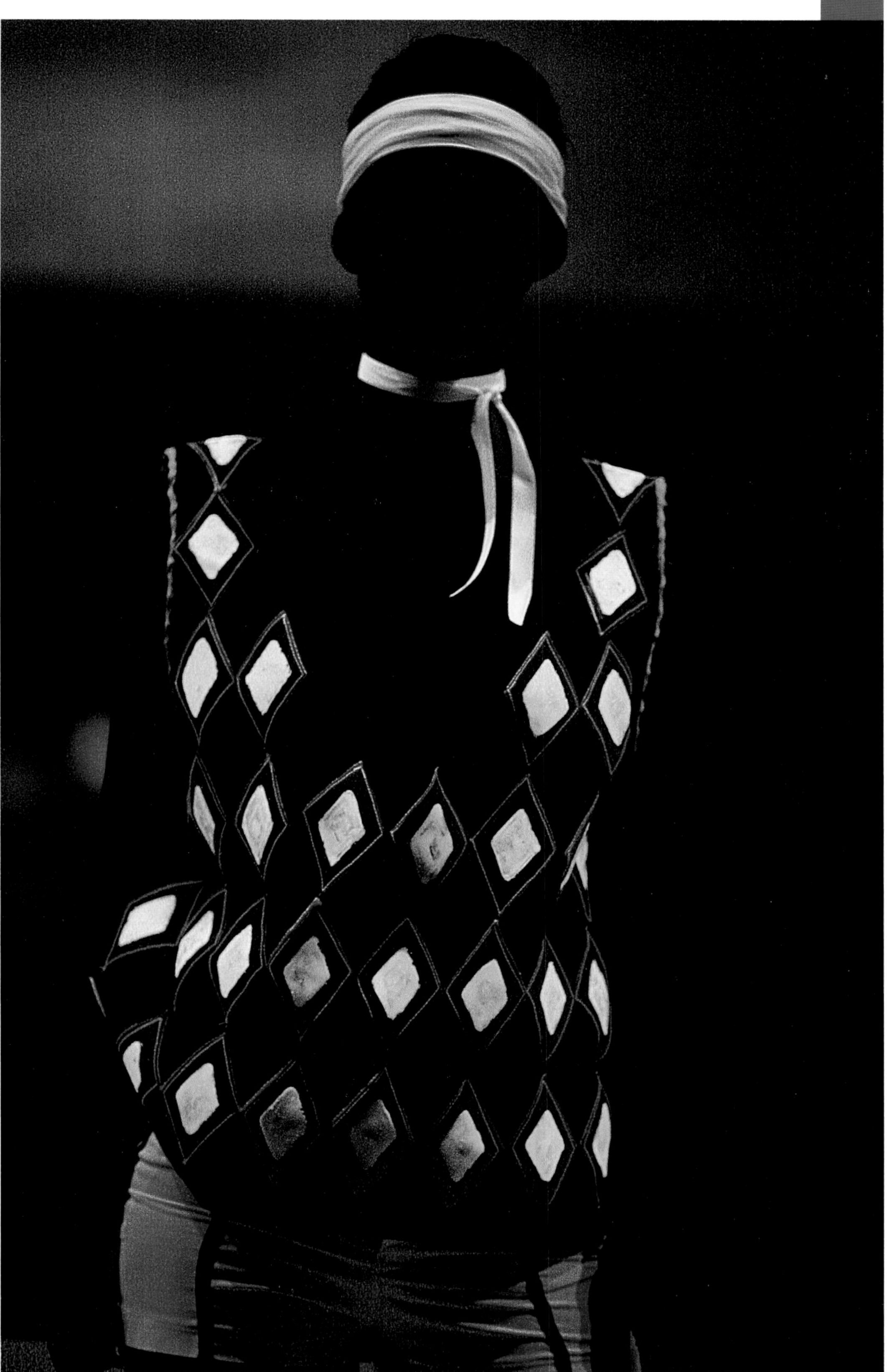

TOYOTA

Agency: Leo Burnett Colombiana, Bogotá
Colombia – 2006

Readers of the Colombian magazine *Semana* were no doubt surprised when they received their December 2006 issue, which contained an insert made of banana leaves. The single-page advert for the new special edition Land Cruiser Prado was designed to encourage Colombians to keep in touch with nature.

The logistical effort required to produce this innovative insert was considerable. Two-metre (6-foot) banana leaves, destined to be thrown away in any case, were bought from the country's leading suppliers. Eight adverts could be cut from a single leaf, although the leaves had to be hand-printed within five days of receipt to ensure that they reached *Semana* readers in perfect condition. Twenty thousand subscribers in Bogotá and Medellín received the issue.

ECONOMÍA

◀ El proyecto contempla la posibilidad de extender las preferencias hasta diciembre de 2007, siempre y cuando para el mes de junio el TLC haya sido aprobado por los Congresos de Colombia y Estados Unidos

COMERCIO EXTERIOR

Regalo de Navidad

El Congreso de Estados Unidos radicó un proyecto para extender por seis meses más las preferencias arancelarias a Colombia y Perú. Ahora la pelota quedó en el campo colombiano.

AUNQUE FALTAN 15 DÍAS PARA Nochebuena, el Niño Dios ya les adelantó el regalo a los exportadores del país: la extensión de las preferencias arancelarias, más conocidas como Atpdea. Estos beneficios, que les permiten a Colombia y a otros países de la región ingresar cientos de productos al mercado estadounidense sin pagar aranceles, caducan el próximo 31 de diciembre. Por eso el aguinaldo navideño es que quedarán vigentes por unos seis meses más.

En efecto, el jueves de la semana pasada, el Comité de Medios y Árbitros de la Cámara de Representantes de Estados Unidos radicó un proyecto de ley para extender el Atpdea hasta el 30 de junio de 2007. El proyecto también tiene el apoyo de los líderes de los partidos en el Senado. Los beneficiaros con la medida son Colombia, Perú, Bolivia y Ecuador. Para estos dos últimos países, sin embargo, se trata de un paño de agua tibia. Y la razón es que ninguno de ellos se trae entre manos un Tratado de Libre Comercio (TLC) con Estados Unidos que les permita reemplazar esas preferencias temporales y volverlas permanentes.

Otro cuento muy diferente es la extensión del Atpdea para Colombia y Perú.

Los gobiernos de ambos países ya firmaron un TLC con los norteamericanos y ahora sólo están a la espera de su aprobación por el Congreso de Estados Unidos. En el caso peruano, el Congreso de ese país ya aprobó el tratado, pero aún falta que lo haga el de Estados Unidos. En el caso colombiano, este trámite todavía falta por surtirse en ambos lados.

La idea es lograr empatar el final del Atpdea con el comienzo del TLC. Y justamente por eso es que el proyecto radicado en la Cámara de Representantes la semana pasada contempla la extensión del Atpdea por otros seis meses más. Según el proyecto, una vez terminado el primer semestre de 2007, las preferencias se podrían extender hasta fin de año, siempre y cuando el TLC ya haya recibido para entonces la bendición por parte de los Congresos de Colombia y Estados Unidos. En otras palabras, amarra la extensión del Atpdea por un año a la aprobación del TLC.

Eso es bueno y es malo. Bueno, porque le tira la pelota a Colombia y deja sin excusas a quienes dicen que el problema está sólo en el Congreso de Estados Unidos. Hace más factible que el Congreso colombiano cumpla con la aprobación del TLC en el primer semestre del año y no se extienda eternamente en los debates. Además, de alguna manera obliga al Congreso gringo a votar el tratado antes de junio 30, porque las condiciones aplican para ambas partes. Había preocupación de que la presentación del TLC al Congreso se dilatara indefinidamente por diferencias entre republicanos y demócratas.

EL PROYECTO PONE UNA ENORME PRESIÓN SOBRE EL GOBIERNO COLOMBIANO

▶ El mejor aguinaldo que les pudieron dar a los exportadores del país fue la extensión del Atpdea hasta junio del año entrante

Pero es malo porque pone una enorme presión sobre el gobierno colombiano, que debe finiquitar en una carrera contrarreloj, algunos anexos laborales que aún están pendientes y que son clave para que los demócratas aprueben el tratado.

En definitiva, si no está aprobado el TLC para junio de 2007, no habrá prórroga del Atpdea hasta diciembre del año entrante. Por el momento, la noticia de la ampliación de las preferencias por seis meses más es el mejor regalo de Navidad que le hayan podido dar a los exportadores del país. ■

130 DICIEMBRE 11, 2006 Semana

VIRGIN ATLANTIC/TEA & SYMPATHY
Agency: The Joneses
United States – 2007

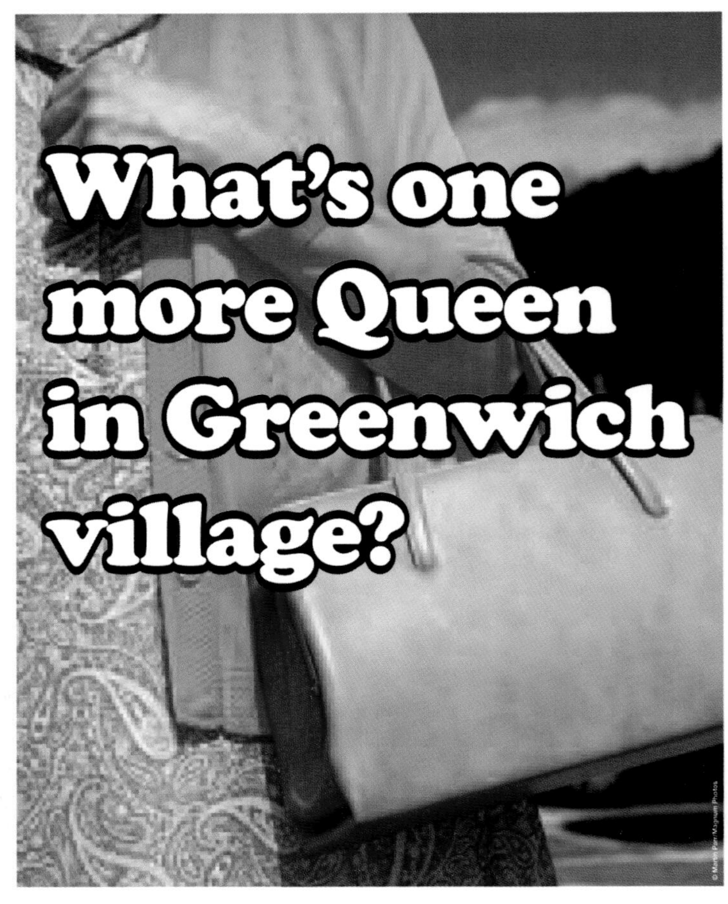

What's one more Queen in Greenwich village?
© Martin Parr/Magnum Photos

Vote for Little Britain in the Big Apple
www.campaignforlittlebritain.com

The different communities that characterize pockets of New York City have been officially recognized for many years through neighbourhoods such as Little Italy, Chinatown, Spanish Harlem, Little Brazil and Koreatown. But despite the number of British residents in New York City, and the large number of travellers between New York and the United Kingdom, there is no Little Britain.

Tea & Sympathy, a British café in the city's Greenwich Village, teamed up with Virgin Atlantic to petition New York City to formally recognize the stretch of Greenwich Avenue between West 12th and 13th Streets as a new neighbourhood in Manhattan and rename it 'Little Britain'. Both Tea & Sympathy and Virgin Atlantic are no strangers to the neighbourhood. The airline company had its first US office on Perry Street and drew up its preliminary US business plan on a napkin in the White Horse Tavern on nearby Hudson Street, while Tea & Sympathy is known as the unofficial British Embassy. Both wanted to draw business into the area, and help preserve the charm of the neighbourhood.

The tongue-in-cheek campaign consisted of a 'party political broadcast' on the campaign website, flyers all over the city, posters and postcards distributed through British retailers, canvassing in corporate restaurants with British food as the day's 'special', a launch press conference held on Greenwich Avenue and ongoing coverage and debate both online and offline.

With Tea & Sympathy acting as the campaign headquarters, other British brands and icons soon joined forces. Fashion company Ben Sherman created a special T-shirt for the cause. Celebrities with strong British roots, such as Kiefer Sutherland (*opposite, centre*), Joss Stone, Sir Paul Smith, Mischa Barton, Billy Connolly and Mike Myers willingly signed the petition. In less than one month the campaign had won the support of more than 6,000 people (57 per cent of whom were New Yorkers) and news media from all over the world reported on it.

Vote for
Little Britain
in the
Big Apple
www.campaignforlittlebritain.com

The proposal was shot down in a first phase by local authorities, as they saw only commercial rather than historical reasons in the name change. Other objections included the lack of any real British presence in the area, in contrast to, for instance, Little Italy and Chinatown. But this first setback didn't discourage the campaigners, who are still eager to see Little Britain come to life. As a direct result of the campaign, several British businesses are looking for space in the proposed area and two are negotiating new leases. The campaign met Virgin's marketing objective to be the airline that brings New York and London together in a cultural sense.

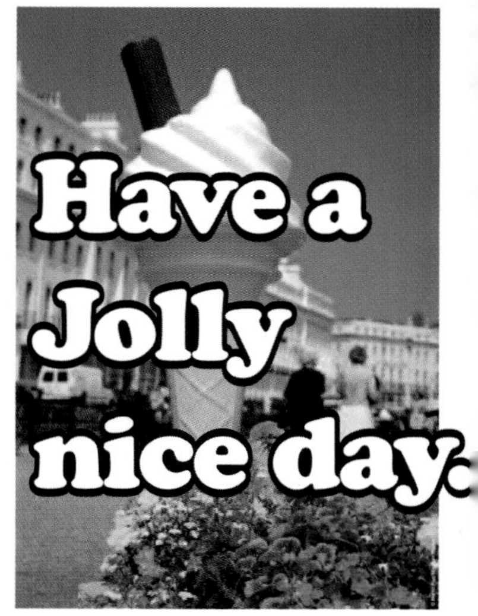

'IN TRUE NEW YORK AND BRITISH FASHION, THIS COMMUNITY WILL CONTINUE TO THRIVE AND GROW, WITH OR WITHOUT APPROVAL FROM THE CITY....'

SIR RICHARD BRANSON

BE PERSONAL

It's not always easy being a marketer these days. On the one hand, people scream out for more personal messages; they want to feel as if brands understand and acknowledge their particular situation and preferences, rather than being treated as a number. In times when people can write their own blogs, create their own profiles or websites, make their personal selection of news and information, and start their own video channels – in short, create their own personal media landscape – their expectations of brands have changed. They don't feel personally addressed by big messages from big brands aimed at big, anonymous audiences. They want big brands to fit into *their* lives, delivering relevant messages and content exclusively to them. On the other hand, those same people don't seem particularly eager to give away too much information about themselves, naturally wary about databases or brands penetrating too deeply into their personal lives.

This is the inherent dilemma with personalization, the tension between increased relevance on the one hand, and reduced privacy on the other. It's as annoying to receive a blunt, anonymous message that does not seem to acknowledge you as an individual as it is to feel a brand is invading your privacy through an overtly personal message that you haven't asked for. Most social networking sites, such as Facebook and MySpace, are constantly involved in this balancing act. They are launching hyper-targeted advertising systems, designed to deliver more personalized adverts to their users, while trying their utmost to safeguard the privacy and intimacy of members. The backlash over privacy levelled at Facebook following the launch of Facebook Beacon, a service tracking members' activities through partners' websites, clearly highlighted this tension.

Online brand 'advocates' or 'evangelists', as they are sometimes called, are well aware of this balancing act. Tasked by brands with listening to and resolving customer complaints, they search for online conversations – in the blogosphere, forums or social networks – relating to a specific brand, and directly and personally engage in those conversations. But even though their intentions are good, there's always the risk of a backlash as they are invading people's private spaces.

Brands can also opt for a less pushy approach, leaving it up to customers to personalize the message or product on their own terms. This could be likened to serving them with a standard dish but providing them with extra ingredients that they can then add themselves. Classic and straightforward personalization tricks include allowing people to add a picture, a spoken message or a few lines of text to a piece of online content, or enabling them to change the sequence or music of a video. As technology continuously evolves and matures, new and more advanced opportunities will arise beyond the simple cut-and-paste nature of early online personalization, as the Verizon case on pages 222–3 already demonstrates.

One step beyond this is the personalization of products. Mass customization allows people to add or change functionalities of a core product or even build custom products from scratch, mostly through software-based product configurators. This combines the best of two worlds: the low unit costs of mass-production processes with the flexibility of individual customization. Mass customization has been made possible through the combination of cutting-edge technology, digitization and databases with detailed information about customers. Although it has only been adopted on a fairly limited scale so far, the more advanced brands are starting to integrate it into their offline offering and develop it as a structural part of their long-term business (see the NikeID Studio case on pages 228–31 and LEGO Factory on pages 226–7).

Whether it's in communication or in product development, personalization tactics should either enhance the entertainment value or relevance of the message, or increase the usefulness of the product or service. Without those clear benefits, brands might as well go back to delivering standard, anonymous marketing messages.

BEPERSONAL
BANCO DO BRASIL
Agency: Artplan
Brazil – 2006

Banco do Brasil, Latin America's largest bank with approximately 23 million clients, rebranded 300 of their entrance banners in nine Brazilian states to include clients' names. The rebranding was part of a bigger campaign to celebrate the fact that (as of January 2007) people were free to change to another bank without paying an additional fee. Banco do Brasil has 15,000 branches, and only a fraction of those were personalized, but the symbolic gesture created the sense that every Banco do Brasil client is unique. The campaign doubled the number of new accounts and spawned spontaneous media coverage.

Monitor Mercantil

PETROBRAS

Mais 2

Estatal informa à AN

MARKETING

BB troca o nome de 300 agências

Fachadas terão nomes tipicamente brasileiros a partir de terça-feira, para reforçar 'vínculos com o cliente'

CONCORRÊNCIA - Modelo do novo letreiro: para segurar os clientes

Gustavo Freire

REASON
Agency: Entremedia
United States – 2004

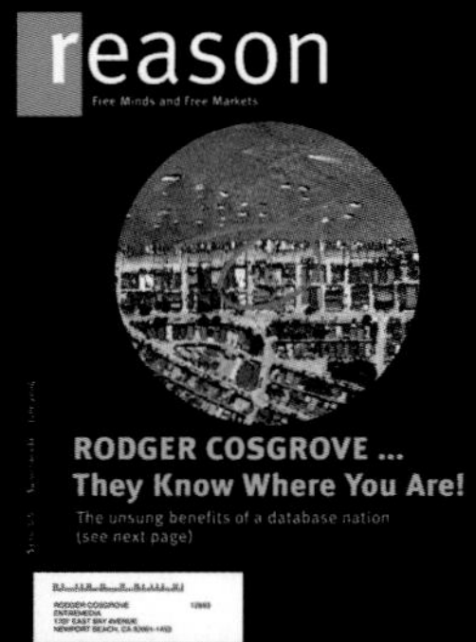
reason
RODGER COSGROVE ...
They Know Where You Are!
The unsung benefits of a database nation
(see next page)

reason
DONNA CHILDS
They Know Where You Are!
The unsung benefits of a database nation
(see next page)

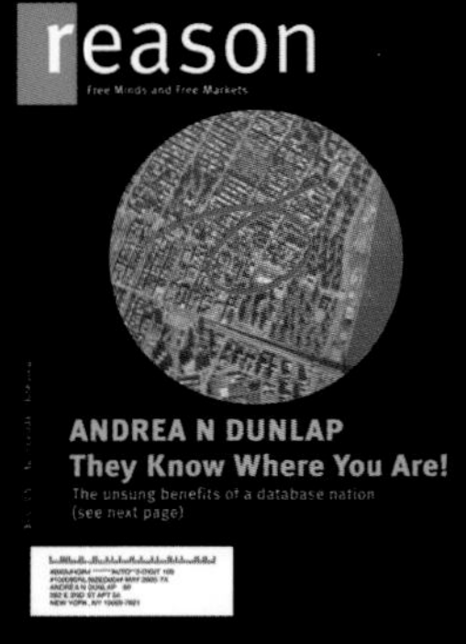
reason
ANDREA N DUNLAP
They Know Where You Are!
The unsung benefits of a database nation
(see next page)

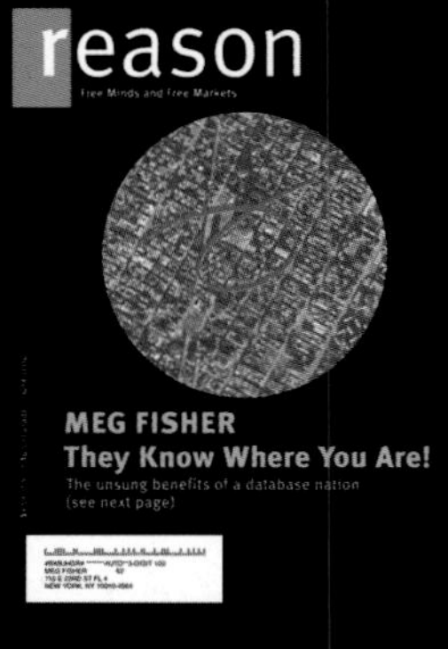
reason
MEG FISHER
They Know Where You Are!
The unsung benefits of a database nation
(see next page)

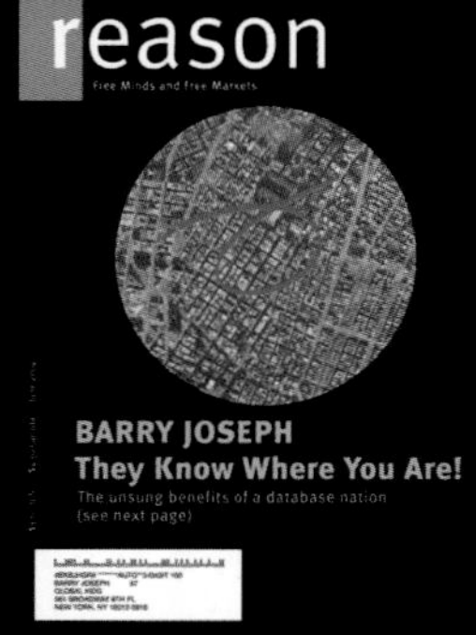
reason
BARRY JOSEPH
They Know Where You Are!
The unsung benefits of a database nation
(see next page)

reason
ELIZABETH KOCH
They Know Where You Are!
The unsung benefits of a database nation
(see next page)

reason
H AVICE LEE
They Know Where You Are!
The unsung benefits of a database nation
(see next page)

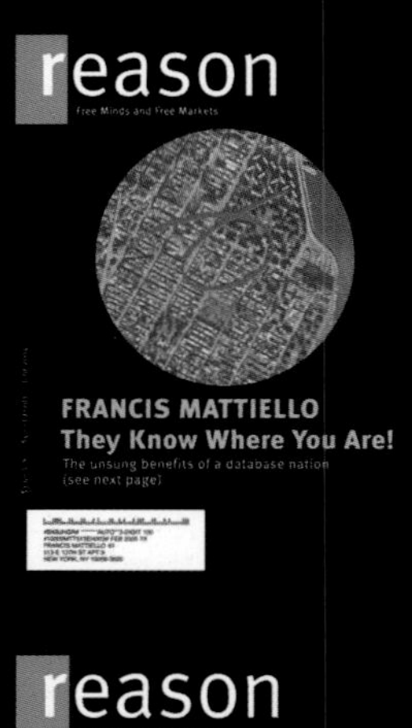
reason
FRANCIS MATTIELLO
They Know Where You Are!
The unsung benefits of a database nation
(see next page)

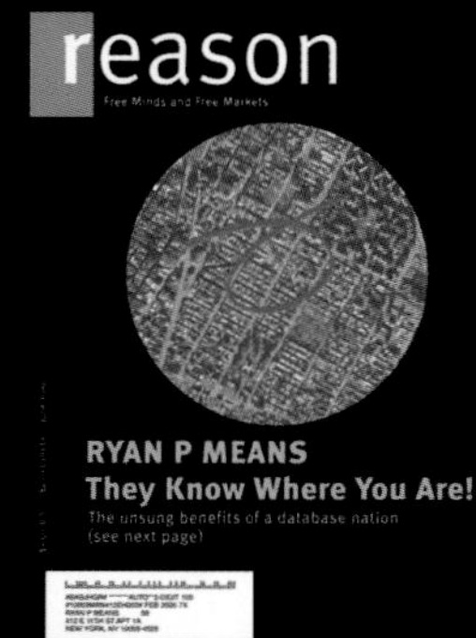
reason
RYAN P MEANS
They Know Where You Are!
The unsung benefits of a database nation
(see next page)

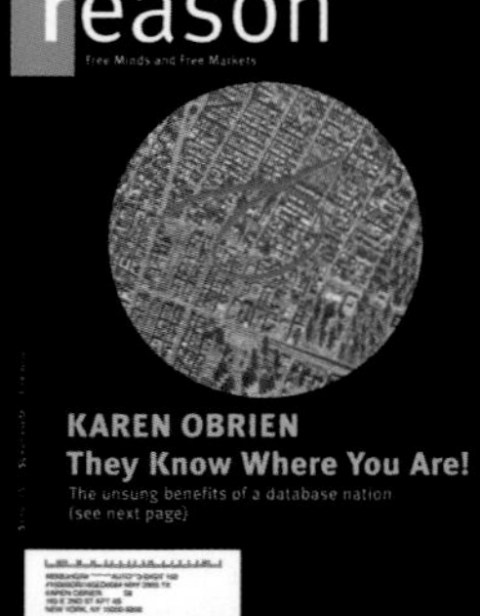
reason
KAREN OBRIEN
They Know Where You Are!
The unsung benefits of a database nation
(see next page)

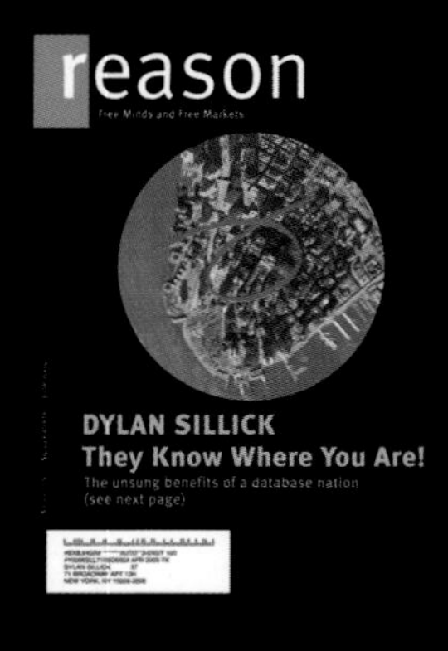
reason
DYLAN SILLICK
They Know Where You Are!
The unsung benefits of a database nation
(see next page)

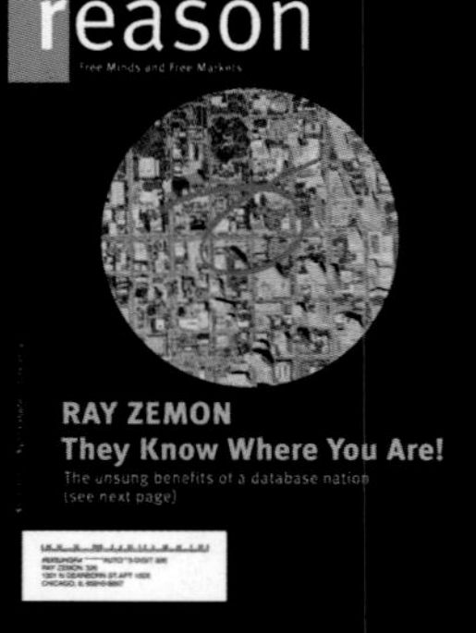
reason
RAY ZEMON
They Know Where You Are!
The unsung benefits of a database nation
(see next page)

'THIS REPRESENTS AN UNPRECEDENTED EXPERIMENT IN HYPER-INDIVIDUALIZING A COMMERCIAL PRINT PUBLICATION.'

NICK GILLESPIE, EDITOR-IN-CHIEF OF *REASON*, IN THE JUNE 2004 ISSUE

Monthly libertarian magazine *Reason* pulled off the ultimate in customized publishing when its 40,000 subscribers received their June 2004 copy with a satellite photo of their own neighbourhood on the cover and their house circled in red. On the back cover, readers found adverts customized to them and their neighbourhood. The stunt accompanied the magazine's cover article about the power and importance of databases to customize information.

reason

Free Minds and Free Markets

$3.50 U.S. $4.50 Canada June 2004

JIM LINTOTT & MAY LIANG
They Know Where You Are!

The unsung benefits of a database nation
(see next page)

#BXBJHGR# *******AUTO**3-DIGIT 220
JIM LINTOTT & MAY LIANG 1165
9811 SUNNYBROOK DR
GREAT FALLS, VA 22066-1908

In an attempt to make British art accessible to the masses, Tate Britain launched the 'Your Collection' campaign and turned its visitors into curators. Visitors to the website could create their own personal collection, reflecting different moods or themes and revealing the extraordinary breadth of work on show at the gallery, which houses British art from 1500 to the present day.

The facility is accessed at www.tate.org.uk/britain/yourcollection. Users are invited to choose a title for their personal collection, select six works of art, and create a theme that links their choices. They can send their completed collection to a friend, print it as a leaflet or put it on their fridge. To give people some inspiration, Tate Britain created a series of sample collections with quirky, playful themes.

The **I HAVE A BIG MEETING** Collection

Meetings, meetings, meetings... all of them important, all of them crucial. How crazy is today's world? Anyway, if you need a hand with a meeting, this Tate Britain Collection is designed to help you look good and ooze confidence. Lesson number one: important matters should be treated as small matters. In Room 6, *Harvest Home* by John Linnell should help you achieve this state of mind. You can almost breathe the fresh air from a stunning golden afternoon. Fill your lungs with its greatness, and always remember to make yourself bigger before entering a room. Now it's time to take a look at a champion. *Teucer* by Sir Hamo Thornycroft, near the Millbank entrance, portrays one of the heroes of Homer's Trojan War. This monumental bronze archer teaches us to never lose focus on what we're aiming for. Now we need to work on your look. Eyes are the most powerful weapons in meetings. Stare at the portrait of *Queen Elizabeth I* in Room 2. Study her eyes and her pose because she's the model to follow. Don't even dare leave the room until you've nailed that look. Finally, spend some time in front of *The Battle of Camperdown* by Philip De Loutherbourg. This breathtaking sea battle dominates Room 9 completely. Meetings are often a lot like this, but take heart from the fact that this painting still depicts the precise moment of victory. So off you pop bravery's the name of the game, and remember, for maximum effect, we suggest you experience this Collection twenty-four hours prior to your meeting.

Create your own Collection

Admission Free
www.tate.org.uk

British Art Displays 1500 – 2006
Supported by BP

The **I'M HUNGOVER** Collection

OK. Right now you're in a very particular emotional state. We understand, so we've put together a mini Collection for you with lots of stops for a sit down. Firstly, we need to run a check on you. Are we talking about a *Cholmondeley Ladies* hangover or a *Heads of Six of Hogarth's Servants* hangover? A *Cholmondeley Ladies* hangover is fine as it is a portrait of identical twins and means you are just seeing double. The other is slightly more serious as Hogarth painted six portraits swirling around on a single canvas, and if this is what your head feels like then you're in trouble. If you are feeling some guilt, a visit to the Vatican might help redeem your soul. Have a look at Richard Wilson's picture of the Vatican in Room 6, showing a splendid morning view from a hill above the Tiber. (Stand still until you see just one Vatican). Now, let's ease your headache. What you need is a strong dose of the *The Plains of Heaven* by John Martin in Room 9. This hypnotizing image oozes tranquillity and harmony, whilst the blissful landscape represents salvation. You should be feeling better now. Just to make sure that the symptoms are completely gone, we need to run another quick check. The painting of *The Cock Tavern* in Room 7 is a good test as it portrays a classic English country pub. If you can bear to stare at it for a decent amount of time, it means you're cured. Don't get any ideas about going out again though; it's an eight o'clock bedtime for you tonight.

Create your own Collection

Admission Free
www.tate.org.uk

Pimlico
Millbank Pier

British Art Displays 1500 – 2006
Supported by BP

BRITAIN
TATE

The **I'VE JUST SPLIT UP** Collection

We know how it feels. You don't even want to wake up in the morning. Your confidence has taken a bit of a knock and we understand. So much so we've prepared a little Collection to cheer you up. Especially, since you have a little more time on your hands now. (Sorry). Ready to feel better? First, stand in front of the Pre-Raphaelite masterpiece *Ophelia from Hamlet* by Millais. See? Someone else went through that too. Her loneliness should make you feel... less lonely, strangely enough. Maybe it's not the end of the world for you. Actually, you should look at the monumental *The Last Judgement* by John Martin in Room 9. Now, that is the end of the world, quite literally. This painting will help you put things in perspective, so no more sobbing, alright? Now we should talk about your future. Think about it, you're facing a moment of endless possibilities, a bit like Simon Patterson's contemporary work *The Great Bear* in Room 26. (You know, the one with the underground map.) It means that anything can happen. So comb your hair because you never know who's around. Now, you're ready for a Turner Stand in front of *Sunrise, with a Boat between Headlands*. Its highlights represent the idea of a bright new beginning. Everything will be okay. And remember, we're always here for you (10.00 – 17.50 daily).

Create your own Collection

Admission Free
www.tate.org.uk

Pimlico
Millbank Pier

British Art Displays 1500 – 2006
Supported by BP

BRITAIN
TATE

■ Agency: TEQUILA\Digital
■ Australia – 2005

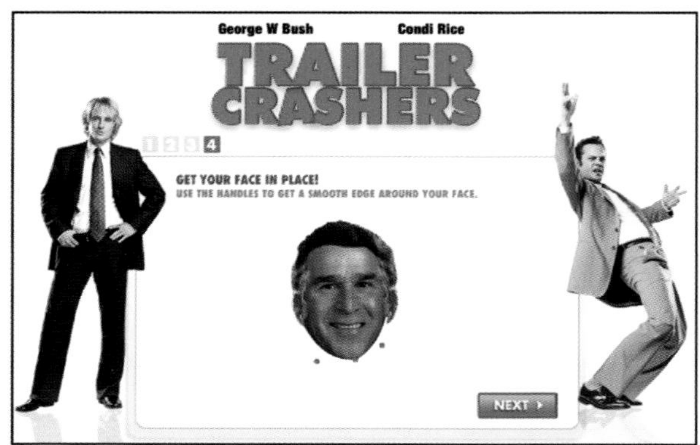

For the promotion of the movie *Wedding Crashers*, starring comedy duo Vince Vaughn and Owen Wilson, people could crash the movie's official trailer and create their own version. By entering their name, a friend's name and uploading their head shots, their faces were superimposed over those of Wilson and Vaughn and their names appeared throughout the trailer.

Around 200,000 people made their own trailer, and while the official trailer was watched one million times, the personalized versions were viewed 3.3 million times. Although the concept has been adopted many times since, *Wedding Crashers* was one of the first to use it successfully.

Enter Your Zip Code For Showtimes & Tickets

TYPE HERE

GO

WEDDING CRASHERS

LIFE'S A PARTY. CRASH IT. OUT NOW.

TRAILER | IMAGES | PRODUCTION | DOWNLOADS | CRASHER KIT | QUAIL SHOOT | SOUNDTRACK

WWW.FILMRATINGS.COM | WWW.PARENTALGUIDE.COM

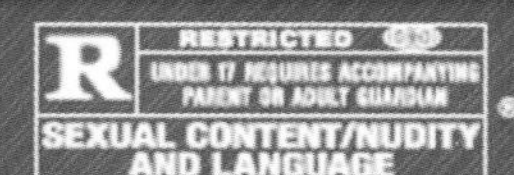

REGISTER FOR UPDATES!

■ **MTV NETWORKS**
■ Agency: EVB
■ United States – 2007

'WE ARE TRYING TO CREATE A SOCIAL COMMUNITY AROUND THE SHOW'S FRANCHISE. WE WANT VIEWERS TO LIVE WITH THE BRAND EVEN WHEN THE SHOW IS NOT ON AIR. WE'D LOVE IT TO BE SELF-SUSTAINING.'

GAURAV MISRA, VICE-PRESIDENT OF PROGRAMMING FOR MTV AND VH1

MTV's *Yo Momma* is a reality contest that sees the toughest jokesters from major cities insulting each other to comic effect. Promotion for the show revolved around an online contest, 'Let's Bully', in which viewers were encouraged to compete in their own slanging matches by creating characters and personalized jokes to send to friends. The site invited users to select a competitor, answer a series of questions and upload a photograph of themselves. Armed with personal info, the site developed trash-talking videos pasting the challenger's oversized headshot onto the bodies of dancing hip-hop figures. Videos were sent to the selected rival via email. Following the video, viewers were invited to 'Let's Bully' online to fight back.

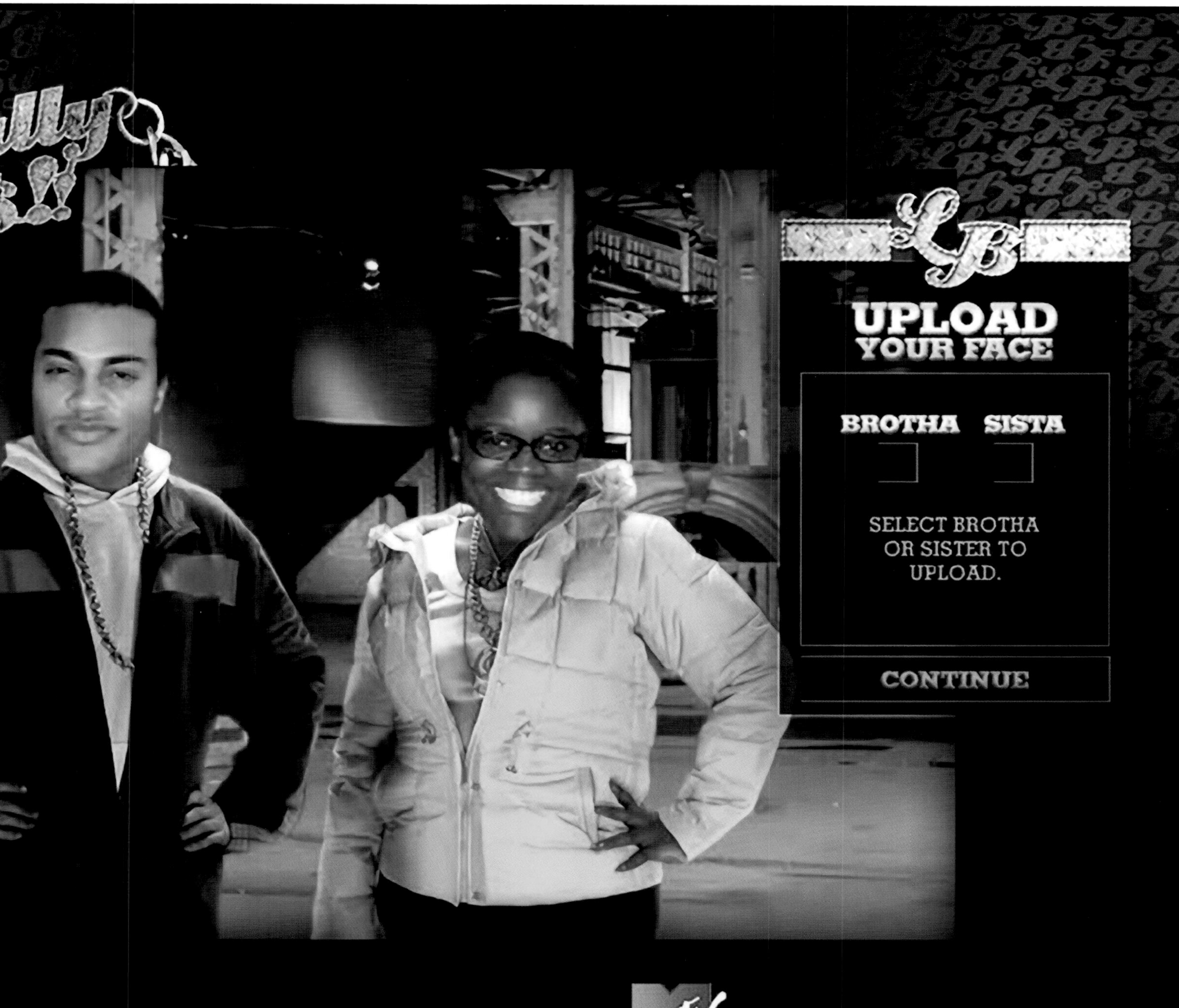
LB
UPLOAD
YOUR FACE
BROTHA
SISTA
SELECT BROTHA
OR SISTER TO
UPLOAD.
CONTINUE
MTV
MUSIC TELEVISION
YO MOMMA.tv

■ BEPERSONAL
■ VERIZON
■ Agency: R/GA
■ United States – 2007

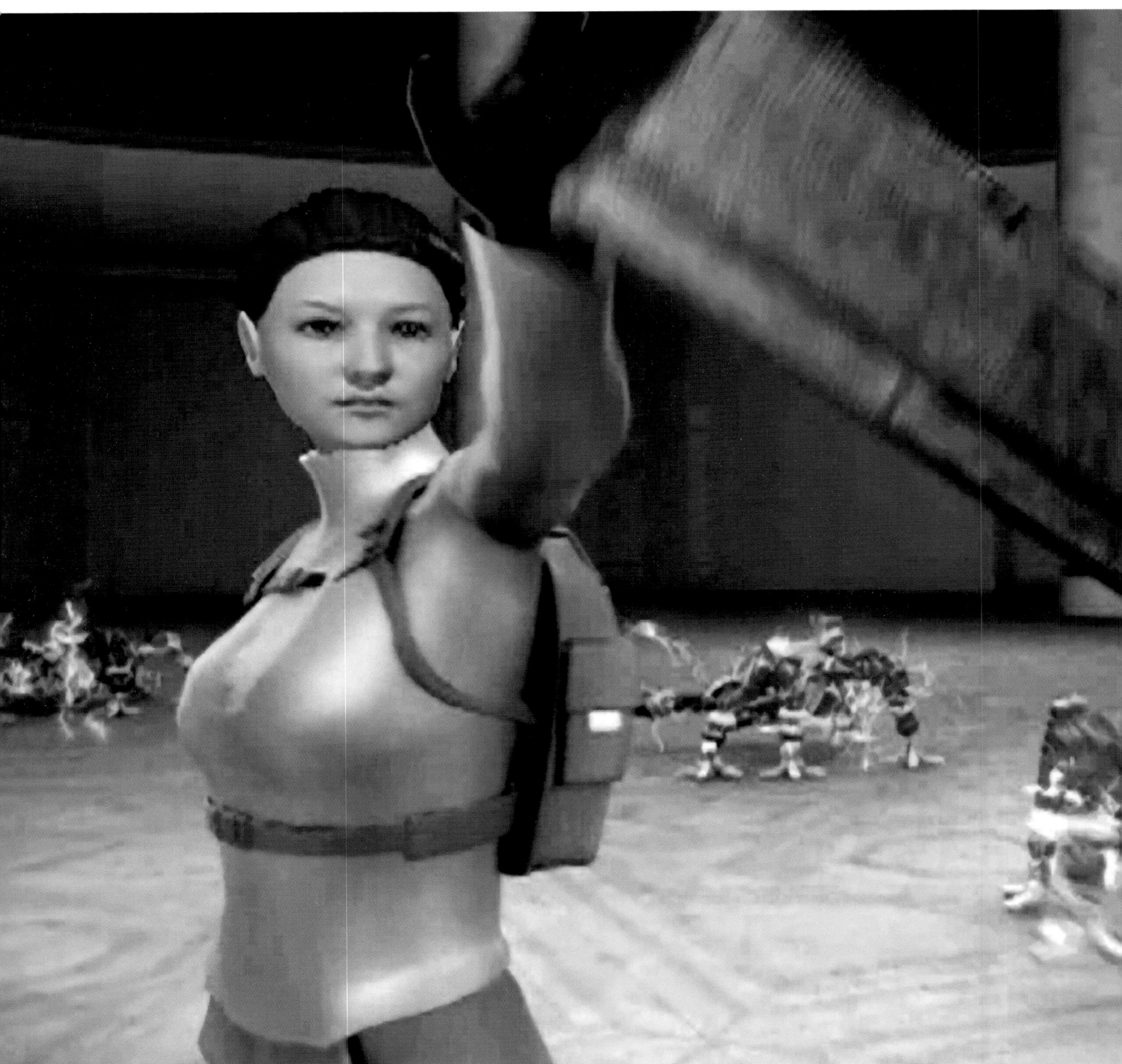

'VERIZON IS HANDING CONSUMERS THE REINS OF A STATE-OF-THE-ART, HOLLYWOOD-STUDIO-QUALITY ANIMATION AND SPECIAL-EFFECTS FACILITY.'

TARAS WAYNER, EXECUTIVE CREATIVE DIRECTOR AT R/GA

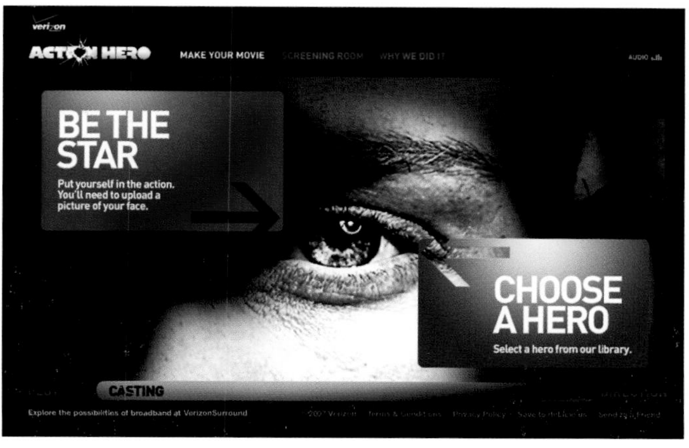

Verizon took the potential of online personalization to new heights with the launch of Action Hero, a free online tool enabling anybody to become a computer-generated character and take the lead in a personalized action movie. Designed to showcase the power of broadband and highlight Verizon's focus on entertainment, Action Hero gives users the opportunity to direct their own Hollywood-style action clip, in the style of a video game, and cast themselves as the hero who has to save the world from killer bugs, mad scientists or insane robots.

The process is simple. Users first upload a photo of themselves, which is modelled in 3D using computer graphics; scenes, character dialogue, music and a title can then be selected. Clicking on the 'go' button confirms the selection, and within 12–24 hours the movie is done and ready to view. The personalized clip can be saved, shared, posted or emailed.

According to Brian Price, executive director of Verizon's Online Center of Excellence, 'Action Hero is more than just a novelty. It delivers an experience to people who make their own movies that they can't get from online games, video uploads or Java animations. It's total immersion in modern creative arts, made possible by the magic of broadband.'

'IN OUR SEVEN-YEAR HISTORY, THIS WAS THE FIRST TIME WE HAD THE PLEASURE OF CREATING OUR OWN MOVIE THAT WOULD BE RENDERED AND SENT TO US FOR OUR PERSONAL AND SHARED VIEWING PLEASURE.'

ROB FORD, FOUNDER AND PRINCIPAL OF FAVOURITE WEBSITE AWARDS

■ BEPERSONAL
■ **BMW GROUP**
■ Agency: Butler, Shine, Stern & Partners
■ United States – 2007

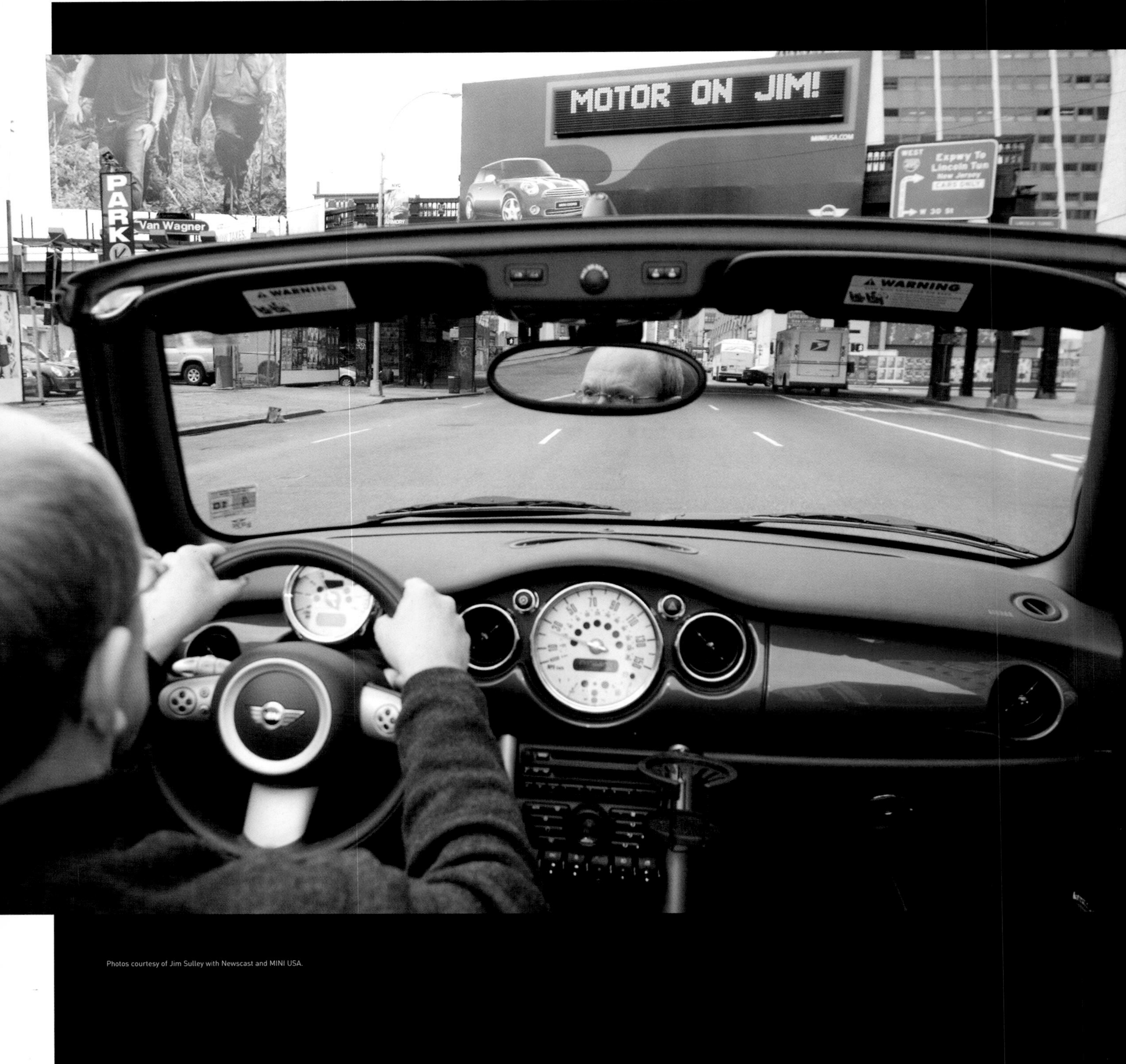

Photos courtesy of Jim Sulley with Newscast and MINI USA.

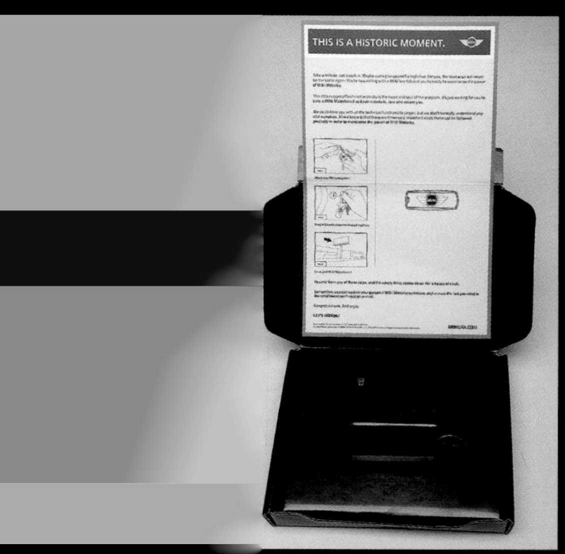

Through clever use of advanced technology, MINI was able to turn standard billboard advertising into personal messages for selected MINI owners. MINI Motorby, as the initiative was dubbed, started out with an email to pre-selected MINI owners asking them random questions about themselves. Some were as straightforward as a profession, while others were more detailed, including 'What adjective best describes how you motor?' and 'What is your MINI's nickname?'.

Four to six weeks later, the respondents received an electronic key fob, a small hardware device with built-in authentication mechanisms, which could be attached to a regular MINI keychain. Four interactive billboards in Chicago, New York, Miami and San Francisco were set up to detect any key fobs within a 150-metre (500-foot) range using RFID (Radio Frequency Identification) technology. Whenever a participating MINI owner drove by one of the billboards (which ordinarily showed content that was relevant to MINI or the location), a personal message would flash up on screen based on the information supplied. The personalized content was based on a number of factors, including the information provided by the owners, the location of the board and the time. The result was an ever-changing array of unique, personal and unexpected messages targeted at and triggered by MINI owners.

BE PERSONAL
LEGO GROUP
Agency: n/a
Denmark – since 2005

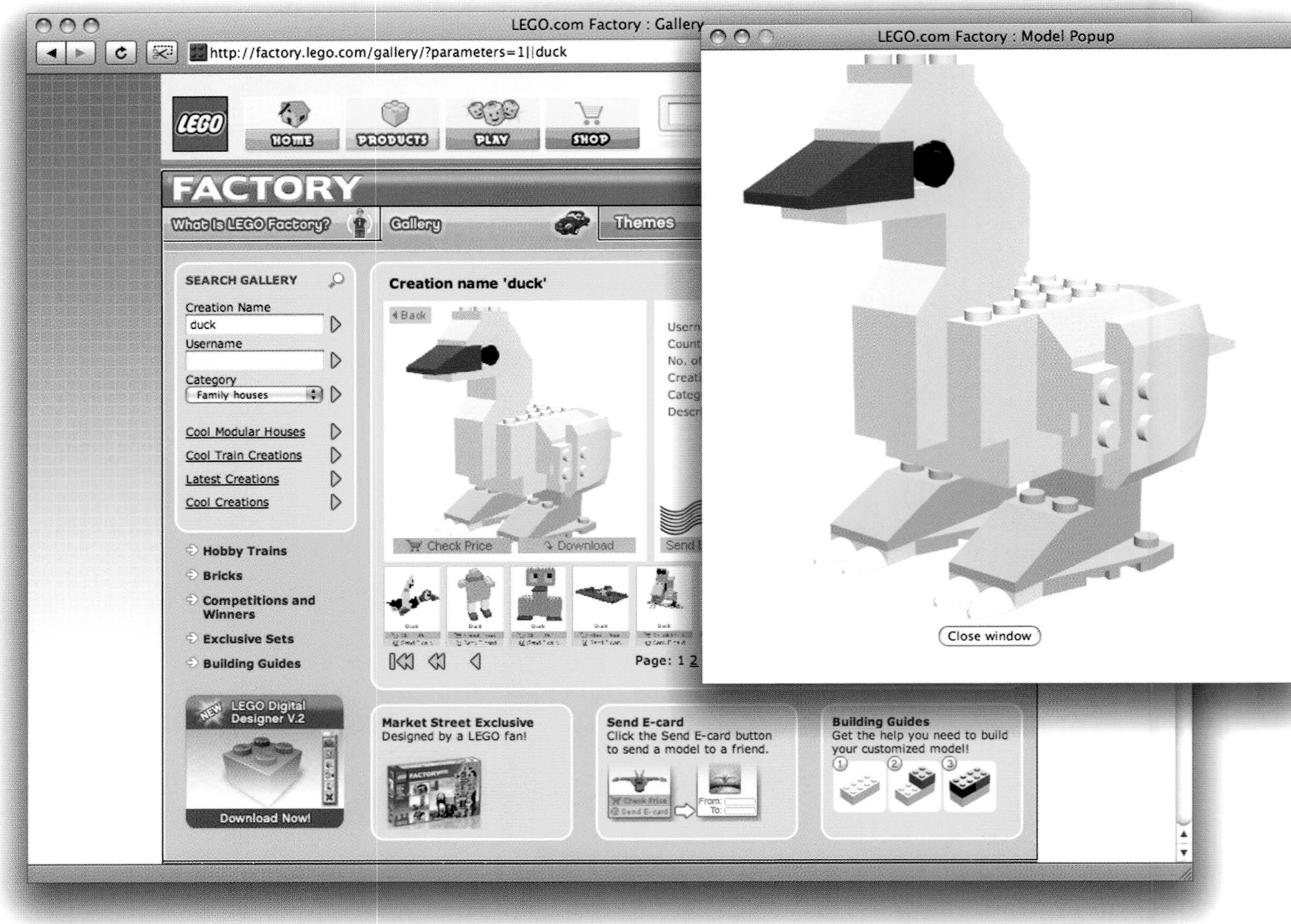

'LEGO FACTORY IS A TRUE LONG TAIL BUSINESS, CATERING FOR SEGMENTS OF ONE.'

HELENE VENGE, DIRECTOR OF LEGO FACTORY

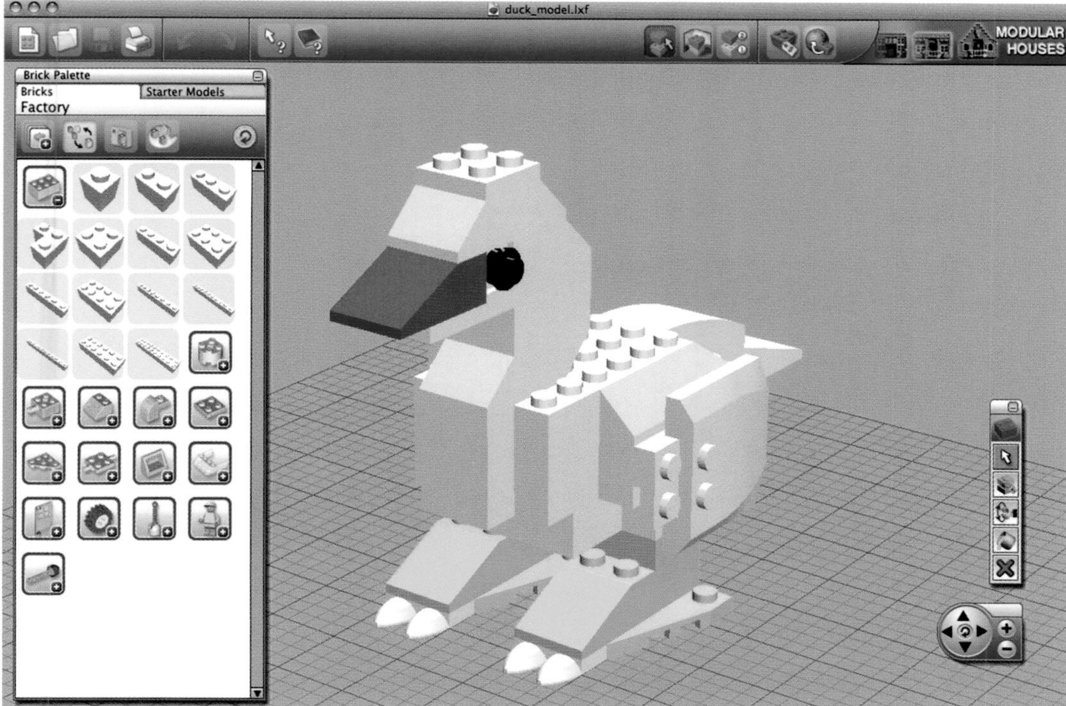

LEGO Factory is the Danish company's audacious venture into consumer customization, enabling anyone to design their own LEGO model. LEGO fans can download the free 3D modelling software LEGO Digital Designer from the LEGO Factory website (www.LEGOFactory.com) and then use it to design, build and upload virtual LEGO creations, dragging and dropping as many bricks as they want. The LEGO creation can also be ordered online and comes in a box labelled with an image of the custom design. Building guides are also available online.

The idea started in autumn 2005 when LEGO launched a competition in which the ten best consumer-designed LEGO models were manufactured and sold as real sets. The company then extended the concept to incorporate a consumer customization platform and service from which consumer-designed models have already been handpicked and turned into official LEGO products, called LEGO Factory Exclusives.

The hard part of LEGO Factory lies in managing the complexity of the logistical process, as one might expect given the single-brick nature of the service and the 998 different bricks available in the LEGO Digital Designer brick palette. The picking and packing process proves to be a complex challenge – as all the custom designs are produced on a 1:1 basis. Today, about 200,000 designs are displayed in the gallery, with 4,000 to 5,000 new models uploaded every single week.

Agency: n/a
United States – 2007

'THE NIKEID STUDIO ENABLES CONSUMERS TO CREATE THEIR EXPRESSION OF THE NIKE BRAND WITH THE GUIDANCE OF A SKILLED DESIGN CONSULTANT.'

TREVOR EDWARDS, VICE-PRESIDENT, BRAND AND CATEGORY MANAGEMENT FOR NIKE

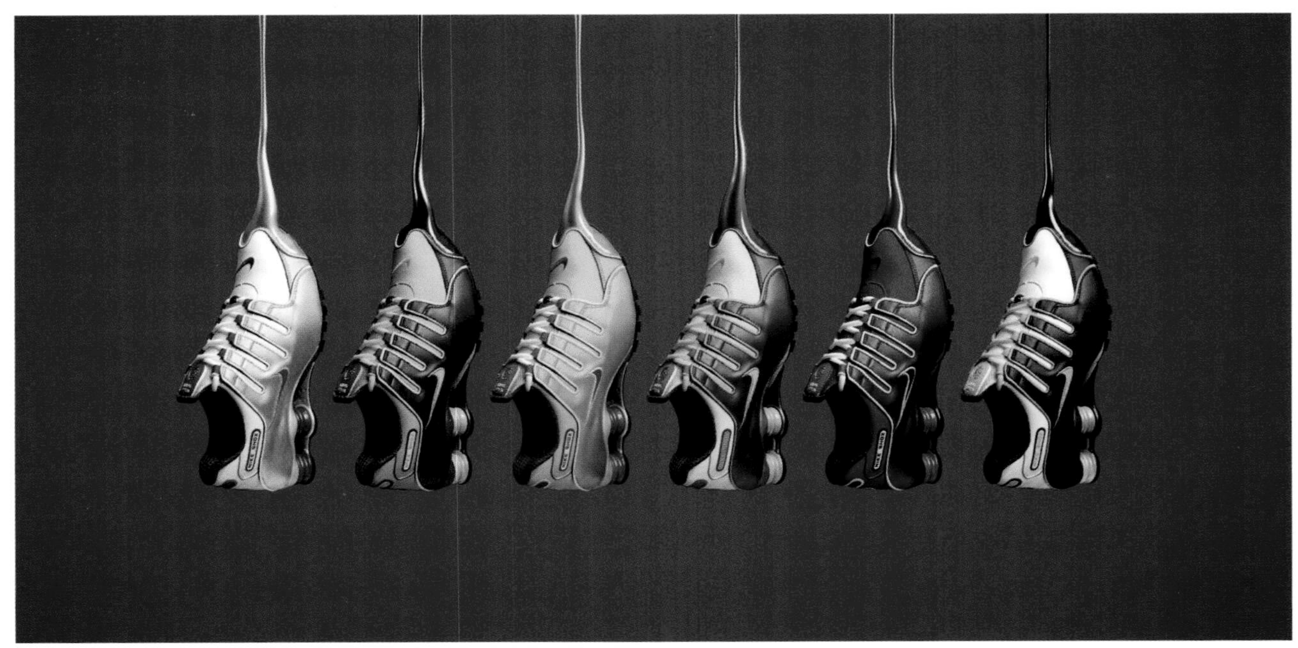

Due to the success of NIKEiD.com, which since its launch in 1999 has enabled consumers to create their own customized footwear and now attracts more than 3 million visitors every month, Nike decided to expand its custom service by offering an in-store alternative. Pilot NIKEiD Studios were unveiled in Paris and Osaka, and the first comprehensive spaces were opened in New York and London in autumn 2007.

The NIKEiD Studio is a design studio environment where people can create a near-endless array of customized products from 105 key styles and a handful of items that are exclusive to the NIKEiD Studio. People are greeted by a concierge and have an appointment with a Design Consultant, who assumes the role of personal advisor, sounding board and confidant(e) all rolled into one. He or she will help the consumer tap into their design potential during a 45- to 60-minute session. Once complete, designs can be purchased and delivered either to the store for collection or directly to the consumer's home address. A select few designs are chosen throughout the year to be produced as limited editions and sold at Niketown.

With no more than four customers allowed in the space at one time and sessions limited to hour-long appointments, Nike ensures that the experience remains both exclusive and highly memorable.

The New York NIKEiD Studio features a touch screen in the front window of the store where consumers are able to design on the street in front of an audience. They are also able to email their designs from the touch screen or even purchase the design inside at Niketown.

The screen displays a sequence of shoe designs from around the world that have been made by people at NIKEiD.com within the past hour. Each shoe posted has the designer's name and nationality, the name of the shoe and the time it was designed.

NIKE

Agencies: Naked Communications/AKQA/Freud Communications
United Kingdom – 2007

To promote the NIKEiD Studio in London, three 'digital dispensing cubes' appeared at key London sites (*below*) enabling people to win fast-track Bluetooth appointment tickets on their mobile phones. Screens on the sides of the cubes showed near real-time images of the NIKEiD shoes being created by real customers in the NIKEiD Studio. The display also featured the customers' names and a few words about their shoe.

NIKEiD.com/londonstudio acts as a window into the NIKEiD Studio with real-time footage. Customers can make appointments and a digital guestbook allows them to share their creations. To generate word-of-mouth and boost appointments, 1,000 mini aluminium cubes (*right*) containing unique fast-track appointment codes were released to London's cultural elite, including graffiti artists, musicians and sneaker freaks.

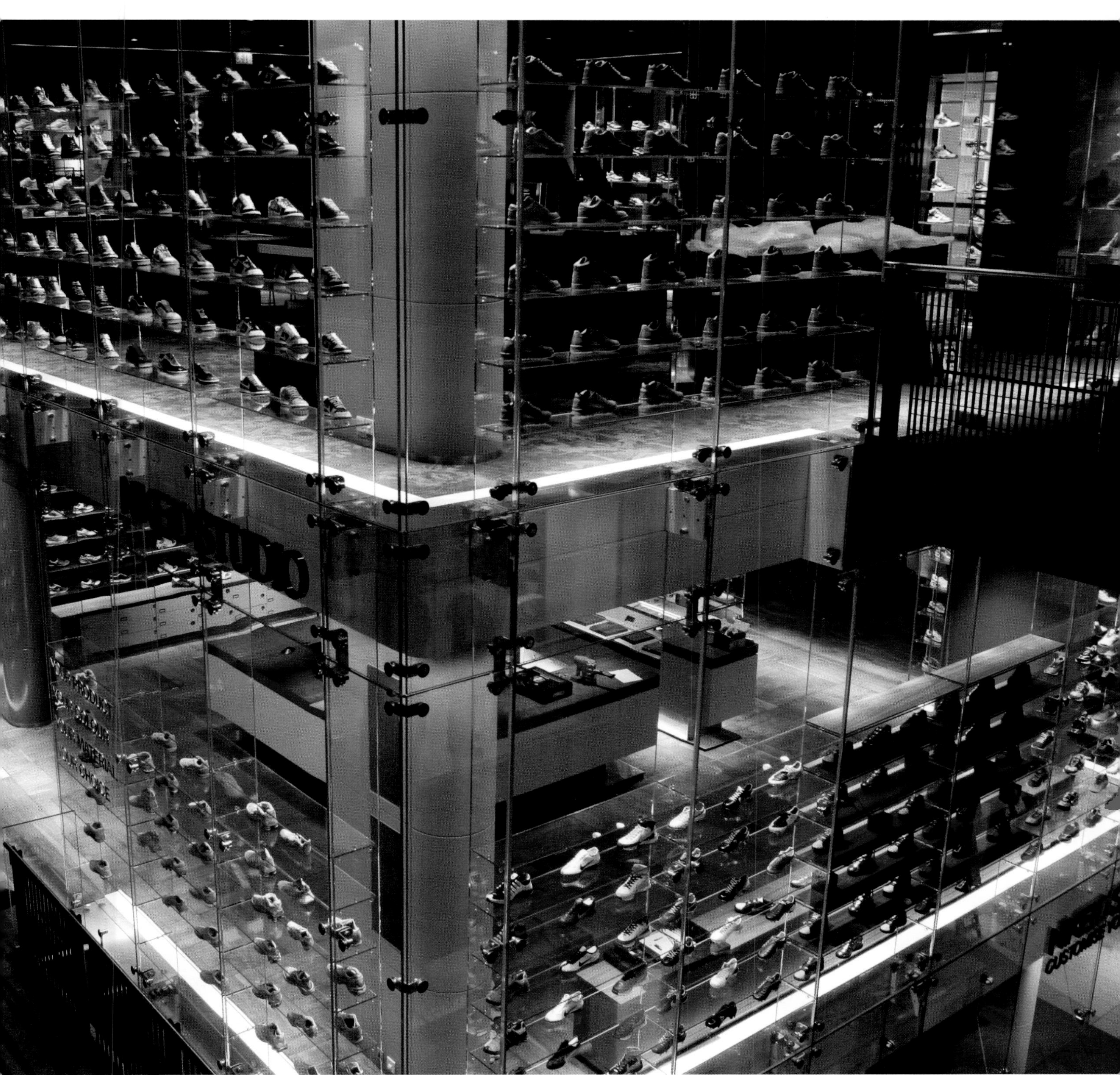
YOUR PRODUCT
YOUR COLOUR
YOUR MATERIAL
YOUR CHOICE

BESOCIABLE

If a person is sociable, he or she is inclined to seek or enjoy companionship. Sociable brands, in turn, are inclined to seek or enjoy the companionship of people, in particular of their customers. Rather than speaking to them from a distance, sociable brands go out of their way to meet their customers, whether it's in the real or the virtual world.

While the real world is more or less familiar terrain for brands, virtual socializing brings with it a new set of conventions and potential embarrassments. People already find it hard to find their way through the minefields of online social networking, which have blurred the lines between friend, acquaintance and complete stranger. For a brand, it's all the more tricky to enter this arena. Especially for brands with little experience of online social mingling, and more comfortable communicating with their audiences from a safe distance, the experience might initially prove awkward. In an environment where friendship is now unequivocally quantifiable and exposed for everyone to see, a brand's popularity – or lack of it – can become painfully obvious once it starts mixing with the crowd.

Yet the sheer and overwhelming popularity of online social networking has left brands with no other choice than to enter the playing field. As a result, they need to adopt a new language and adhere to the rules prevalent in these spaces. One of the first questions any brand that wants to socialize online should ask itself is why anybody should or would care about its presence. Global research by The Future Laboratory revealed two major reasons why anyone would want to socialize with a brand online. Either social-networking users are simply interested in 'associating' themselves with their favourite brands, or they would like to hear about free giveaways or exclusive events. This seems pretty straightforward. But another way for brands to find a place within the online social fabric is by adopting the role of social facilitator. Rather than trying to be the most popular, it's about trying to help others become more popular. The challenge shifts to: How can a brand enable conversations among people? How can it become the social glue that people need? To this end, brands need to provide people with content and tools that can stimulate social interaction. It's essentially not that much different from how they would approach real-world events, where it's a matter of creating opportunities for people to meet each another and have a good time.

The more self-confident brands don't just mix in existing social networks but start their very own, branded versions. It's a risky strategy, as there are so many online platforms out there, including niche areas aimed at specific age groups or interests. Starting a platform from scratch also requires a huge effort, as people are reluctant to visit places without the reassurance that like-minded people are already hanging out there. So there's always the nightmare of ending up with an empty platform, lonely and unloved. But successful cases prove that it is possible.

The most exciting opportunities, however, lie in the crossover between online and offline socializing. In *The Philosophy of Friendship* (2005), Mark Vernon argues that the digital age has renewed our interest in friendship. This manifests itself in the rising phenomenon of real-world gatherings of online groups or communities, which allow friends, acquaintances and strangers to find out the real faces behind the virtual profiles and further solidify and deepen their online bonds. It provides brands with the opportunity to encourage and facilitate social-networking users to keep investing in real-world relationships. Stormhoek, the South African wine brand that got its reputation from its experiments in the online sphere, played with this inherent online–offline duality when it started sponsoring so-called geek dinners (gatherings of bloggers) by providing them with free wine (pages 250–1).

BE SOCIABLE
LEVI'S
Agency: TEQUILA\Hong Kong
Hong Kong/China – 2007

'LEVI'S WORLD COMBINES ENTERTAINMENT, SOCIAL INTERACTION AND THE ABILITY FOR MEMBERS TO CREATE THEIR VERY OWN AND ORIGINAL VIRTUAL SELF.'

VINCY HO, MARKETING MANAGER OF LEVI'S GREATER CHINA

To raise brand awareness and draw people into its shops, Levi's created Levi's World, a virtual environment where members can create their own avatar and customize their look (including gender, body shape, facial features, hair colour, skin tone and Levi's wardrobe and accessories). They can chat with each other, invite their friends to join, try to snap up the latest Levi's collections using virtual coins they have earned, and participate in a host of daily online events including DJ music nights, singles beach parties and celebrity nights. Participants get the chance to win real limited-edition items, and VIP members of real-world stores can also exchange their Levi's reward points for virtual coins.

In Hong Kong, the site went live with an online 'red carpet' launch party, where members were able to meet real local celebrities, create and customize their own online characters, and engage with each other through public and private chats in a series of ongoing virtual events. Within seventy-two hours, the Hong Kong red carpet launch event had received over 6,000 RSVPs. In its first week Levi's World generated 10 million hits, 150,000 visits and over 10,000 registered members from Hong Kong and China. It also created a huge buzz in the local press, including *New Monday* and a ten-page spread in *Face*.

BESOCIABLE
LEVI'S
Agency: TEQUILA\Hong Kong
Hong Kong/China – 2007

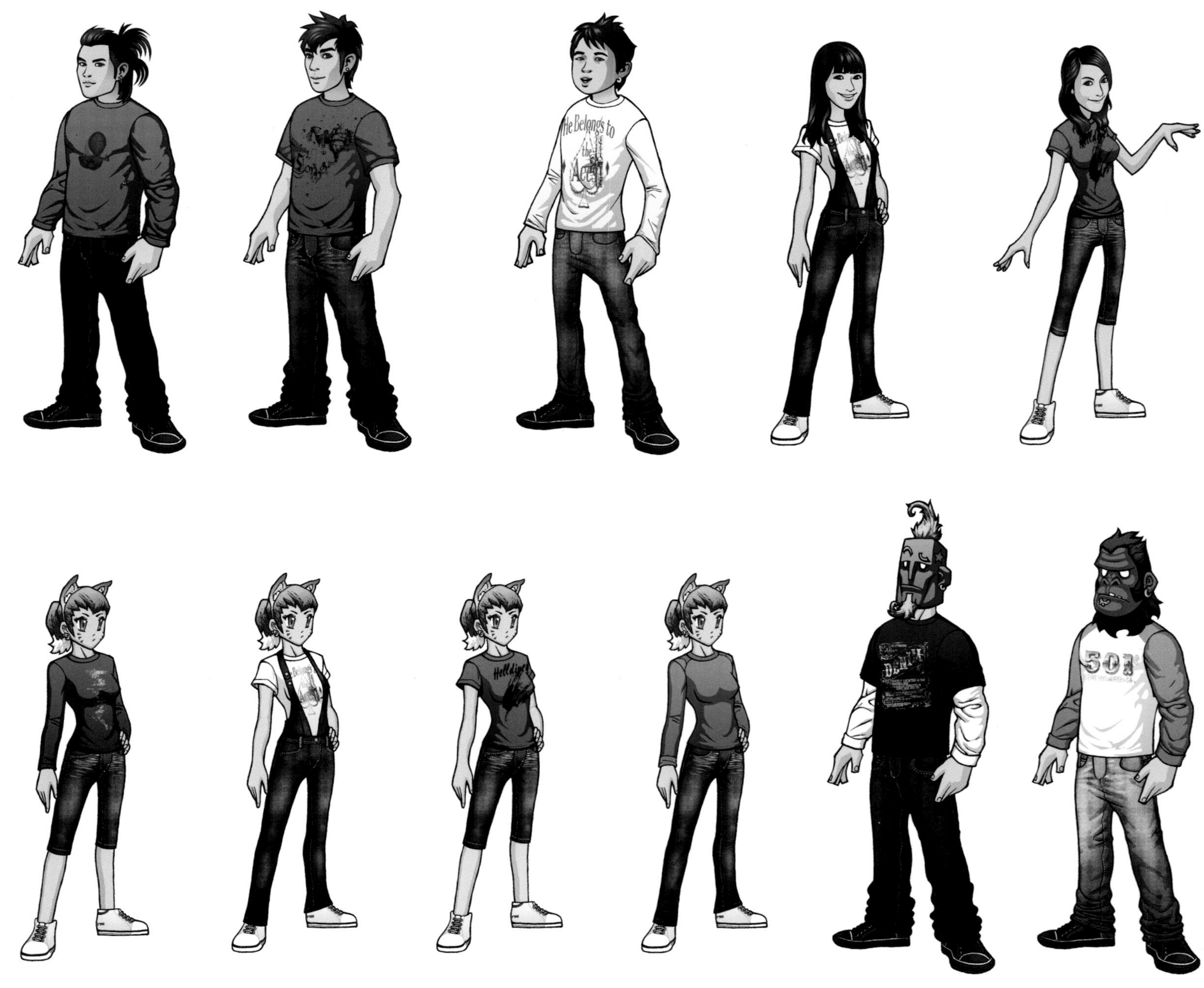

OUT OF THE BLUE
OUT OF THE BLUE
He Belongs to
the
Aces

PROCTER & GAMBLE – CLEAN & CLEAR

Agency: Tribal DDB London
United Kingdom – 2006

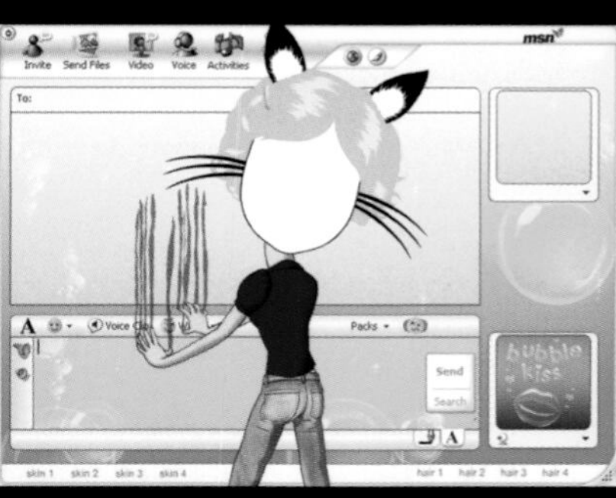

Clean & Clear's cheesy television campaign seemed to fall short of what teenage girls expected from the UK's number one medicated skin care brand. So the brand ventured into new territory by partnering with MSN Instant Messenger in an attempt to add a bit of fun to young girls' online conversations.

The result was 'Clean & Clear Personalised Winks'. Girls could select one of ten characters, such as 'Angel', 'You Rock' and 'Whatever', upload a photo of their choice and then send their own animated 'wink' to a friend during their next Instant Messenger chat. There were also emoticons and backgrounds for the IM window. By developing these tools, Clean & Clear was able to adopt a relevant role within the MSN Instant Messenger environment.

Girls sent 200,000 winks to each other using the Clean & Clear tool, in addition to an ongoing branded presence on desktops and in Messenger windows.

msn
Invite
Send Files
Video
Voice
To:
Voice Clip
Winks
Packs
Send
Search
bubble kiss
skin 1
skin 2
skin 3
skin 4
hair 1
hair 2
hair 3
hair 4

Agency: n/a
Worldwide – since 1983

In 1983 the Harley-Davidson Motor Company launched H.O.G. (Harley Owners Group®), responding to a growing call among riders for an organized network through which they could share the passion and pride they felt for their bikes. H.O.G. is the largest manufacturer-sponsored bikers' organization in the world. Its aim is to enhance the experience of owning a Harley-Davidson by offering access to a host of benefits and services associated with ownership of the world's most famous motorcycle. These include the club magazine *Hog Tales*, the Touring Handbook, access to emergency roadside recovery services, rental schemes, discounts on goods and services, and much more. If a member travels to practically any major city in the US, Australia or Europe they can rent a Harley-Davidson on a daily or weekly basis under the exclusive and inexpensive Fly & Ride and Harley-Davidson Rentals schemes.

Since the organization was formed in 1983, membership of the Harley Owners Group has grown rapidly. It now has over a million members around the world, with over 90,000 in Europe. As well as joining their national H.O.G. organization, members have the option of joining their local H.O.G. chapter, which is sponsored by the local Harley-Davidson dealer. Most chapters hold monthly meetings, organize regular recreational and touring rides and take part in fundraising activities. Chapters are invited to join in friendly competitions with each other at national and international H.O.G. rallies and events. There are currently over 1,500 H.O.G. chapters around the globe. To recognize and encourage the increasing role played by women in the world of Harley, female enthusiasts can become members of Ladies of Harley (L.O.H.).

In 2007, H.O.G. organized many major events throughout Europe, including European Bike Week in Austria; Touring Rides in France, Spain, Germany and many other countries; Harley-Davidson Euro Festival at Port Grimaud in the Gulf of St Tropez; and the year's flagship event, the European H.O.G. Rally at Fuengirola, Spain.

RIGA CHAPTER
LATVIA
HARLEY OWNERS GROUP

BALI CHAPTER
INDONESIA
HOG
HARLEY OWNERS GROUP

WEST SIDE CHAPTER
POZNAN
POLAND

SÃO PAULO - BRASIL
CHAPTER
HARLEY OWNERS GROUP

MOTOR
HARLEY-DAVIDSON
CYCLES

2007
HARLEY OWNERS GROUP®
MEMBERSHIP MANUAL
ENGLISH

When the annual Fruitstock music festival in London became a little too crowded, organizer Innocent Drinks launched a much smaller alternative. The Innocent Village Fete, which toured the UK during the summer period, was a more family- and community-orientated event, and visitors were charged an admission fee to keep down the numbers and raise money for charity. As well as music from unplugged bands, the event offered all the traditional country fete attractions: homemade cakes, a coconut shy, maypole dancing, ferret racing, duck herding, fruit and veg competitions, theatrical performances and lots of bunting. Among the free attractions specifically geared to younger visitors were face painting, storytelling, miniature JCB racing and train rides. Free yoga sessions were also open to people of all ages.

'...A COMPLETE BRAND WORLD CREATED FOR THE EXPLICIT PURPOSES OF CONSUMER IMMERSION....' ADLITERATE.COM

BESOCIABLE
LINCOLN
Agency: Kirt Gunn & Associates
United States – 2006

Home Page :: My DREAM

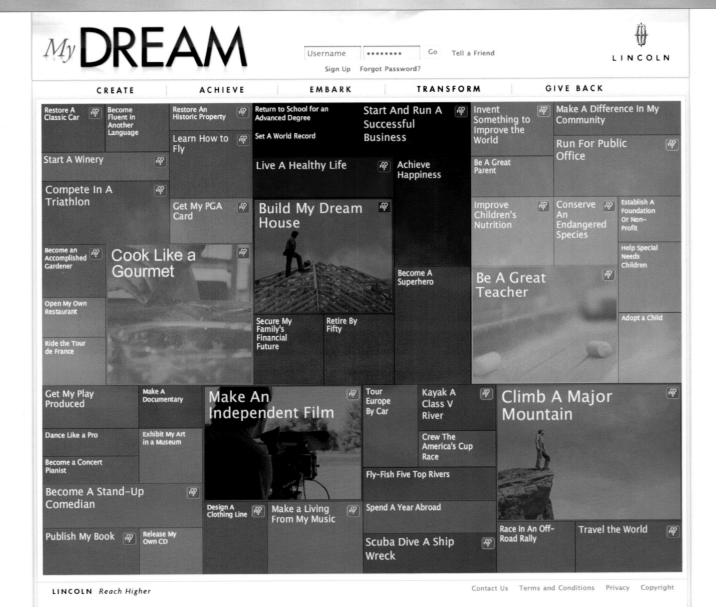

http://www.mydream.tv/

Username Go Tell a Friend
Sign Up Forgot Password?

LINCOLN

CREATE | ACHIEVE | EMBARK | TRANSFORM | GIVE BACK

Restore A Classic Car
Become Fluent in Another Language
Restore An Historic Property
Return to School for an Advanced Degree
Set A World Record
Start And Run A Successful Business
Invent Something to Improve the World
Make A Difference In My Community
Learn How to Fly
Start A Winery
Live A Healthy Life
Achieve Happiness
Be A Great Parent
Run For Public Office
Compete In A Triathlon
Get My PGA Card
Build My Dream House
Improve Children's Nutrition
Conserve An Endangered Species
Establish A Foundation Or Non-Profit
Become an Accomplished Gardener
Cook Like a Gourmet
Help Special Needs Children
Become A Superhero
Be A Great Teacher
Open My Own Restaurant
Secure My Family's Financial Future
Retire By Fifty
Adopt a Child
Ride the Tour de France
Get My Play Produced
Make A Documentary
Make An Independent Film
Tour Europe By Car
Kayak A Class V River
Climb A Major Mountain
Dance Like a Pro
Exhibit My Art in a Museum
Crew The America's Cup Race
Become a Concert Pianist
Fly-Fish Five Top Rivers
Become A Stand-Up Comedian
Design A Clothing Line
Make a Living From My Music
Spend A Year Abroad
Race In An Off-Road Rally
Travel the World
Publish My Book
Release My Own CD
Scuba Dive A Ship Wreck

LINCOLN *Reach Higher*

Contact Us Terms and Conditions Privacy Copyright

In its 'Dreams' campaign, US car manufacturer Lincoln drew an association between the brand and the accomplishment of major life goals. In order for people to share their aspirations and learn from each other's experiences, an online social network was launched called MyDream.tv.

MyDream.tv featured about fifty short documentary films starring real people who have achieved their greatest dream in life – dreams that lay far outside the conventional mould, such as opening a school in a deprived area, publishing a novel, climbing Everest, building a dream house or making an independent film.

The participants in the documentaries took on the role of 'Dream Experts', helping others to pursue their dreams, answering questions, giving advice and holding online chats. Next to each dream, there were relevant Amazon links to get people started. Visitors could submit their own dreams and ambitions, blog about their experiences and connect with like-minded dreamers.

The site spawned numerous vibrant online communities, and Lincoln successfully connected the brand with a modern definition of success and achievement by offering a window into people's deepest passions.

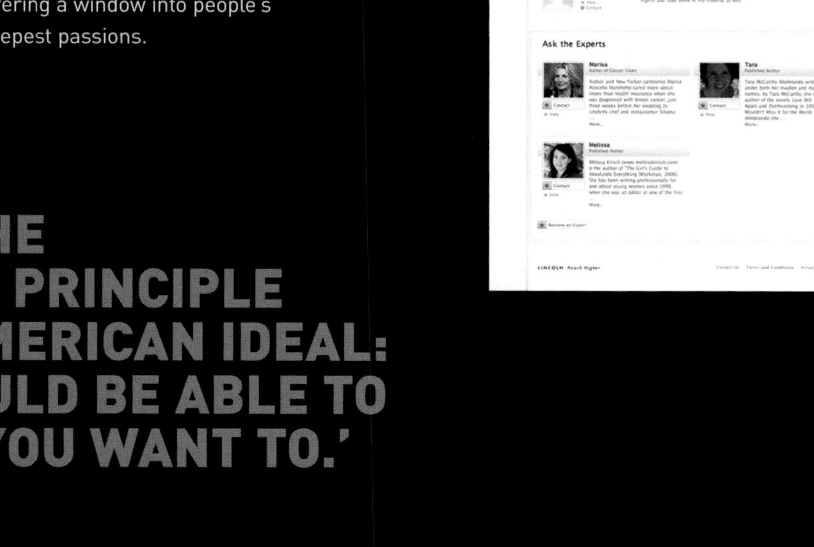

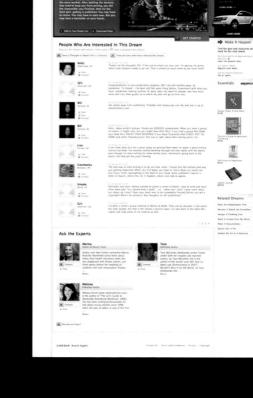

'IT'S REALLY THE FUNDAMENTAL PRINCIPLE BEHIND THE AMERICAN IDEAL: THAT YOU SHOULD BE ABLE TO DO ANYTHING YOU WANT TO.'

KIRT GUNN ON ADCRITIC.COM

MSNBC.COM
Agency: SS+K
United States – 2007

During the summer blockbuster season MSNBC.com entertained cinema audiences as they waited for the film to start. *NewsBreaker Live* was a participatory and above all social video game. Working as a team, the audience directs the on-screen action using a ball and a long paddle (as in the classic Atari game *Breakout*). As filmgoers sway, swing and rock in their seats, motion-sensor technology dubbed 'Crowd Gaming' tracks the entire audience's collective movement. The audience's goal is to move in sync and break MSNBC.com's colourful brick wall of news. Each brick they break earns them points. Some of the bricks contain real-time MSNBC.com headlines that the audience can 'catch' with the paddle as they fall from the broken bricks, which also earns them points. For people who couldn't get enough of the game, MSNBC.com also created an online version.

'INSTEAD OF WAITING IMPATIENTLY FOR MOVIES TO START, MSNBC.COM'S *NEWSBREAKER LIVE* LETS MOVIEGOERS IN ON THE ACTION.'

CATHERINE CAPTAIN, VICE-PRESIDENT OF MARKETING AT MSNBC.COM

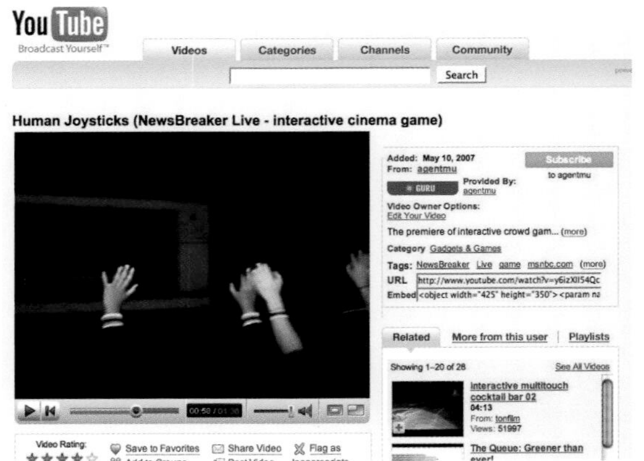

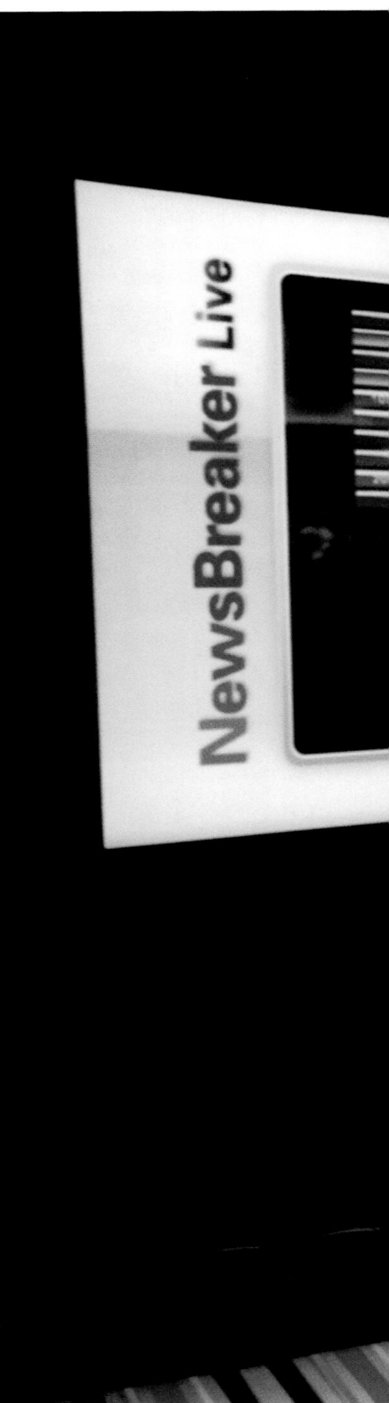

msnbc.com
A Fuller Spectrum of News
Score 12850
High Score 14400
'American Idol' cuts cast to four

BESOCIABLE
NOKIA
Agency: Contra
Finland – 2007

To showcase the music capabilities of the Nokia N91, a specially designed mobile sound system was created that was reminiscent of an old-school ghettoblaster but played music directly from a Nokia device. The portable, transparent ghettoblaster was taken on tour by the Blaster Crew, a handpicked group of people who were already heavily involved in the music scene. They went wherever the target audience congregated: at festivals, on the streets, at the beach, in shopping centres or in cinemas. They arranged street-dance shows, BBQs and DJ sessions, spreading the word via SMS. Online seeding on Flickr and MySpace also drummed up support for the Blaster Tour. More than 80,000 young people actively participated in the Blaster Tour, with a further 400,000 spectators.

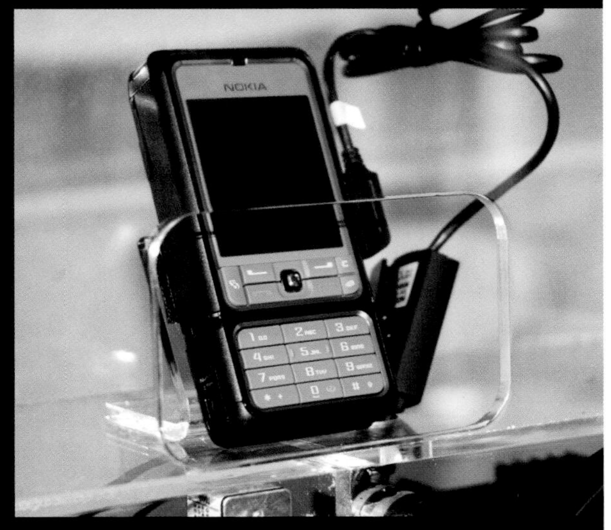

'THE BLASTER TOUR WAS A TRULY INNOVATIVE AND HIGHLY EFFECTIVE WAY TO BUILD CREDIBILITY FOR THE NOKIA BRAND AMONG A VERY IMPORTANT GROUP OF CONSUMERS.'

PEKKA RANTALA, SENIOR VICE-PRESIDENT OF NOKIA

STORMHOEK

Agency: n/a
South Africa – since 2005

Before it became a blogosphere phenomenon, Stormhoek was just one of many niche wine brands around the world. Hugh MacLeod, part-time cartoonist, part-time blogger and part-time marketer, helped the South African wine brand to embrace the social value of its product. He recognized that the interesting thing is not so much the intrinsic characteristics of the wine, but what people do with it.

Stormhoek started out by sending free bottles of wine to about a hundred bloggers in the UK, Ireland and France, with each of the bottles carrying a customized label. Although they were not asked to do so, a lot of those bloggers ended up writing about Stormhoek wine.

The most overtly social initiative was Stormhoek's sponsorship of '100 Geek Dinners in 100 Days' in the US. The initiative, which accompanied the brand's US launch, was orchestrated through a wiki, inviting every blogger to sign up and announce their dinner. Stormhoek simply supplied the wine, and threw a free limited-edition cartoon into the bargain, but demanded nothing in return. Organizers of the dinners could set their own rules for the event, and participants were equally free to blog about it or post pictures online.

Stormhoek's activities in the blogosphere put the brand on the global map and led to a five-fold increase in sales in less than two years.

'PEOPLE GATHERING AND TALKING ABOUT WHAT MATTERS TO THEM – I FRANKLY CAN'T THINK OF A BETTER REASON TO OPEN A BOTTLE OF WINE.'

JASON KORMAN, HEAD OF MARKETING AT STORMHOEK

Wine Blogging as Marketing Disruption

'THE CAMPAIGN HAS ALLOWED US TO GO TO THE TRADE WITH AN INTERESTING PERSPECTIVE.'

NICK DYMOKE MARR, STORMHOEK SPOKESMAN

BE COLLABORATIVE

In Jamaica, mash-up (or 'mash it up') means 'to destroy'. Yet paradoxically, in many other parts of the world the term also indicates the birth of something new as elements from different sources are 'mashed up' and reformulated, whether it's in music, video or web applications. By taking the best bits of different, often completely opposing things and mixing them together, mash-ups hope to create something refreshing, useful or entirely original. And often, the more polarized the different elements, the better the end result. As one blogger, Sarah Morning, points out, 'The beauty of the music mash-up is that the more diverse and polarized the collaborations are, the better they tend to work. It is a medium set up to bring the polarized together.'

The habit of remixing sits at the heart of digital culture. Architect and computer scientist Nicholas Negroponte pointed out the recombinant nature of the internet in the book *Being Digital* (1995) in which he states that 'bits commingle effortlessly. They start to get mixed up and can be used and reused together or separately.' This recombinant climate of mash-ups and open source has a major impact on how brands think about and approach collaborations. In a world where bits can mingle effortlessly, to paraphrase Negroponte, so can brands. They are increasingly forced to step outside the box in order to stand out in their own highly competitive category, and do so by collaborating with new and refreshing partners of all kinds. Of course, most brands have always had ongoing collaborations with a range of partners on different levels, from product development to retail, from joint events to content deals. But only a selection of those partnerships is generally able to transcend business-as-usual and truly spark the imagination of audiences.

In essence, a partnership is a relationship based on mutual cooperation and responsibility for the achievement of a specified goal. As long as the outcome makes sense to people, they will accept the puzzle brands have created to get there. According to Trendwatching.com, brand alliances will continue to grow, because people 'know which brands have a competency in what area, and they are relentlessly looking for the best of the best'. Much like mash-ups, it's a matter of admitting what you're genuinely good at, and finding the complementary bits elsewhere.

Although in theory any collaboration is feasible, there are a few golden rules when it comes to choosing partners. Firstly, where possible, brands should look to collaborate with partners that are well established in people's minds and understood by the target audience. If people are familiar with the separate ingredients, they are more likely to appreciate the resulting meal. Secondly, brands should always seek to partner with companies or organizations that will echo and enhance the positive attributes of the brand. If the partner also plugs a negative gap, that is an added bonus.

As brands come to realize the value of strong partnerships, they are increasingly opting for full integration. Rather than restricting partnerships to specific areas, the most audacious brands are stretching them as far as possible, through different media channels, packaging, content deals or product development. By leveraging the partnership in different ways, both partners maximize the value of the joint effort as well as its impact. The examples in this chapter represent some of the most outstanding and memorable collaborations in recent years, whether they are global or local, short-term or long-term, or with a focus on communication or on product development.

H&M/THE SIMS
Agency: n/a
United States – 2007

'WE COULDN'T IMAGINE A MORE PERFECT MATCH. FASHION INSPIRES CREATIVITY IN THE SAME WAY VIDEOGAMES DO. THIS BRINGS NEW AND EXCITING GAME CONTENT FROM TWO TRUSTED BRANDS THAT SHARE THE SAME GLOBAL FOOTPRINT AND CUSTOMER PROFILE.'

STEVE SEABOLT, VICE-PRESIDENT OF GLOBAL BRAND DEVELOPMENT AT ELECTRONIC ARTS

This special collaboration between the clothing company H&M and *The Sims 2* (developed by Electronic Arts) brought together the real world of fashion and the virtual world of gaming. To dress their Sims characters in the latest H&M designs gamers purchase *The Sims 2: H&M Fashion Stuff*. More adventurous players can also design their own creations and enter them into the Fashion Runway online competition, with the possibility of having their design made and sold in real H&M stores. H&M is the first brand to enter into the Sims world in this way.

H&M
H&M
H&M
09

H&M
H&M

'Old masters meet new technology' captures the essence of Hewlett-Packard's long-standing collaboration with the National Gallery in London. HP's sponsorship enables high-resolution reproductions of the gallery's paintings to be made and examined in minute detail.

The Grand Tour celebrated the collaboration in a highly imaginative way. Forty-four high-quality reproductions were framed and mounted around central London for a twelve-week period, turning the city streets into an open gallery. It gave both partners what they wanted, attracting hordes of visitors to the National Gallery's collection of Western European art, and highlighting HP's high standards in colour reproduction.

Each picture had a plaque next to it and a phone number that people could call to listen to a pre-recorded guide to the work of art. A Grand Tour microsite (www.thegrandtour.org.uk) featured all forty-four locations on an interactive map, allowed people to select a walking tour and contained a picture gallery. There was also a Flickr group for Grand Tour pictures. The gallery was inundated with requests from the public for maps and information as the project was unveiled, with the website receiving well over a million hits.

'IF WE CAN'T BRING PEOPLE TO THE ART, WE'LL BRING THE ART TO THE PEOPLE.'

CHARLES SAUMAREZ SMITH, FORMER DIRECTOR OF THE NATIONAL GALLERY

'MY OPINION – IN ANSWER TO THE YOUNG MAN WHO ALMOST FELL OFF HIS BICYCLE WHEN HE MET *THE AMBASSADORS* IN BERWICK STREET, BLURTING OUT "WHAT THE FUCK IS THAT?" – IS IT'S THE BEST NATIONAL GALLERY EXHIBITION I'VE EVER SEEN.'

MAEV KENNEDY, IN *THE GUARDIAN*

Fire escape Keep clear
Fire escape Keep clear

■ **BE COLLABORATIVE**
■ **NIKE/APPLE**
■ Agency: RG/A
■ United States – since 2006

Nike+ is a unique concept – a Nike running shoe that communicates with an iPod Nano to give feedback on aspects of performance such as distance covered and speed. A sensor makes it possible to transfer data wirelessly from Nike+ footwear to the Nano. Runners can sync the iPod with their computer and compare their performance on different runs (by distance or time, for example), chart their progress and set themselves goals. They can also interact with a global community of runners and compete against them.

Users can also challenge each other and participate in 'virtual' marathons, choosing their own theme, setting their own rules, and selecting the number of participants and team names. Pictures can be uploaded on the Nikeplus.com homepage.

Another additional feature is the Nike+ Distance Club where runners who have achieved certain milestones – 100, 500 or 1,000 miles, for example – can be initiated into the club.

Running used to be a largely solitary sport for dedicated health-conscious athletes, with each outing relegated to memory the instant it was completed. Nike+ turns running into a fun, social, digitally enhanced sport.

Prior to its collaboration with Apple, Nike had attempted to link up with electronics producer Philips instead, but it was not a success. Apple came to Nike after it separated from Philips.

Collectively, the Nike+ community has run millions of miles. Nike attributed much of its 8.1 per cent Q2 increase in profits in the second quarter of 2007 to the success of the Nike+ platform.

'WE KNOW THAT THESE TWO BRANDS WORK REALLY WELL TOGETHER. WE SHARE THE SAME TYPES OF CONSUMERS.'

TREVOR EDWARDS, NIKE'S VICE-PRESIDENT OF GLOBAL BRAND MANAGEMENT ON BBC.COM

Opposite, second from top: Runners can compare their runs by distance or time week-on-week or month-on-month.

Opposite, second from bottom: The Nike+ community shares favourite runs using the Map-it tool.

Above: The Nike Women's Marathon in San Francisco sold out within days, so to handle the demand Nike+ hosted the first-ever virtual marathon. Over 3,400 'virtual' runners joined the 20,000 in San Francisco on 21 October 2007 and logged their miles from anywhere in the United States using Nike+.

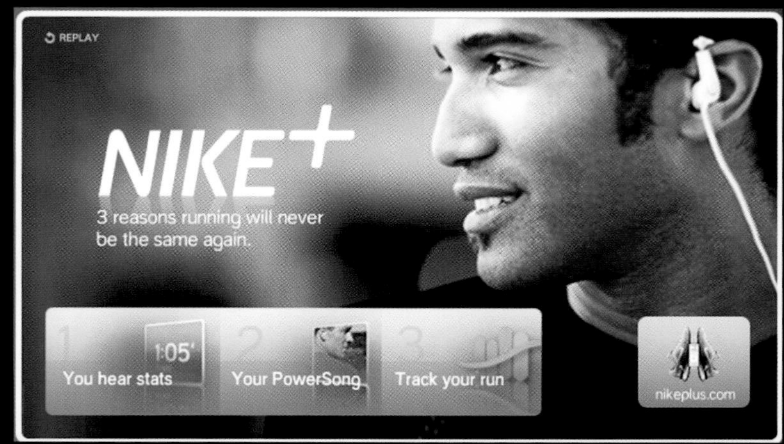

Agency: Shine Communications
United Kingdom – 2007

PlayStation Season London is a unique series of events and exhibitions for which PlayStation teamed up with selected public arts institutions that are known for an innovative approach to arts programming, whether it's in art ('Kozyndan' at BALTIC, Gateshead), design ('Volume' at the V&A, London, *top left and opposite*), performance ('Inside Out' at the English National Opera, London, *centre left*), dance ('Sampled' at Sadler's Wells, London, *bottom left*) or audiovisual experience ('Optronica' at the British Film Institute, London). Rather than opting for passive sponsorship, Sony PlayStation gave these five prestigious organizations an equal, undisclosed sum so that they could develop projects with an interactive element (audience participation). Common themes running through the events and exhibitions are interactivity, appeal to young and new audiences and technological sophistication. In each collaboration, Sony PlayStation was used to broaden and enhance the available content.

'WE HAD TO CHANGE [THESE ORGANIZATIONS'] BEHAVIOUR. THEY ARE USED TO GETTING A CHUNK OF MONEY FROM A BANK WHICH JUST WANTS ITS LOGO DISPLAYED, AND THE CORPORATE HOSPITALITY, AND THEN DISAPPEARS. THAT WAS NOT OUR CONCERN. AS A BRAND, WE DON'T BADGE.'

CARL CHRISTOPHER, HEAD OF SPONSORSHIP AND EVENTS AT SONY PLAYSTATION, IN THE *FINANCIAL TIMES*

■ Agency: TracyLocke
■ United States & Canada – 2007

'WE'VE NEVER KNOWN A COMPANY THAT HAS SO FULLY EMBRACED A PROMOTION.'

LISA LICHT, 20TH CENTURY FOX'S EXECUTIVE VICE-PRESIDENT OF GLOBAL MARKETING PARTNERSHIPS ON ITS PARTNERSHIP WITH 7-ELEVEN

Some of the collaborations surrounding the release of *The Simpsons Movie* perfectly reflected the cleverness and irreverence of the global television hit. Airline company JetBlue labelled itself as the 'official airline of Springfield', sending out a direct mailing to its five million members, creating an in-flight *Simpsons*-only channel and launching the 'Woo-hoo JetBlue!' *Simpsons*-themed plane.

Undoubtedly the most audacious collaboration, however, was the temporary rebranding of a dozen 7-Eleven stores as Kwik-E-Marts, Springfield's one and only convenience store. As part of this promotion, several real-life versions of famous fictional *Simpsons* products were sold across almost 6,400 7-Eleven stores in the US and Canada, including Buzz Cola, Squishees, Krusty O's, pink-frosted Sprinklicious doughnuts and a special edition of Radioactive Man. The only product clearly missing was Duff Beer, which didn't seem appropriate in light of the movie's PG-13 rating.

Those involved spent months examining every piece of communication in 7-Eleven stores and finding ways to bring a *Simpsons* tone of voice to the shopping experience. Original art was created for points of sale. All 7-Eleven logos were replaced with those of Kwik-E-Mart. Store associates were given hand-made Kwik-E-Mart uniforms and nametags. Life-size Springfield characters were placed all over the stores. To make the transformation of the twelve 7-Eleven stores complete, brick facades were created, walls were painted yellow, 5-metre (18-foot) backlit Kwik-E-Mart pole signs were erected, and fictitious Springfield Bank signs and 'Violators Will Be Executed' parking signs were displayed.

If all of that wasn't enough, the store's 'Get Animated' promotion gave one lucky shopper the chance of being animated and 'appearing' as a character in the show. Woo-hoo indeed!

7-Eleven may have carried all the costs of the initiative, which executives of the retail chain put at somewhere in the single millions, but the collaboration led to a steep increase in traffic and sales. Throughout the month, 7-Eleven sold out of all proprietary products, sold more than 1 million doughnuts, and more than 3 million pieces of *Simpsons* merchandise. Kwik-E-Mart products soon started to show up on eBay, with a uniform selling for more than $500 (£250), and products selling for three or four times their retail price.

TATE MODERN

Agency: Fallon, London
United Kingdom – 2006

'Tate Tracks' was an initiative by Tate Modern to attract young inner-city Londoners to the gallery. Well-known musicians were invited to walk around the museum and pick out an artwork that would inspire them to write a track. Chemical Brothers, Graham Coxon from Blur, Klaxons, Union of Knives and Roll Deep were among those that took part. Each month, a new track was released exclusively in Tate Modern at listening posts placed in front of the artwork that had inspired the song. The tracks could be accessed exclusively in the gallery for one month and were then made available on Tate.org, drawing fans to the website. Tate Modern also promoted the project outside clubs by giving away free A2 posters.

Two thirds of the people that listened to a track on one of the listening posts had visited Tate Modern specifically for that purpose. The collaboration received an estimated £2.1 m ($4.2 m) worth of coverage across a wealth of media channels, both in London and beyond.

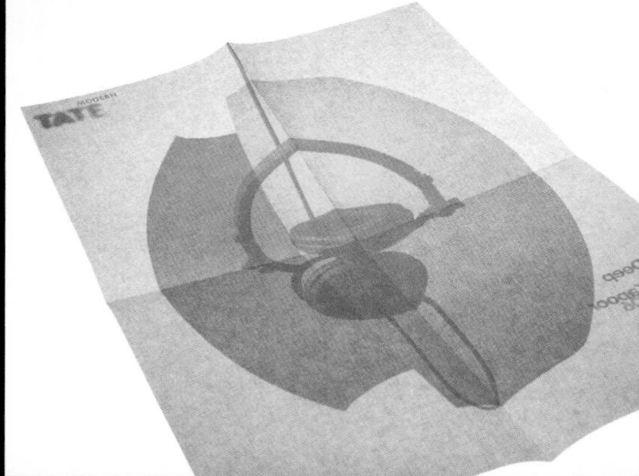

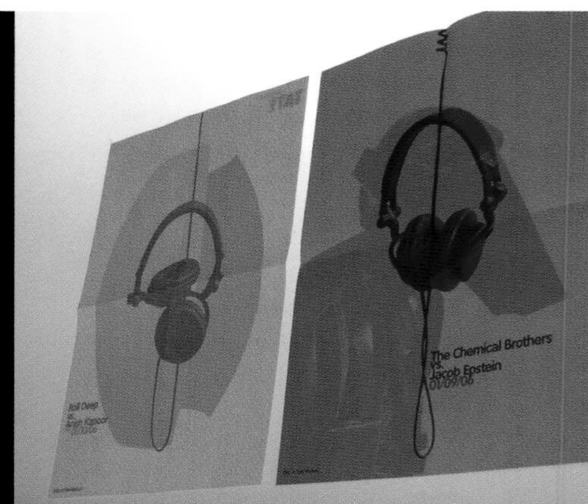

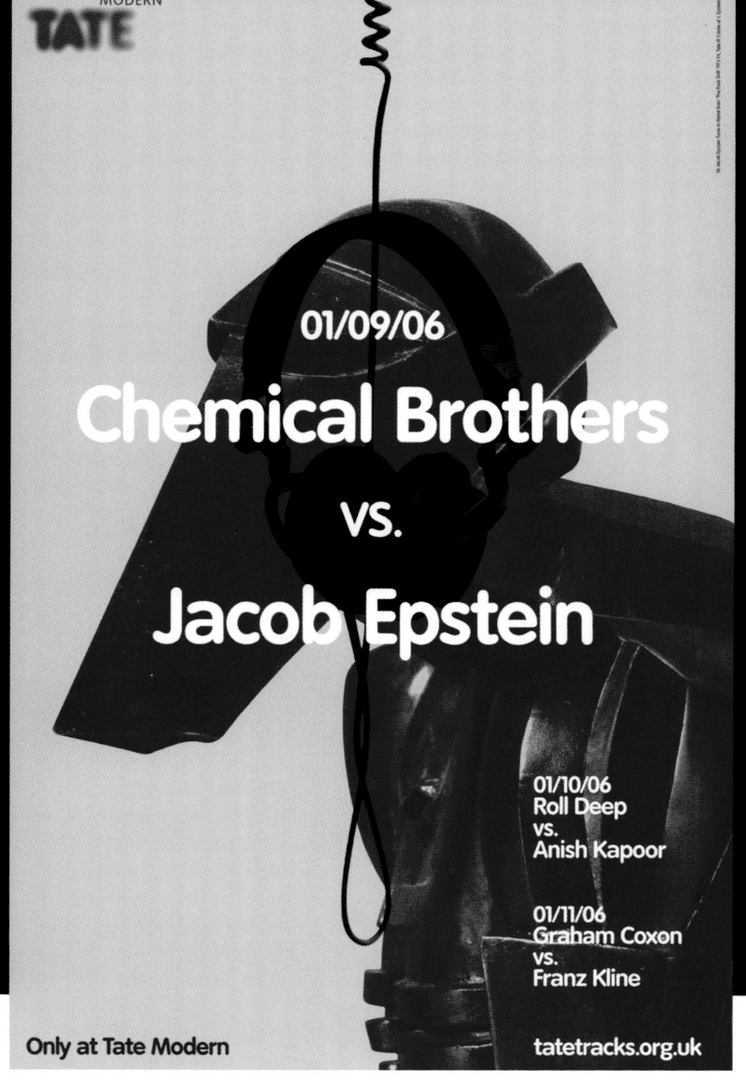

Tate Tracks Union of Knives vs. Cy Twombly

Exit X

© Cy Twombly, from Quattro Stagioni (A Painting in Four Parts), Quattro Stagioni 1993–4
More info >

Play track

< Previous

Next >

Hide controls

Credits >

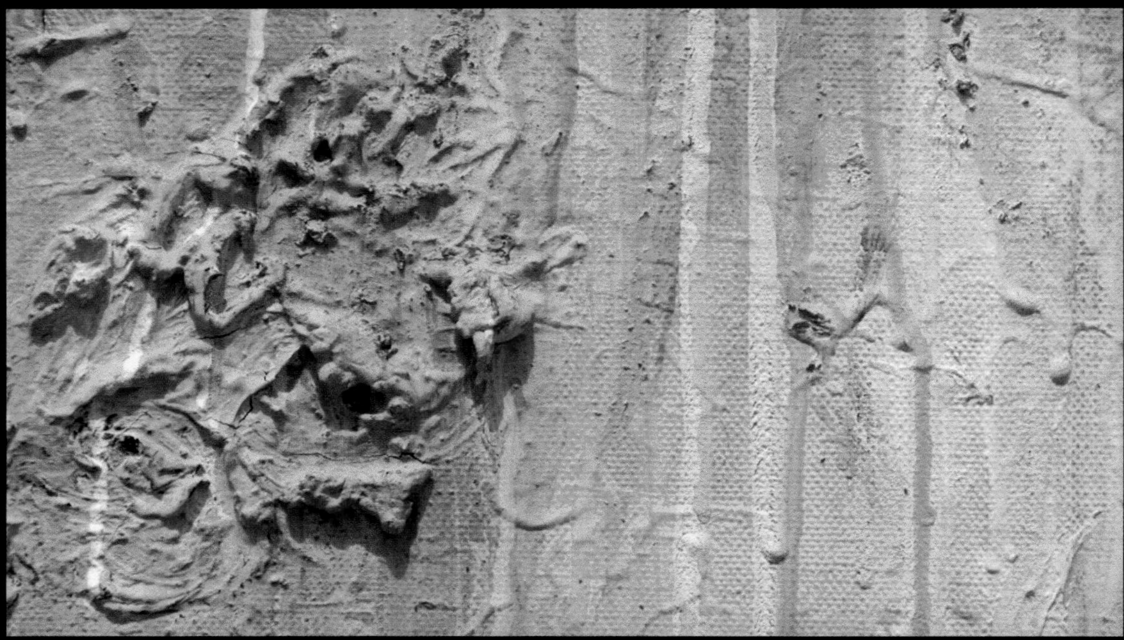

Show controls

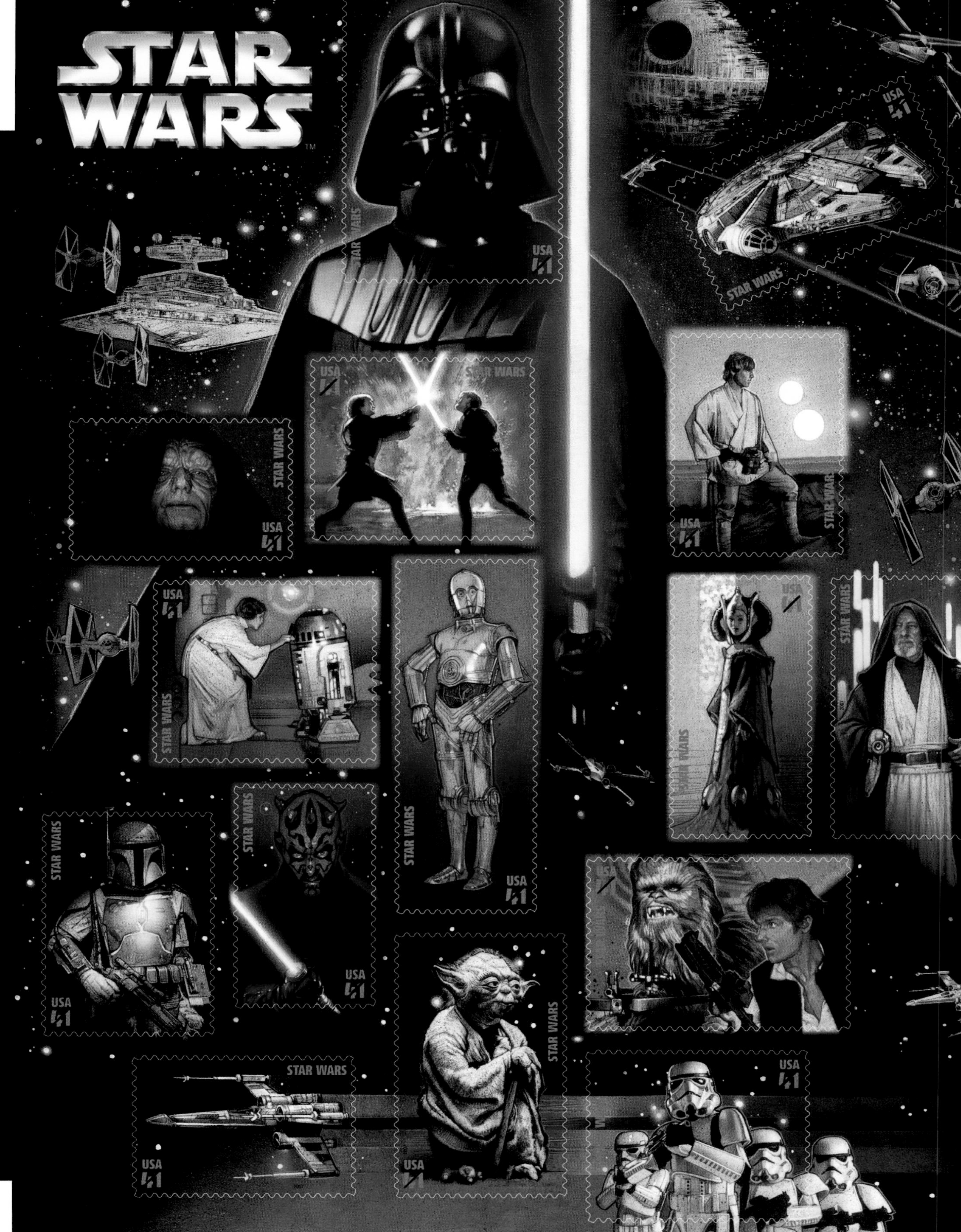
STAR WARS™
STAR WARS
USA 41

US POSTAL SERVICES/LUCASFILM
Agency: n/a
United States – 2006

US Postal Services partnered up with *Star Wars* to release commemorative stamps featuring images from all six films. Mailboxes around the United States were also redesigned to look like R2-D2.

BE CO-CREATIVE

There are two schools of thought when it comes to involving people in a company's or a brand's creative process. According to one, the democratization of content is a good thing – it's about time brands gave over some control to people, and digital tools are opening up their creativity. According to the other school of thought, talent is scarce, the majority of people create, at best, mediocre content and there should be a clear distinction between authors and audience. This latter school is openly nostalgic about a world where true authorship and expertise are valued, and finally got its own spokesperson with the publication of Andrew Keen's book *The Cult of the Amateur: How Today's Internet is Killing Our Culture and Assaulting Our Economy* (2007).

As is often the case, the truth lies somewhere between the two. Any company looking to involve people creatively as a quick, stress-free and cheap ticket to success is betting on the wrong horse; any company that disregards or is completely oblivious to negative opinions or feedback, or cannot live with an expression that does not perfectly reflect the brand's predefined values and character, is better off leaving things as they are.

One question arises from all this: How can we optimize the benefits and minimize the risks involved with co-creation initiatives? In other words, how can we relax our guard and leave our brand defenceless but prevent scavengers from picking away at it? After all, you may want to invite as many people as possible to the party, but you don't want a few drunken louts spoiling the fun for everyone else. There are a few simple rules when tapping into other people's creative flair, which the cases in this chapter adhere to: community-building, rule-setting and/or long-term thinking. By sticking to one or more of these guiding principles, the chances are that brands will be rewarded accordingly.

The first rule is about the importance of community-building. The co-creation initiatives that have been most successful and worthwhile in the long term are the ones that have succeeded in building a community of like-minded individuals, whether it's on their own or in partnership with existing social networks, and have embedded their requests for creativity within that community. Because they consist of a complex web of relationships, communities take away a sense of anonymity and act as a form of self-regulation, a safety blanket against scavengers. Members who step out of line risk being reproached by their peers. There is a greater degree of openness and transparency, and a heightened sense of long-term commitment. As a result, communities lead to quality over quantity, to commitment over opportunism, to group-thinking over selfish individual impulses. Greenpeace's call for a greener Apple (see pages 288–9), Boeing's development of its Dreamliner plane (pages 278–9), Nikon's 'Picturetown' campaign (pages 294–5), Penguin's *MyPenguins* series (296–7) and E4's launch of *Skins* (pages 280–1) are examples of co-creation where a central community formed an integral part of the approach.

The second rule highlights the need for authorship. Co-creation is not just about handing over creativity and passively watching how people take over. There is still a need for a primary author, a centrally conceived concept, but its distribution happens much more easily and much quicker by inviting people to help bring it to life. A kitchen that allows the guests to determine the menu and play with the ingredients still needs a visionary chef to bring it all together. The Absolut (pages 272–5), Beastie Boys (pages 276–7), E4 (pages 280–1), Nike (pages 292–3) and Red Bull (pages 298–9) concepts in this chapter were all presented to audiences with a clearly defined creative framework. This allows a more mainstream crowd to join in, rather than just the creative elite.

The third rule establishes the need for long-term thinking. If co-creation is ultimately about establishing a closer and more intimate rapport with people, it's only natural to strive for more structural, long-term co-creation initiatives. There's not much sense in initiating a dialogue but not maintaining it. Both Electrolux (pages 282–5) and MUJI (pages 290–1) have turned their design competitions into long-term properties.

So, there are thoughtful and cautious ways for brands to hand over creative control to a larger group of people. With co-creation entering a more mature phase, there's one thing that brands can no longer afford to do – to control their brand from A to Z.

In collaboration with The Lomographic Society, Absolut invited both dedicated Lomo artists and the general public to interpret Absolut Vodka with Lomography. This form of snapshot photography takes its name from the Lomo, a low-quality camera that is known for its tendency to oversaturate or overexpose shots, with potentially fascinating results.

Pictures by the six Lomo artists featured in a print campaign, and the photographs from people around the world were posted online. In line with the Lomographic philosophy, the website used printed photographs. Every picture that was sent in was printed out on paper and glued onto a massive wall in a real gallery in central Stockholm. Every half an hour, a fixed camera took a high-resolution image of the wall, which was put on the Absolut Lomo website, so that people could see the exhibition evolve day by day. Every time a picture was placed on the wall, its coordinates were mapped with custom-built software, and a digital version was made available online. Around 30,000 people from all over the world uploaded pictures.

BECO-CREATIVE
V&S ABSOLUT SPIRITS
Agency: Great Works
Sweden – 2006

On 9 October 2004, the Beastie Boys handed out fifty-five Hi-8 videos and six digital video cameras to audience members at their sell-out gig in New York's Madison Square Garden. These untrained videographers were given simple instructions: do whatever you want, rock out, act like a filmmaker, try to sneak backstage, but keep the tape rolling.

When the show was over, band member Adam Yauch (aka MCA, aka Nathaniel Hörnblowér) spent a year editing the many different perspectives into the grainy, disorientating, explosive film, *Awesome; I Fuckin' Shot That!* Yauch wanted to produce something very different from the typical 'standardized' concert footage, with its slick camerawork and predictable sequence of edits. *Awesome* contains 6,732 edits or an average of 75 cuts per minute, taking the viewer deep inside the world of a live Beastie Boys show and capturing the experience of a music event like never before. The multiple points of view simulate that sense of shared experience that make concerts much more than a live rendition of recorded music. The Beasties describe *Awesome* as an 'authorized bootleg', aimed at capturing the DIY spirit of the early punk and hip-hop movements.

'WHAT I REALLY LIKE ABOUT THE MOVIE IS THAT THE PEOPLE SHOT IT. THAT'S THE ESSENCE OF HIP-HOP OR PUNK. IT'S NOT LIKE "THESE PEOPLE MADE IT". WE ALL MADE IT TOGETHER.'

ADAM YAUCH, DIRECTOR OF *AWESOME; I FUCKIN' SHOT THAT!*

...FINALLY, HöRNBLOWéR IS TAKING BACK WHAT'S HIS
THINKFILM IN ASSOCIATION WITH OSCILLOSCOPE PICTURES PRESENT
BEASTIE BOYS STARRING IN
AWESOME;
I FUCKiN' SHOT THAT!
THINKFILM In Association With OSCILLOSCOPE PICTURES Present
A NATHANIAL HöRNBLOWēR Film AWESOME; I FUCKIN' SHOT THAT! (An Authorized Bootleg) Starring MIKE D ADROCK MCA as the BEASTIE BOYS
Shot by A BUNCH OF PEOPLE Edited By NEAL USATIN Produced By JON DORAN Produced And Directed By NATHANIAL HöRNBLOWēR
OSCILLOSCOPE
COMING TO A THEATER NEAR YOU IN 2006
oscilloscope.net thinkfilmcompany.com beastieboys.com hollywoodandvine.com
TH!NKFilm INTERNATIONAL

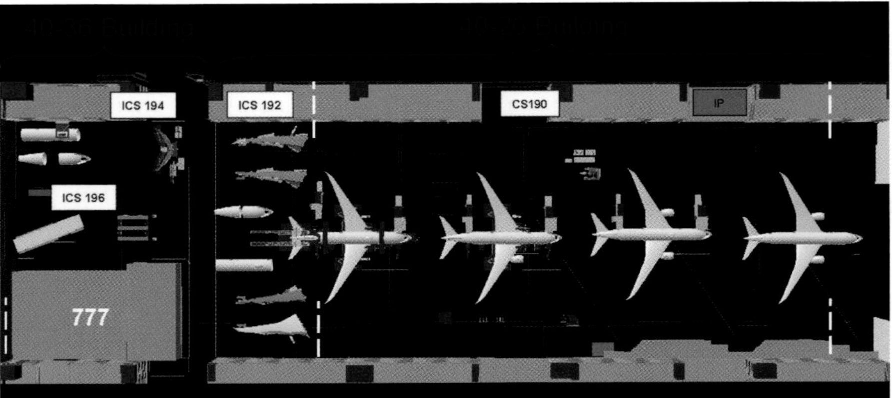

Boeing sought outside help for each stage in the development of its groundbreaking and audacious Dreamliner aeroplane, from the initial concept and name to the external design, interiors, materials and final assembly processes.

An external consultant and Boeing employees were invited to suggest names in line with the company's vision for the brand. The four best suggestions (Dreamliner, eLiner, Global Cruiser and Stratoclimber) were included in a 'Name Your Plane' promotion in alliance with AOL Time Warner Inc., in which people could vote for their favourite. There was a particular effort to involve children at the naming stage. A special issue of *TIME For Kids*, sent to more than 2 million children, featured the history of flight, introduced its readers to the new aeroplane and invited them to join in. Nearly 478,000 people in 166 countries around the world voted, and more than 7,100 Boeing employees took part in the internal sweepstakes. The grand prize was a two-hour full-motion flight in a Boeing flight simulator.

Aircraft enthusiasts and industry professionals were also invited to join the World Design Team. This virtual community of more than 120,000 members was involved in the design of the aeroplane, contributing not only on a basic level (such as the colour of the seats) but also with complex technological issues. In order to keep the World Design Team involved, Boeing conducted surveys about design elements and gave sneak peeks as the design of the exterior and interior evolved.

The company sourced two thirds of the invention of its new 787 Dreamliner jet from a global network of partners, all collaborating over a secure Boeing-operated site. By tapping into the ideas of an external network of inventors, Boeing gained considerably in time-to-market and kept development costs to a minimum.

'WE ARE LOOKING AT OUR NEW AIRPLANE AS AN OPPORTUNITY TO CHANGE THE WAY WE DO BUSINESS.'

ROB POLLACK, VICE-PRESIDENT OF BRANDING FOR BOEING COMMERCIAL AIRPLANES MARKETING

E4

Agencies: Naked Communications/Holler

United Kingdom – 2007

Two months before the first episode of the teen drama *Skins* aired on E4, young people were invited to join a *Skins* community across E4.com and MySpace, offering them free exclusive content and updates on the show. Members were also invited to submit content for use in *Skins* or other aspects of the programme. They could create music for a scene in the show, style a fashion shoot with the cast, re-design the logo or make a short film based around one of the characters. The number of MySpace friends grew to more than 50,000 after the first series and *Skins* proved to be the most successful launch of a drama on multichannel TV.

'OUR *SKINS* ADVOCATES STARTED TO INTERACT WITH THE SHOW AND ITS CHARACTERS MONTHS BEFORE TRANSMISSION, AND THE WORK WE RECEIVED WAS OF AN INCREDIBLY HIGH STANDARD.'

PETER SPIERS, CHANNEL 4 MARKETING MANAGER

skins

skins

skins

skins

e4.com
skins

skins
BRAND SPANKING NEW
BRITISH DRAMA
COMING SOON TO E4

skins

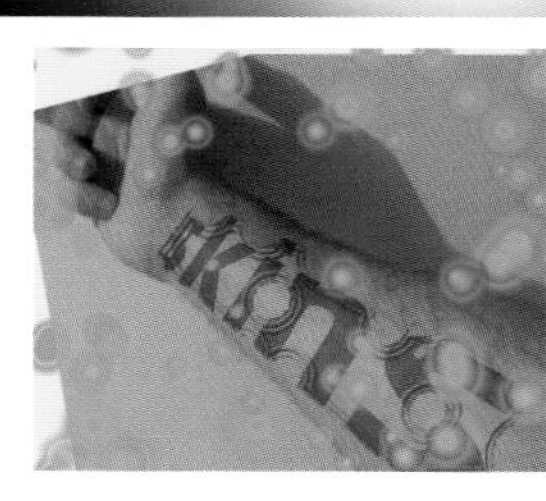

skins

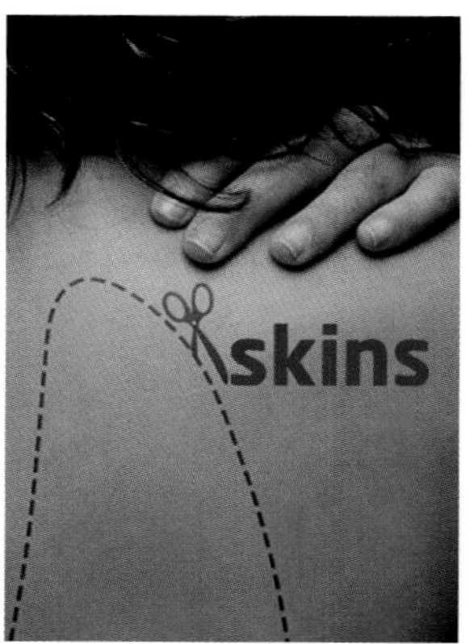
skins

skins

skins

ELECTROLUX
Agency: n/a
Worldwide – since 2003

In 2003 Electrolux proved itself a pioneer of product co-creation with the launch of the Electrolux Design Lab. This global design competition challenges both undergraduate and graduate industrial design students from around the world to create home appliances of the future.

Since then, the Electrolux Design Lab competition has taken place every year, each time with a different theme. In 2006 the focus was on 'Healthy eating habits in 2016', with designers asked to reinvent food preservation and preparation and inspire a more mindful approach to the way we eat, while the theme in 2007 was eco-friendly and sustainable household appliances.

The Design Lab winner receives a six-month internship at one of Electrolux's global design centres. The company also offers work and research placements, and is involved in teaching and running projects with a number of design schools. Some of the Design Lab concepts submitted are in the early stages of development and may perhaps be brought to the market in the future.

The Electrolux Design Lab has attracted over 4,000 entries from more than ninety countries in its first five years, with the top three countries from the 2007 competition being China, South Korea and the Philippines. It has also drawn enormous media attention through travelling exhibitions, blogs, a website, word-of-mouth and an awards ceremony that hosts more than a hundred journalists from around the world.

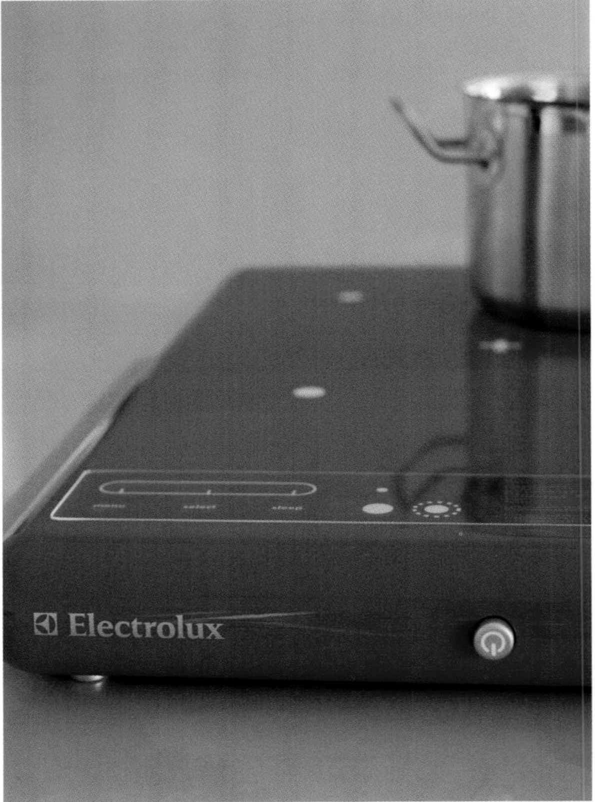

'[ELECTROLUX DESIGN LAB] HAS BECOME SOMETHING OF AN INCUBATOR FOR OUR PRODUCT INNOVATION PROCESS.'

ULRICH GARTNER, ELECTROLUX VICE-PRESIDENT OF COMMUNICATIONS FOR EUROPE

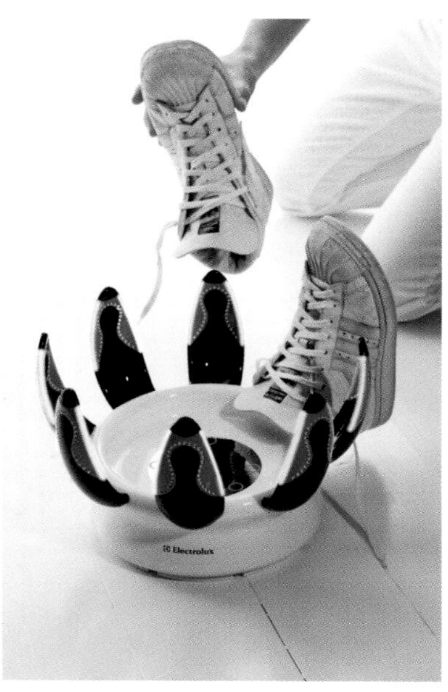

Opposite, top: Vessto, a sleekly designed portable cooker that uses renewable energy to power itself. *Opposite, bottom:* Design Lab 2007 finalists: 'Green solutions for 2020'.

This page, clockwise from top left: The KaionWAVE washing system acts as both a washer and a dryer, using no water or chemicals; With Dustmate, shoes are used as a cleaning apparatus, sucking dirt as you walk about your home; Happy Feet is a solution for cleaning and sanitizing shoes which uses charcoal and ultraviolet rays to eliminate odours and sterilize shoes; The Eclipse Vacuum Cleaner follows you around as you clean, using sensor-controlled navigation; Hydrosphere, a glass sphere that grows vegetables and herbs in the kitchen and is solar-powered.

Electrolux
UV
TEMP

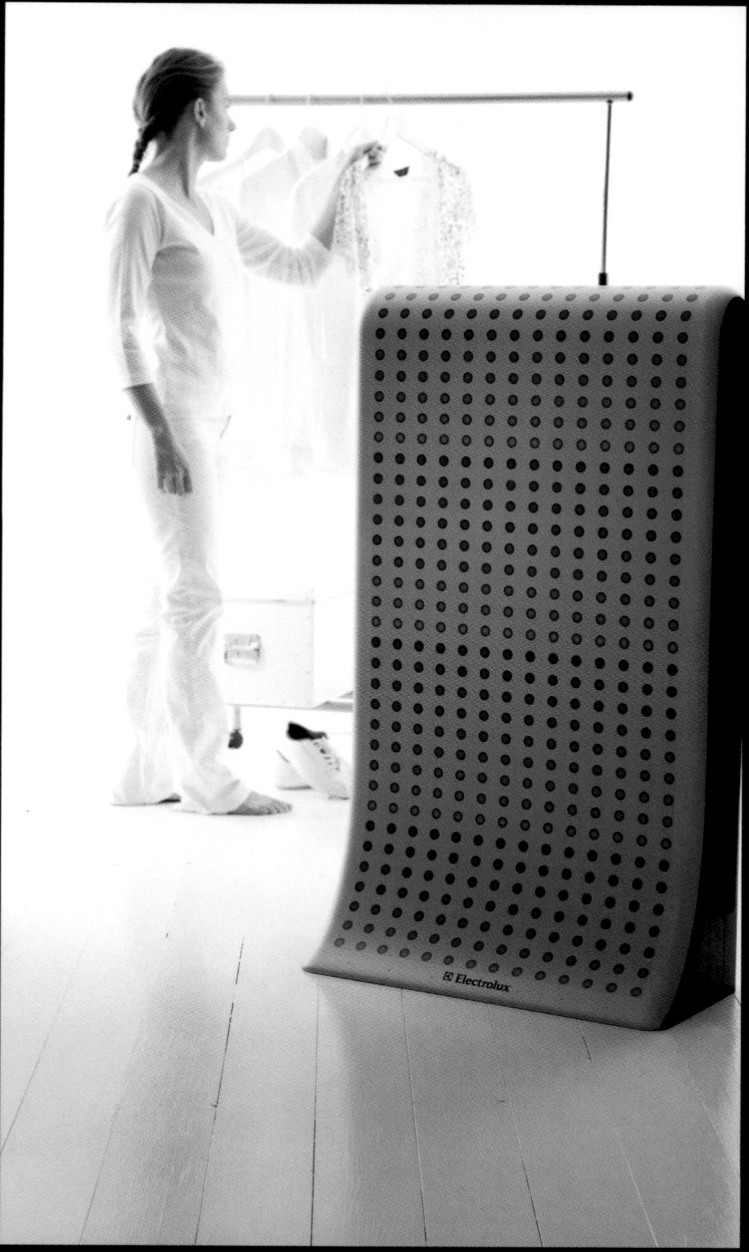

Opposite: Vege is an appliance that allows consumers to grow fresh, healthy vegetables in their kitchens all year round with hydroponics, a crop-production system that cultivates and manages vegetable growth using mineral nutrient solutions instead of soil. Designed to hold up to forty plants, an easy-to-use digital display shows the number of days required to achieve full growth for each row of plants.

Above left: The Soft Refrigerator is a portable refrigerator that expands and folds up to adapt to the amount of food inside the cooling chamber.

Above right: Airwash is a waterless washing machine. By eliminating the use of detergent and precious water resources, it cleans clothes with pressurized air and negative ions – nature's cleansing agent.

Flying Dog is Denver's largest brewery and the second-largest craft brewery in Colorado. 'Purposeful, provocative irreverence' flows through the veins of the brewery's founders, George Stranahan and Richard McIntyre, and exhibits itself in every aspect of the company, from the names of its beers to the labels on its bottles. Stranahan and McIntyre were friends with *Fear and Loathing in Las Vegas* author Hunter S. Thompson, who is credited as the creator of Gonzo journalism and coined the brand's tagline 'Good People Drink Good Beer', as well as the 'Gonzo artist' Ralph Steadman, who illustrates the brand's packaging.

Given their irreverent streak, it comes as no surprise that Flying Dog was the first brewery to embrace the principles of open source – a term that refers to software in which the source code is available to everyone. Flying Dog's Open Source Beer Project encouraged beer drinkers and home brewers to recommend changes and modifications to the recipe via a website, down to the variety of hops, the quantity used and when they should be added. The resulting beer was suitably baptized 'Collaborator'. The beer's final recipe and label are freely downloadable at www.opensourcebeerproject.com – giving home brewers all the information they need.

'THE RESULT IS A DOPPELBOCK THAT HAS A FULL BODY WITH A COMPLEX MALT PROFILE AND A SLIGHT ROASTED CARAMEL CHARACTER. THE KNOWLEDGEABLE FEEDBACK FROM THE HOME BREWERS AND THE PASSION THEY PUT FORTH REALLY MADE THIS PROJECT A SUCCESS.'

MATT BROPHY, HEAD BREWER AT FLYING DOG BREWERY

FLYING DOG BREWERY
When Flying Dog Founder and Owner George Stranahan speaks of his brewery's origins, he tells a far-fetched tale. It started with a trek up the Himalayas that included a Sherpa, donkey and suitcase full of contraband. It continued with George convincing Hunter S. Thompson and Ralph Steadman to help him achieve World Beer Domination. Investigate more at flyingdogales.com.
OPEN SOURCE BEER PROJECT
You are holding what we believe is the first Open Source Beer to hit the market in the United States. We started with a basic Doppelbock recipe and solicited suggestions from homebrewers on our blog. We took your comments and crafted this Doppelbock, aptly named Collaborator. The blog, recipe, and label are online at opensourcebeerproject.com, if you'd like to brew some yourself!
FLYING DOG Brewery
©2007 FLYING DOG BREWERY, DENVER, COLORADO
PRINTED ON 100% POST-CONSUMER RECYCLED PAPER.
WILD DOG
COLLABORATOR
DOPPELBOCK
OPEN SOURCE BEER

'THE OPEN SOURCE BEER IS A TRULY COLLABORATIVE PROJECT AND GIVES OUR LOYAL FANS THE OPPORTUNITY TO BUY A BEER THAT THEY ACTUALLY PLAYED A MAJOR ROLE IN CREATING.'

NEAL STEWART, DIRECTOR OF MARKETING FOR FLYING DOG BREWERY

GREENPEACE INTERNATIONAL
Agency: n/a
Worldwide – 2006

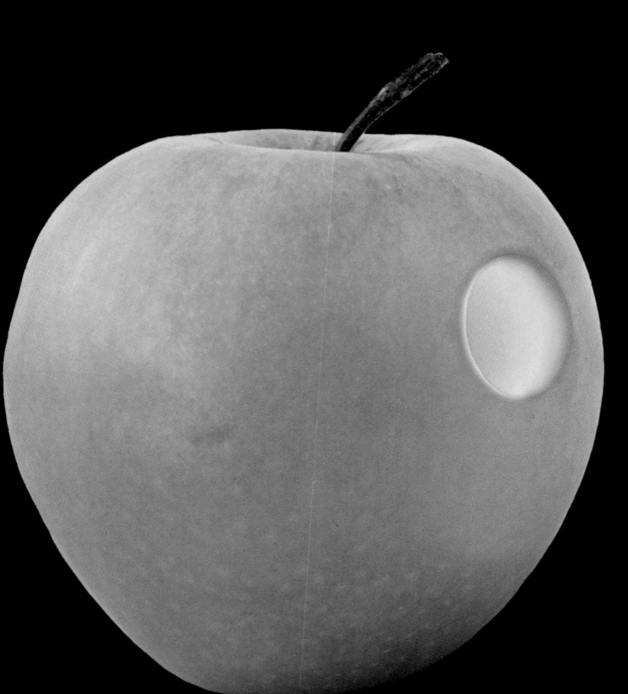

10 9 8 7 6 5 4 3 2 1
5* Woo-hoo! Steve's May 2nd statement means Apple goes greener.
Green my Apple, to the core.

Backed by studies and research, Greenpeace urged Apple to become a greener company. In the *Greenpeace Guide to Green Electronics*, Apple ranked lower than Hewlett-Packard, Dell, Nokia and Sony. Though renowned for being an industry innovator, it was falling seriously behind its competitors on green issues.

Greenpeace claimed it was time for Apple to use clean ingredients in all of its products, and to provide a free take-back programme to re-use and recycle its products wherever they are sold, not just in the US where Apple is legally compelled. They urged co-founder Steve Jobs to do better than 'good enough' and 'amaze us' by turning Apple into a green leader.

Greenpeace decided to 'Think Different' in its campaign approach. Rather than hanging banners off Apple HQ or using their ships to blockade the Apple supply chain or bungee-jumping into the next MacWorld, Greenpeace cleverly called on Apple fans – the people Apple would definitely listen to – to

'THIS IS VIRTUOSO ACTIVISM – WITH THE BEST USAGE OF ONLINE AND DIGITAL MEDIA I HAVE EVER SEEN.'

INTERNATIONAL ASSOCIATION OF BUSINESS COMMUNICATORS BLOG

'WHAT MAKES IT SO BRILLIANT IS THAT THEY ARE TRYING TO MOBILIZE THE PEOPLE THAT APPLE IS MOST LIKELY TO LISTEN TO – THEIR EXTREMELY LOYAL CUSTOMERS. AND THEY ARE DOING SO BY APPEALING TO THEIR PRIDE, AS OPPOSED TO SHAMING THEM INTO ACTION.'

ALISON BYRNE FIELDS, VICE-PRESIDENT/SENIOR STRATEGIST, 360° DIGITAL INFLUENCE AT OGILVY

I just wish it came in green.

demand a new, cool product: a greener Apple. Apple users were asked to submit self-created T-shirt designs, advertisements and videos to promote the 'Green My Apple' campaign.

The hub of the campaign was a parody of the Apple site that added a green spin to the brand's traditional clean look. The site contained all the information and the raw materials Apple fans needed to get started. The best user 'Procreations' were featured on the site. Apple fans sent in over 200 self-made designs, videos and campaign ideas, and more than 1,200 people sent in personal pictures in support of a 'Greener Apple'. The site was viewed over one million times and generated over 3,000 blog links. Almost 50,000 people wrote to Jobs asking him to go green.

About eight months after the launch of the campaign, in May 2007, the words 'A Greener Apple' appeared on the home page of Apple's site, with a message from Steve Jobs saying, 'Today we're changing our policy'. Apple declared a phase-out of the worst chemicals in its product range by 2008, beating the pledges by Dell and other computer manufacturers to phase them out by 2009. As other issues remain unresolved, Greenpeace continues to strive for 'an Apple green to the core', a company that will set the example for a greener electronics industry.

Stylish Japanese purveyor of all things minimalist MUJI has a long tradition of collecting and using input from its customer base. In 1999, for instance, MUJI received a monthly average of 8,000 suggestions for improvements or new product developments through postcards attached to catalogues, emails, calls and letters to customer services. In addition, all MUJI staff members on the sales floor are known for carrying a booklet in which they record notes on customer behaviour or snippets from their conversations with clients.

All this input is collected, categorized and passed on to the departments to help with product development. The best ideas are viewed as starting points for new products, and as a token of appreciation any item originating from a customer suggestion is clearly marked as such in the MUJI catalogue. In 2006, MUJI took this ongoing collaboration with its customers to a new level by launching an annual international design competition, with a top prize of $20,000 (£10,000).

In 2006, the competition theme was 'SUMI' (corner/edge/end). MUJI invited designers to create something 'that is not placed in the middle of the room, but towards the edges, not at the centre and not directly around the centre; you should look for somewhere that evades the eye'. It could be anything from furniture to stationery and office equipment. The winner designed a 'cast of skin', an innovative and environmentally friendly outlet plug designed to do three things: save energy, prevent dust from getting into an outlet, and maintain a connection between an outlet plug and an outlet. The MUJI Award 01 attracted 4,758 entries from fifty-two countries around the world. MUJI's own product development staff selected the winners.

In 2007, the theme was RE, which stands for the reinvention of everyday life. Entries had to embody a new angle on the everyday.

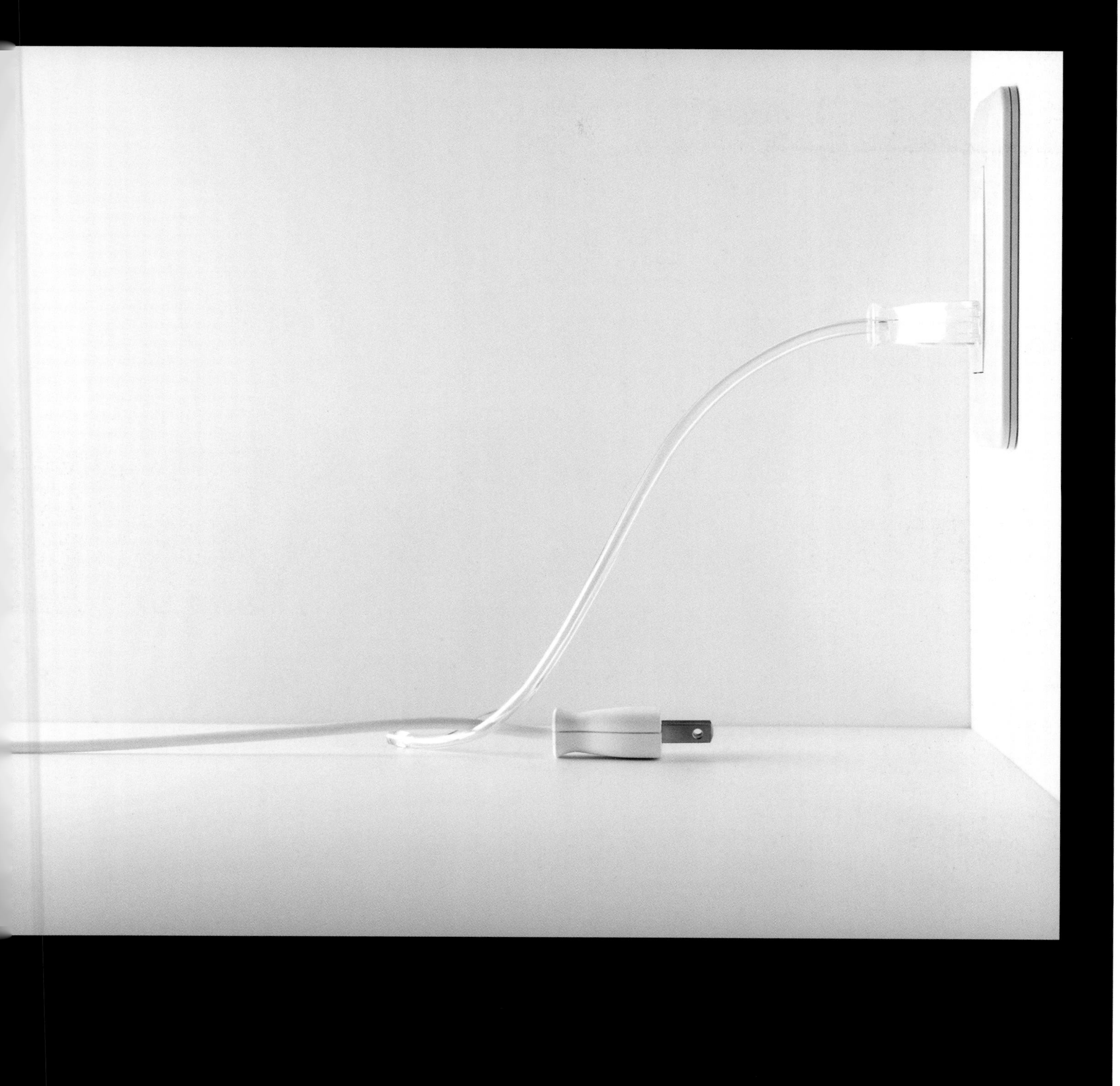

NIKE

Agency: FramFab
Denmark – 2006

As part of its Joga Bonito campaign, Nike wanted to make the longest football video ever and involve fans from across the globe. Anybody could create their own video showing off their ball skills, with the only condition that the ball had to come into the screen from the left and exit to the right. A selection of videos was edited back to back, creating a global chain. Forty thousand videos were sent in, of which 2,000 were featured. The final video lasted several hours and encompassed footage from eighty-three different countries.

NIKON
Agency: MRM Worldwide
United States – 2007

Rather than giving people the usual sales pitch, Nikon distributed two hundred D40 cameras to Georgetown (South Carolina) residents so that they could experience firsthand the superior quality of the device. Under the slogan 'ordinary people taking extraordinary pictures', the campaign involved residents of all backgrounds and ages, from fire fighters and police officers to high-school students and parents. The photographs that people took of their everyday lives were showcased in an online photo gallery called 'Picturetown'.

Nikon also sent its high-end D80 variant to a group of Flickr users for them to play around with. A selection of their pictures was showcased in a three-page spread in major magazine titles, including *BusinessWeek*.

View the Picturetown Gallery
▾ hide
Select a photo from the wall
Just roll over the thumbnails on the wall to see who took each picture. To view a picture full screen, click on it.
Explore more of the Picturetown Gallery
1 of 7

Meet the People of Picturetown
▾ hide
Sara Player
I'll never go back to what I was using, because you miss out and these pictures are priceless.
Nikon
Click to Play
Picture quality you can trust
With Sara's old point-and-shoot, family pictures didn't look as good as she hoped. Her Nikon D40 gets color, exposure and focus right, so now, deleting most of her pictures is a thing of the past.
See how the D40 gets it right ►

Welcome to Picturetown
▾ hide
Nikon
The Story
The People
The Pictures
The Nikon D40

View the Picturetown Gallery
▾ hide
Mark Collins
It's difficult to take pictures of dolphins, but with this camera I was able to just—bam-bam-bam—get the shots.
► Meet Mark Collins
nice birds
pawel t. / nyc / Wednesday, May 09, 2007
I LOVE this picture, it's amazing. I often take pictures of nature and animals too. It's a good feeling to have the opportunity to capture something this brilliant. I would love a camera like this that's for sure!
Kristy C. / St. Thomas, Ontario / Wednesday, May 09, 2007
As a wildlife photographer, I really liked this. A "Once-in-a-lifetime" pose of so many pelicans "standing at attention" in military formation.
► Comment on this photo

BE CO-CREATIVE
PENGUIN
Agency: n/a
United Kingdom – 2006–7

'ANYONE CAN DRAW, SCRATCH OR SCRIBBLE THEIR OWN COVER, AND MAKE THE OUTSIDE OF THE BOOK AS PERSONAL AS THEIR REACTION TO THE INSIDES.'

HELEN CONFORD, EDITORIAL DIRECTOR OF PENGUIN PRESS, IN *THE GUARDIAN*

It's quite a challenge for any book publisher today to attract a young generation raised on instant, online communication and increasingly unfamiliar with linear storytelling. Over the past few years, Penguin has faced that challenge by reinventing itself as an enabler of conversations about books, authors and stories and a firm believer in co-creation.

In 2006, Penguin published *MyPenguins*, a series of six classics with blank front covers, comprising *Emma*, *Meditations*, *The Waves*, *The Picture of Dorian Gray*, *Magic Tales* and *Crime and Punishment*. Under the tagline 'Books by the Greats, Covers by You', people were encouraged to get their creative juices flowing and send in their own cover designs, which were then posted in an online gallery for all to see.

paddy power bookmakers
grand national, aintree
4.15pm
2abeul £50 e/w 66-1
mckelvey £50 e/w 16-1
Gatsby
THE WESTIN MIYAKO
KYOTO

In 2007, Penguin partnered with Mercury Music and invited seven of their bands to select the novel they'd most like to see published as a *MyPenguin* and then design their own front cover. Razorlight selected *The Great Gatsby*, Ryan Adams picked *Dracula*, and *Animal Farm* was chosen by indie band Mr Hudson & The Library. A series of partnerships were set up to promote the collaboration including an exhibition, features in all of the major music magazines and online tie-ins with MySpace and social-networking site Piczo. In this, young people were encouraged to draw, paint or doodle designs for the books chosen by the musicians, using digital tools provided by Piczo. The bands chose the winners, who received sets of the books and the bands' latest albums.

Penguin's most audacious venture in co-creation was the launch of *A Million Penguins*, a wiki-novel experiment where anyone could write and edit a novel-in-progress for a period of six weeks. The wiki was accompanied by a blog where a Penguin editor provided a running editorial commentary on the work in progress.

Penguin collaborated with MA students in Creative Writing and New Media at De Montfort University who contributed to the wiki and formed the seeds of the community. 'The success of a wiki project depends on the commitment of the community,' said Penguin's Digital Publisher Jeremy Ettinghausen, 'and we're very pleased that these most imaginative students are on board.'

Nearly 1,500 individuals contributed to the writing and editing of *A Million Penguins*, resulting in over 11,000 edits, and 75,000 people visited the site. The end novel contained no fewer than 1,030 pages, which Penguin is looking to convert into an ebook.

'AS THE PROJECT EVOLVED I THINK I STOPPED THINKING ABOUT IT AS A LITERARY EXPERIMENT AND STARTED THINKING ABOUT IT MORE AS A SOCIAL EXPERIMENT.'

JEREMY ETTINGHAUSEN, PENGUIN'S DIGITAL PUBLISHER

Who says that you can only drink out of a Red Bull can? You can also bend it into peculiar shapes, paint it, film or photograph it, glue things to it, melt it or turn it into a sculpture. That's what participants of Red Bull Art of Can have been doing since 1997, in a campaign that has had a global reach.

The competition brief is a good reflection of Red Bull's rebellious spirit: no limits, no rules, with just a Red Bull can as inspiration. All entries, both by creative amateurs and professional artists, should reflect the brand's principles of stimulation, enhanced performance and concentration. The result: imaginative, bizarre and witty aluminium art across the spectrum of different media.

'BASICALLY ALL THE ENTRIES ARE MADE FROM THE SAME MATERIAL, SO WHAT YOU ARE REALLY LOOKING AT IS THE INSIDE OF THE ARTIST'S BRAIN AND WHAT HIS CREATIVITY IS AND WHAT HE CAN DO.'

BOBBY HANSSON, ONE OF THE JUDGES OF THE COMPETITION, AS WELL AS A RENOWNED METAL ARTIST AND AUTHOR OF *THE FINE ART OF THE TIN CAN*

Bull
Re
ENERG
ENERG
ENERG

+ Home Stunt Simulator Stunt Demos Behind The Bourne Ultimatum Login / Register
Stunt Gallery Competition

LIKE VOLKSWAGEN CARS, THE SPECTACULAR STUNTS IN THE BOURNE ULTIMATUM ARE THE RESULT OF SOME SERIOUS THINKING.

IT TAKES A LOT OF PLANNING TO ENSURE THEY ARE PERFORMED SAFELY AND WITH MAXIMUM VISUAL

THIS SITE WILL TAKE YOU INSIDE THE WORLD OF CAR STUNT CHOREOGRAPHY AND, USING THE 3D STUNT SIMULATOR, YOU'LL GET SOME HANDS ON EXPERIENCE OF CREATING YOUR OWN.

3D STUNT SIMULATOR

See Films Differently

To promote its tie-in with *The Bourne Ultimatum*, the last film in the Bourne trilogy, Volkswagen offered thrill-seekers the chance to plan, execute and edit their own heart-thumping car chases and stunts. The 3D stunt simulator application, using Adobe's technical Shockwave 3D software, allowed users to add in tricky conditions, explosions, wet weather and a number of different camera angles, giving fans a taste of how high-octane stunts are planned in Hollywood.

The site also featured a Stunt Gallery where people could upload their completed stunt for others to review and vote for their favourite. Winners could receive preview tickets and stunt driving days. 'Backstage' exclusives were also on show, including a behind-the-scenes interview with the stunt coordinator for *The Bourne Ultimatum* and a 'making of' feature on the dynamic New York stunt scene, which sees Matt Damon's Jason Bourne being pursued through the streets by an assassin in a Volkswagen Touareg.

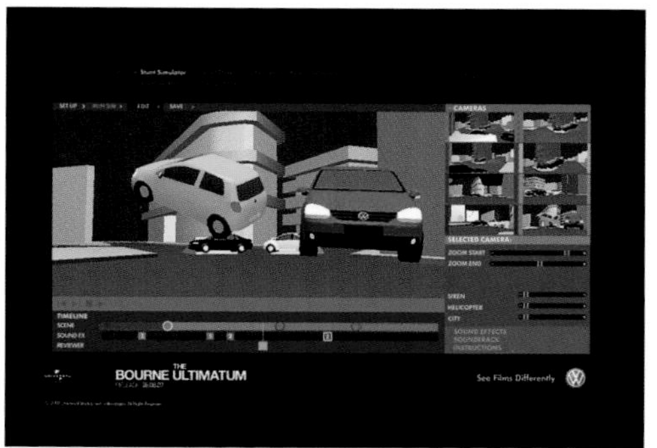

'THE FIRST TWO BOURNE FILMS ARE RENOWNED FOR STUNT WORK AND, JUST LIKE VOLKSWAGEN CARS, THE FANTASTIC STUNTS IN *THE BOURNE ULTIMATUM* ARE THE RESULT OF SOME SERIOUS THINKING.'

SALLY CHAPMAN, COMMUNICATIONS MANAGER AT VOLKSWAGEN

BE OWNABLE

People have an innate desire to materialize their love and admiration for somebody or something. Any half-decent fan will admit to owning at least one tangible item that demonstrates their dedication to their idol, from an exclusive limited edition to a signed T-shirt. Some people are even willing to pay staggering amounts of cash for celebrity memorabilia. Think of the $48,000 (£24,000) that was paid for a lock of John Lennon's hair, or the $27,000 (£13,000) paid for the marriage certificate of Elvis and Priscilla Presley.

In the same respect, people who have an admiration for or loyalty to a brand are eager to materialize those feelings, looking to own something that represents or symbolizes that brand. There is a double motive behind this desire: an internal one, as people want to treasure the brand for themselves, and an external one, a desire to show off their connection with the brand to others. Youth subgroups, for instance, use brands as identity badges to distinguish themselves from one another.

Most marketing doesn't fulfil that need for materialization. The majority of marketing and communication is merely talk. It's a bunch of words, slogans, moving or still images, websites. It comes and goes. It's completely obsolete in nature. Yet in a communications landscape that is becoming increasingly digital and virtual, actually developing tangible and real assets is gaining in value. For one, tangible assets have the benefit of entering people's homes and lives for a potentially longer period of time. If brands are able to create something that people are eager to own, those objects have the potential of penetrating people's private spaces and becoming a lifelong brand asset.

On the most basic level, there's the product itself – for every brand or organization that has a tangible product at least – and linked to that, its packaging. One step beyond this is merchandising of any kind, from simple T-shirts to pins, badges and whatever else. Some (mostly long-lasting or iconic) brands have a thriving subculture of merchandise and collectors' items. Coca-Cola, for instance, has fans across the world collecting a vast array of tangible Coke-branded products. In America there is even a non-profit Coca-Cola Collectors Club that is not affiliated with the company, with no fewer than 4,000 members, fifty local chapters and Annual National Conventions.

The cases in this chapter demonstrate more elaborate and interesting ways for brands to materialize what they stand for, beyond the straightforward and conventional merchandising tricks we're all familiar with. One route that many brands take in order to cultivate people's search for tangible items is the creation of limited editions. By making their products more exclusive and harder to get hold of, brands hope people will make an extra effort not only to obtain the item but also to hold on to it for longer. It becomes a design item rather than a functional commodity that gets thrown away after it has performed its duty. But beyond mere limited editions, this chapter highlights remarkable ways in which brands have been able to create tangible, ownable assets, fuelling people's desire to own something linked to the make.

Agency: n/a
Worldwide – since 1964

'MOST OF US HAVE A BETTER CHANCE OF FINDING THE ARK OF THE COVENANT THAN GETTING ON THE MAILING LIST FOR THE ANNUAL PIRELLI CALENDAR.'

AUTOBLOG.COM, 6 DECEMBER 2007

It's rare to come across an object that hangs both on garage walls and in museums around the world. The Pirelli Calendar is not available by purchase or subscription, and is sent to an exclusive Who's Who of movers and shakers. Over the years it has featured the world's most beautiful women, including Kate Moss, Sophia Loren, Naomi Campbell, Christy Turlington, Nastassja Kinski and many others. The exclusivity of the calendar, which has always been carefully planned and maintained by Pirelli, has made it into a cult object for fashion aficionados and photography buffs everywhere, and a prized collectors' item.

The first international edition of the Pirelli Calendar came out in 1964, a product of the cultural revolution of the 1960s. The marketing department of Pirelli Ltd in the UK had decided to issue a calendar for their top UK customers as a New Year gift. Every year since, the company has called upon world-renowned photographers such as Richard Avedon, Mario Testino, Herb Ritts, Norman Parkinson, Bruce Weber and Annie Leibovitz to photograph the world's most beautiful women. The photographers delivered their own visions of beauty while tracing the history of design, costume, fashion, photography and more.

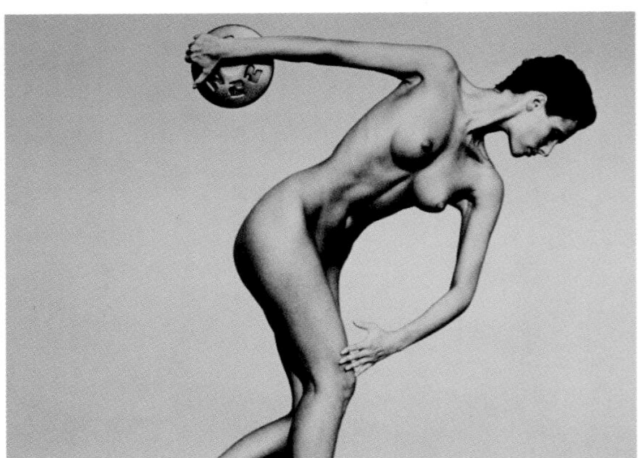

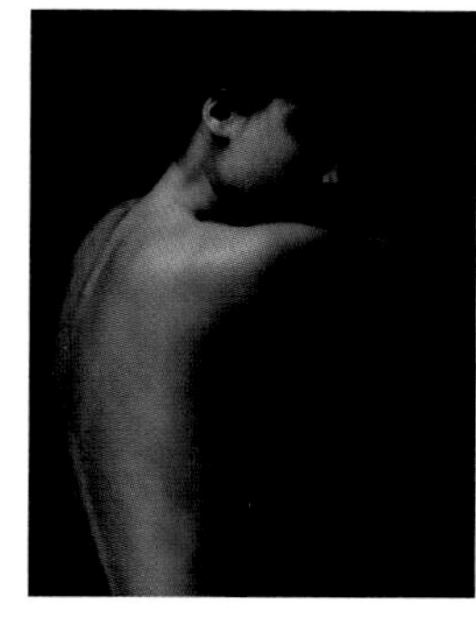

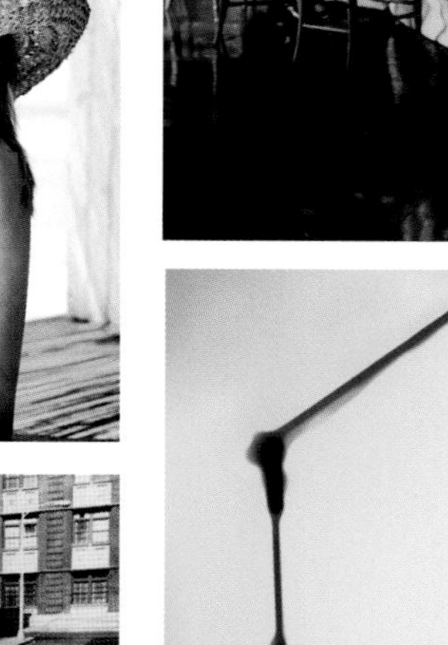

BEOWNABLE
ADIDAS
Agency: TBWA\Whybin
New Zealand – 2006

Each year, Adidas prints a commemorative poster to celebrate the announcement of the new All Blacks squad. In 2006, Adidas wanted a concept that would reflect the powerful bond between the All Blacks and their fans.

The solution was a world-first: they created a limited-edition poster that not only featured the players but also included their actual DNA. Each player in the forty-strong squad donated blood which was sterilized and then embedded into the paper during the printing process. Eight thousand were made and the poster, suitably named *Bonded by Blood*, was displayed at points of sale and was available only to those fans who bought an All Blacks jersey. Each poster came with a numbered certificate of authentication.

All 8,000 posters quickly sold out and appeared on auction sites around the world. It was featured on TV news programmes, in *The Wall Street Journal* and other newspapers around the world. If rugby is a blood sport, these posters proved its ultimate celebration.

ALL BLACKS
adidas
BONDED BY BLOOD
This limited edition poster
was produced using the actual DNA
of the 2006 All Blacks
8000/8000

UNILEVER – LYNX/AXE
Agency: AKQA
Worldwide – 2006

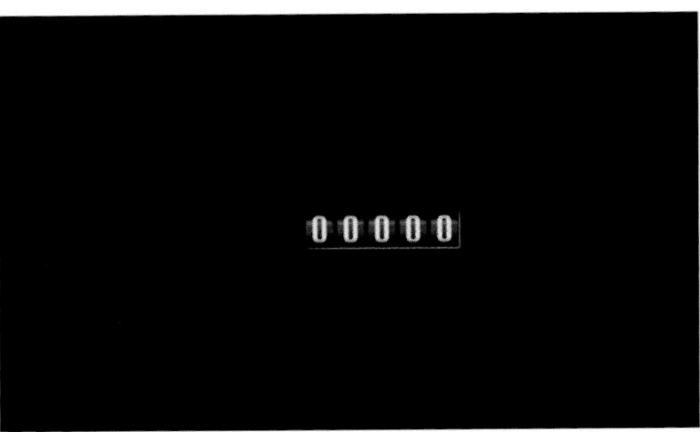

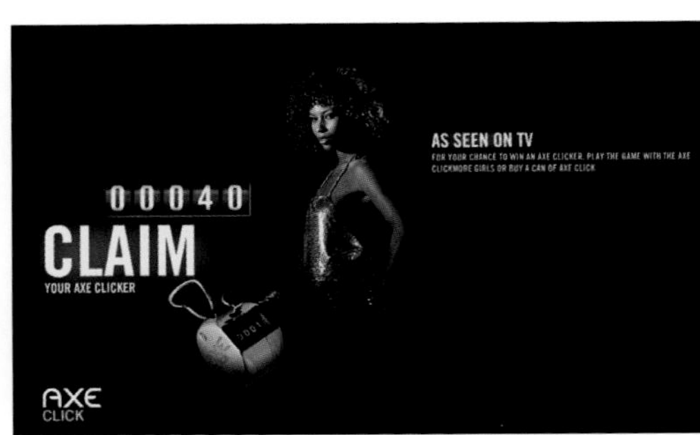

Lynx (aka Axe) took the 'Lynx Effect' to new levels in 2006 with the launch of a new fragrance, Click. Their key objective was to get young guys around the world – with their knowledge of 'flirting', 'pulling' or 'scoring' – to start engaging with the brand by 'clicking'. Featured in a high-profile television ad with Ben Affleck, the 'clicker' looked like the device that club doormen use to keep track of numbers on a Saturday night. Instead, men used the 'clickers' to count flirtatious glances from the opposite sex.

In order to turn clicking into a craze, Lynx distributed the clicker to lads around the world to help them do what they love best – eyeing up girls and keeping score of their tally. Clickers could be ordered on www.clickmore.com, where there was also a facility for visitors to practise their clicking with real Lynx girls through rich video and audio. In total, 2.3 million clickers were ordered.

00040
CLAIM
YOUR AXE CLICKER
AXE

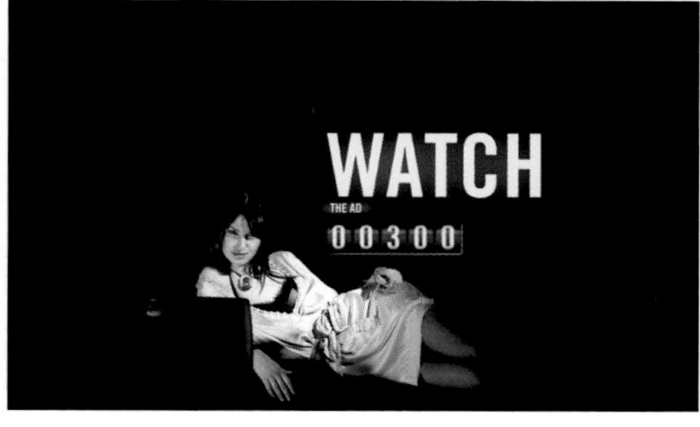
WATCH
THE AD
00300

LEARN
WHAT MAKES GIRLS CLICK
02000

Kiss = 2 Clicks
WHEN SHE BLOWS A KISS GIVE HER 2 QUICK CLICKS.
NEXT »
SHOW ME AGAIN »
AXE
CLICK

Reveal = 3 Clicks
GIVE A GIRL 3 QUICK CLICKS WHEN YOU SEE HER FLASH SOME FLESH.
AXE
CLICK

Touch = 4 Clicks
GIVE A GIRL 4 QUICK CLICKS BEFORE SHE FINISHES THIS MOVE.
AXE
CLICK

Level 1
TIME
00:01
0000
SCORE
0000
AXE
CLICK

keeping score on the click tour...
WEAPON X
& KEN HELL
CLICK TOUR
www.clickher.com
0206

In Australia, a thirteen-gig Click Tour was organized, with two hip-hop rappers glamorizing clicking in their performances and song lyrics. Each male attendee received a free clicker.

evian 2005

'IT SEEMS THAT EVIAN NATURAL SPRING WATER HAS BEEN THERE ALL MY LIFE, I REMEMBER THE CURLY LABEL OF MY CHILDHOOD...IN THE HOTELS BY THE LAKE WHERE OUR FAMILY USED TO SPEND HOLIDAYS.... IT IS THEREFORE AS AN AMUSED AND RATHER PROUD OLD FRIEND THAT I DESIGNED THE 2007–2008 BOTTLES.'

CHRISTIAN LACROIX

The world-famous natural mineral water brand Evian has developed a tradition of limited-edition bottles, many of which have become collectors' items and decoration pieces in interiors worldwide.

In 1999, Evian created its infamous Millennium Bottle, celebrating the turn of the millennium. The bottle came in the shape of a droplet of water, and different variations have since been created (*top left*).

Evian's mountain-shaped bottle (*opposite*) was produced for three consecutive years to mark the end of each year. The mountain-shaped bottles are meant to conjure up the legendary peaks of the French Alps where Evian is sourced, celebrating the water's essentiality and eternal perfection. In 2007, the limited edition was individually numbered for the first time.

For 2008, Evian teamed up with Christian Lacroix, who designed two very distinctive Evian bottles for the holiday season (*bottom left*). For his pret-à-porter bottle, Lacroix used snowy crystals to symbolize the purity of Evian water. The bottle was adorned with what Lacroix described as 'the flowers of success, those that adorn the "paseo" parade capes, like snowy crystal garlands or frost-frozen alpine flowers'. The haute couture bottle, with its subtle, transparent and elegant figure, is Lacroix's ode to femininity.

A limited series of ninety-nine numbered and handmade bottles were auctioned at selected charity events around the world, with proceeds going to charity.

In 2004, Heineken created a promotional item for the UEFA European Football Championship in Portugal that hit the mark with Dutch football fans and became a national craze. The highly visible hat could be turned into a loudspeaker, enabling Dutch football fans to voice their excitement and participate in the game. It came to be known as the 'loudspeaker hat'.

Four hundred thousand loudspeaker hats were distributed and sold through various channels, including competitions in newspapers and on radio stations and 'fan packs' in shops (the joint promotion of loudspeaker hats and cans of beer).

But because the Danish beer brand Carlsberg was lead sponsor of the championship, Dutch fans were stopped at the entrance to the stadium and asked to hand over their precious hats. After the game, some of the Portuguese with an eye for a deal sold the hats back to the Dutch fans for €1.

During the 2006 World Cup in Germany, the same idea was applied but given a German twist. In order to prevent a similar ban at the entrance to the stadium, Heineken made the hat look as German as possible, creating a copy of the iconic German hunting hat.

The company also produced unbranded versions of the hat, which were available inside the stadium in case anyone was banned from taking theirs inside. The hat, which was named 'the Dutch secret weapon', came with special pins representing the countries Holland had to face during the World Cup. For every match the orange national team won, people could attach a country pin to their hat.

Legioen strijkt met duizenden neer

'Toeterhoeden' Oranje mogen stadions niet in

ORANJE-LEGIOEN KAMPIOEN!

et Nederland in beweging

De Telegraaf

DE STAMGASTEN

Agency: TBWA\NEBOKO
Netherlands – 2004 & 2006

Agency: TBWA\Brussels
Belgium & Netherlands – 2006

It might seem odd for a multimedia device such as PSP to bring out good old-fashioned wallpaper, but it was the perfect way to meet a fashion-conscious audience in their own environment. The range of wallpaper designs was based on PSP's different applications – music, gaming, movies, pictures and browsing – and was sold by the coolest shops in major cities in Belgium and the Netherlands. The designs, which were also featured in an outdoor and print campaign, were available to download as desktop wallpaper.

Fish
Chips
Exclusive @ Fish
PLAYSTATION WALLPAPER
Amazing wallpaper!

Feedtheenthusiasts andtheybecomemedia

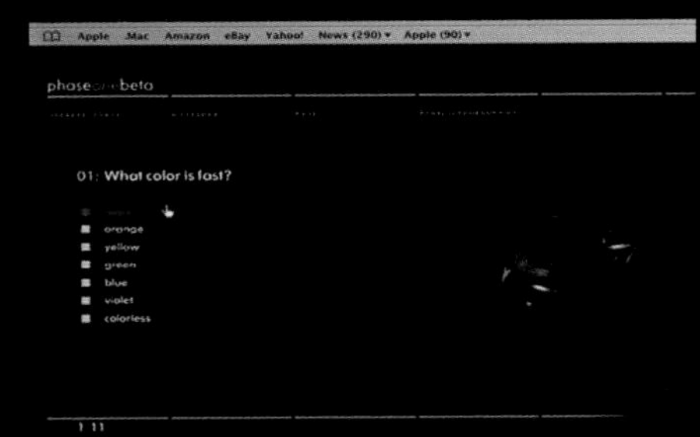

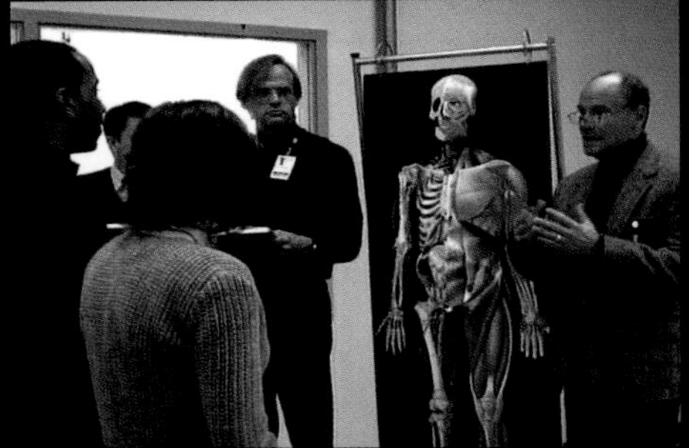

In order to recapture GTI's former cult following of young car enthusiasts, Volkswagen gave 17,000 owners of the new sports model an exclusive limited-edition toy called the 'Fast': an evil-looking vinyl bunny with a red smile (replicating the trim around the car's grille), four interchangeable tails and a care-and-feeding manual. The mascot draws inspiration from the iconic VW Rabbit, the North American car that is known elsewhere as the VW Golf. The campaign theme 'Make friends with your Fast' was also used in television ads.

Listed in category: Collectibles > Advertising > Cars > European > Volks
gen GTI FAST VW limited collectible! 1 of 600
Current bid: US $710.00
No payments for 3 months -
End time: Mar-27-06 18:30:36 PST
Shipping costs: US $10.00 (discount available)
US Postal Service Parcel Post
Ships to: Worldwide
Item location: Nicholasville, Kentucky, United
History: 41 bids

GTI

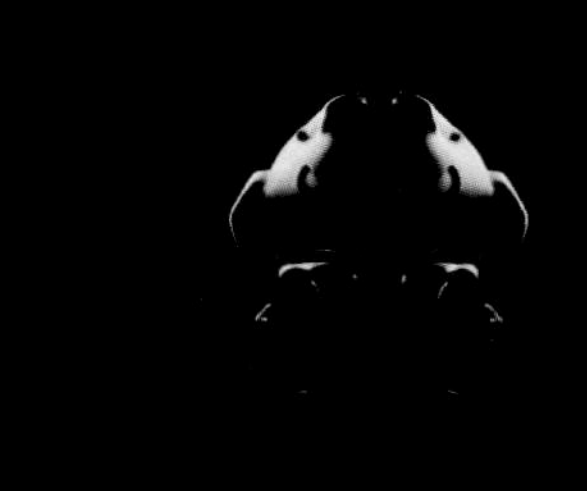

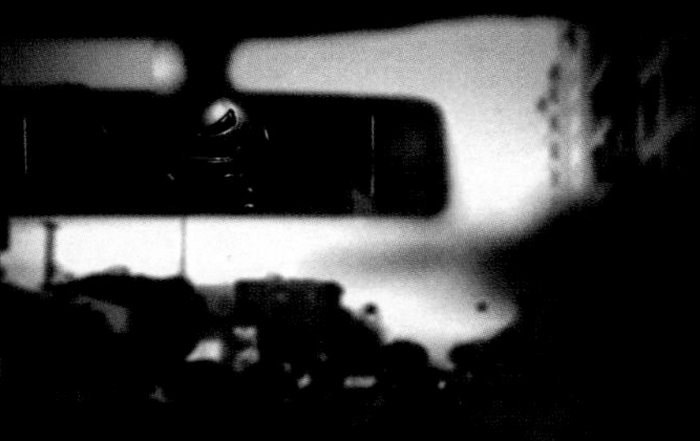

makefriendswithyourfast
GTI Mk V

Inside most, but not all of us, there is a fast. And according to data we collected from thousands of respondents it looks a little something like this. Maybe you've never thought about what your fast looks like. But when we designed the GTI Mk V, we did. We thought about what fast smells like and how much it weighs and what it eats for breakfast. It's all we thought about. Because we wanted this GTI to make your fast happy.

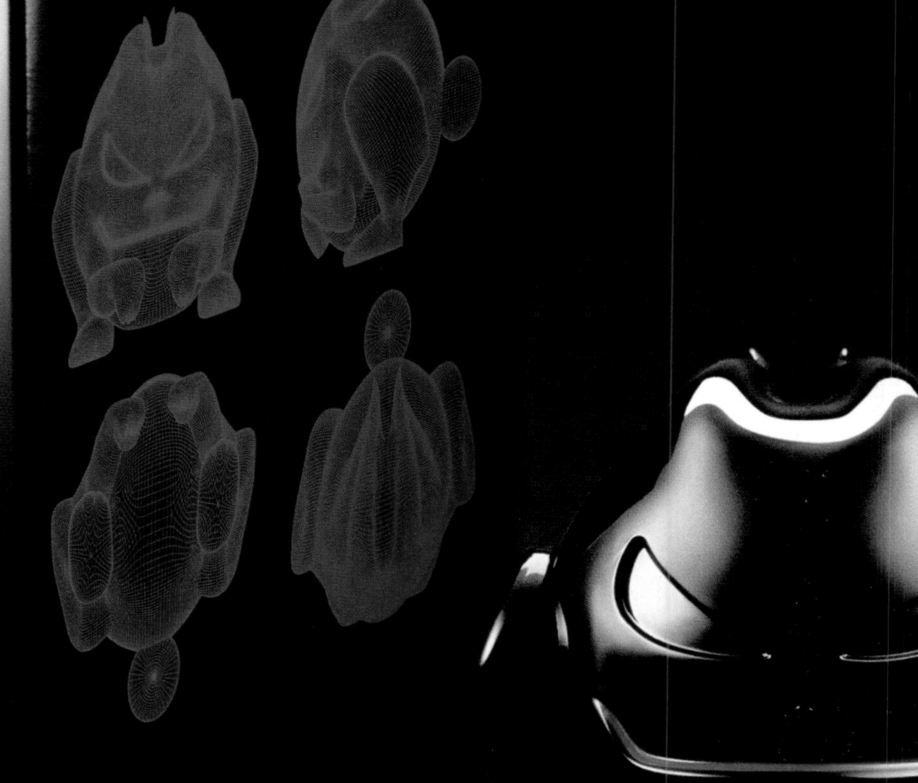

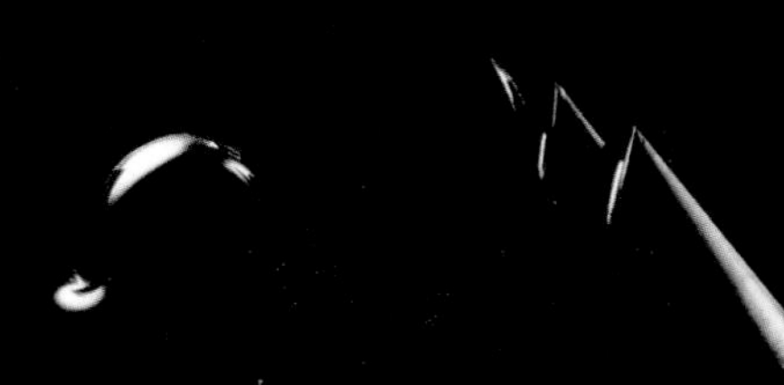

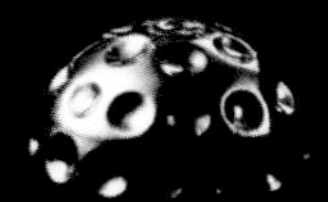

makefriendswithyourfast

fast features

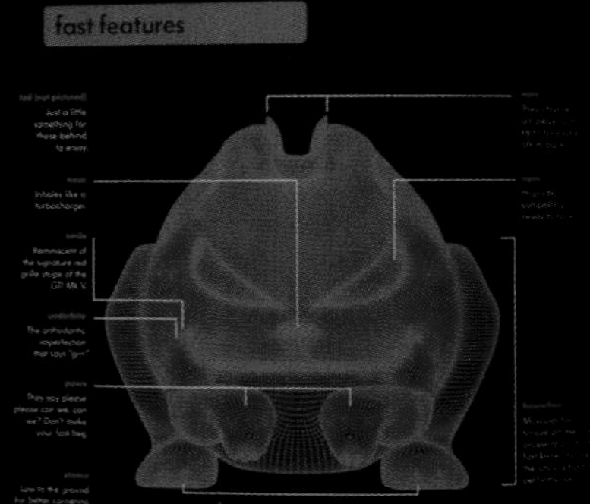

interchangeable tails

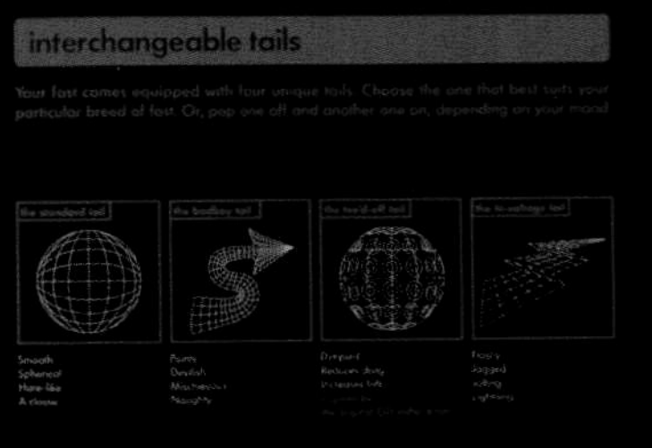

Your fast comes equipped with four unique tails. Choose the one that best suits your particular breed of fast. Or, pop one off and another one on, depending on your mood

installing your fast

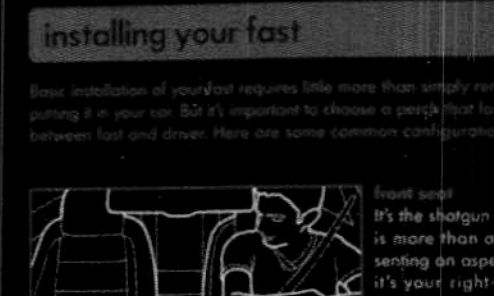

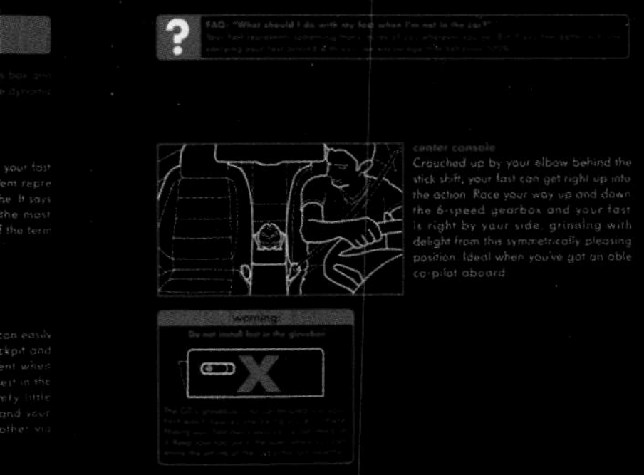

FAQ: "What should I do with my fast when I'm not in the car?"

center console

Crouched up by your elbow behind the stick shift, your fast can get right up into the action. Race your way up and down the 6-speed gearbox and your fast is right by your side, grinning with delight from this symmetrically pleasing position. Ideal when you've got an able co-pilot aboard.

warning:
X

customizing your fast
Your fast is not bound by any dealer lease or service agreement. Feel free to modify and personalize your fast as you see fit without voiding your warranty.
65
65
DEUTSCHLAND

1. choose a design from below and trace it
2. tape your traced artwork to a thicker piece of paper
I ♥ AUTOBAHN

BE USEFUL

You can't blame people for not particularly looking forward to advertising messages. Apart from the occasional spot of entertainment, generally they aren't particularly useful. Advertising is keen to grab people's time and attention, but what do they get in return? It doesn't seem like a fair deal. It's not an equal trade-off. Most brands would of course argue that they are communicating about a product or service that is of great use to their target audience. The truth of the matter is that advertising, in most cases, is there to cover up a lack of true product differentiation. In a sea of sameness, advertising creates the impression that one product is actually different or more effective than another.

The bad news for advertisers is that online access has finally allowed people to look behind the curtains of advertising, and see products and services for what they really are. Every day, the internet exposes the real opinions and genuine experiences of millions of people around the world, through reviews, comments, blogs and articles. This results in a complete transparency and undermines advertising's ability to distract people from the truth or amplify minor differences to fictional proportions.

Rather than spending huge budgets on backing mediocre products and services, wouldn't the money be better spent on actually turning that product or service into something genuinely different (read: useful), or at least create marketing that in itself becomes useful and has an actual function in people's daily lives? After all, even the most brilliant or entertaining ad won't win over a negative or mediocre product review.

Apart from creating an increasingly transparent marketplace, online has also spawned a new generation of brands that are first and foremost rooted in usefulness. Most online success stories from the last decade, from YouTube to Wikipedia, from eBay to Amazon, from Google to Technorati, from MySpace to Facebook, have gained their status by simply providing people with free useful services. All these brands have utility at their very heart, and their best ongoing communication is the constant development and updating of their services and applications. As a result, these brands fade away or lose momentum from the moment they stop adding value to people's lives (and there are plenty of players in the online graveyard to prove it).

This online usefulness has infected people's expectations of brands in the offline environment. More than ever, people expect brands to fit into their lives, not the other way around. As most brands are hardly at the epicentre of people's lives, they need to develop a more humble and facilitating attitude. If people's attention is what brands are after, they'd better give something in return that is equally valuable.

This movement from message-driven marketing to product- or service-driven marketing has been baptized by some as 'brand utility', and requires a completely different mindset from marketers. Rather than asking themselves 'What is the best message to communicate this product or service?', brands should be tackling the question 'How can I be of use in the everyday life of the group of people I'm going for?' The main challenge is to find a solution that is both useful to people and relevant for the brand. Whatever form the 'useful marketing' takes, from a mobile application to an online service, from a retail experience to an online widget, from a relevant partnership to embracing existing grassroots initiatives, it needs to be closely linked to the actual product or service. The mission: to create marketing that people seek out and – most importantly – are thankful for.

'WE ARE CONVINCED THAT ANYONE CAN GET FIT IF THEY HAVE THE RIGHT KNOW-HOW, AND WHO BETTER TO LEARN FROM THAN THE TERRITORIAL ARMY WHO ARE THE EXPERTS AT COMBINING FITNESS WITH BUSY SCHEDULES.'

LIEUTENANT COLONEL PHIL WATKINS, THE ARMY PHYSICAL TRAINING CORPS

In the second week of 2007, the Territorial Army (TA) launched a fourteen-week 'Fitness That Works' programme, timed to coincide with people's New Year's resolutions. The programme was aimed at people between the ages of seventeen and forty who want to get fit but are struggling to find the time.

The fitness programme was launched after a survey revealed that 80 per cent of the UK population most admired trained army instructors for their fitness prowess – more than popular TV presenters or celebrity fitness videos. Although 70 per cent of people in the survey said that getting fit was their number one priority the previous year, nearly half the respondents said that work or family commitments had stopped them fitting in their workouts.

The programme, which is based on the TA's own fitness regime, was designed to get office workers moving with exercises like chair dips and running, encouraging them to exercise during their lunch hours, breaks and journeys to and from work. A television, radio and press campaign prompted people to download a comprehensive training programme from the army's fitness website, with fitness and nutritional advice.

The initiative was clearly aimed not only at improving the fitness of the nation, but at encouraging serious participants to consider a career in the Army or TA. Those who adhered to the programme could get themselves fit enough to join the Territorials, irrespective of previous fitness levels, and even become part-time soldiers if they wanted. More than 200,000 visitors were interested and over 50 per cent signed up. Registrations to join the TA were up by 223 per cent.

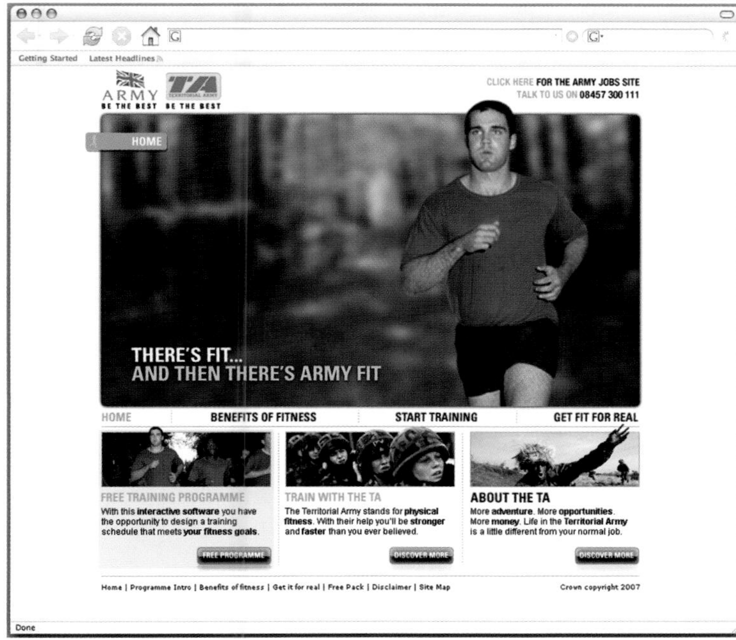
Getting Started
Latest Headlines
ARMY
BE THE BEST
TA
BE THE BEST
CLICK HERE FOR THE ARMY JOBS SITE
TALK TO US ON 08457 300 111
HOME
THERE'S FIT...
AND THEN THERE'S ARMY FIT
HOME
BENEFITS OF FITNESS
START TRAINING
GET FIT FOR REAL
FREE TRAINING PROGRAMME
With this interactive software you have the opportunity to design a training schedule that meets your fitness goals.
FREE PROGRAMME
TRAIN WITH THE TA
The Territorial Army stands for physical fitness. With their help you'll be stronger and faster than you ever believed.
DISCOVER MORE
ABOUT THE TA
More adventure. More opportunities. More money. Life in the Territorial Army is a little different from your normal job.
DISCOVER MORE
Home | Programme Intro | Benefits of fitness | Get it for real | Free Pack | Disclaimer | Site Map
Crown copyright 2007
Done

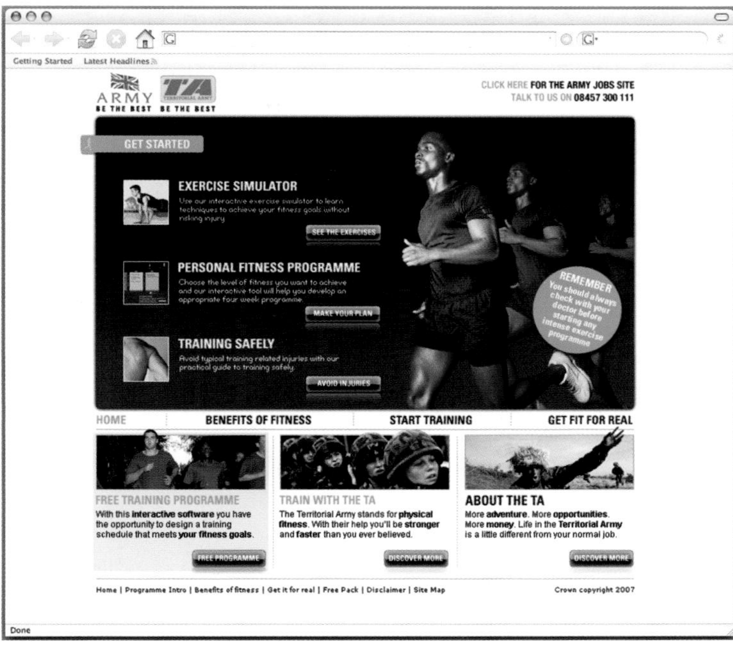
Getting Started
Latest Headlines
ARMY
BE THE BEST
TA
BE THE BEST
CLICK HERE FOR THE ARMY JOBS SITE
TALK TO US ON 08457 300 111
GET STARTED
EXERCISE SIMULATOR
Use our interactive exercise simulator to learn techniques to achieve your fitness goals without risking injury
SEE THE EXERCISES
PERSONAL FITNESS PROGRAMME
Choose the level of fitness you want to achieve and our interactive tool will help you develop an appropriate four week programme.
MAKE YOUR PLAN
TRAINING SAFELY
Avoid typical training related injuries with our practical guide to training safely.
AVOID INJURIES
REMEMBER
You should always check with your doctor before starting any intense exercise programme
HOME
BENEFITS OF FITNESS
START TRAINING
GET FIT FOR REAL
FREE TRAINING PROGRAMME
With this interactive software you have the opportunity to design a training schedule that meets your fitness goals.
FREE PROGRAMME
TRAIN WITH THE TA
The Territorial Army stands for physical fitness. With their help you'll be stronger and faster than you ever believed.
DISCOVER MORE
ABOUT THE TA
More adventure. More opportunities. More money. Life in the Territorial Army is a little different from your normal job.
DISCOVER MORE
Home | Programme Intro | Benefits of fitness | Get it for real | Free Pack | Disclaimer | Site Map
Crown copyright 2007
Done

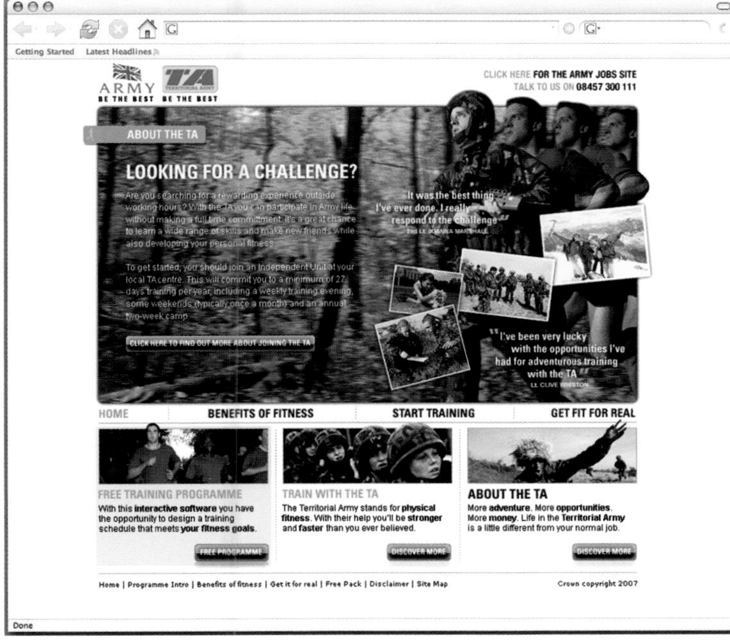
Getting Started
Latest Headlines
ARMY
BE THE BEST
TA
BE THE BEST
CLICK HERE FOR THE ARMY JOBS SITE
TALK TO US ON 08457 300 111
ABOUT THE TA
LOOKING FOR A CHALLENGE?
Are you searching for a rewarding experience outside working hours? With the TA you can participate in Army life without making a full time commitment. It's a great chance to learn a wide range of skills and make new friends while also developing your personal fitness.
To get started, you should join an Independent Unit at your local TA centre. This will commit you to a minimum of 27 days training per year, including a weekly training evening, some weekends (typically once a month) and an annual two-week camp.
CLICK HERE TO FIND OUT MORE ABOUT JOINING THE TA
"It was the best thing I've ever done. I really respond to the challenge"
"I've been very lucky with the opportunities I've had for adventurous training with the TA"
Lt. CLIVE WINSTON
HOME
BENEFITS OF FITNESS
START TRAINING
GET FIT FOR REAL
FREE TRAINING PROGRAMME
With this interactive software you have the opportunity to design a training schedule that meets your fitness goals.
FREE PROGRAMME
TRAIN WITH THE TA
The Territorial Army stands for physical fitness. With their help you'll be stronger and faster than you ever believed.
DISCOVER MORE
ABOUT THE TA
More adventure. More opportunities. More money. Life in the Territorial Army is a little different from your normal job.
DISCOVER MORE
Home | Programme Intro | Benefits of fitness | Get it for real | Free Pack | Disclaimer | Site Map
Crown copyright 2007
Done

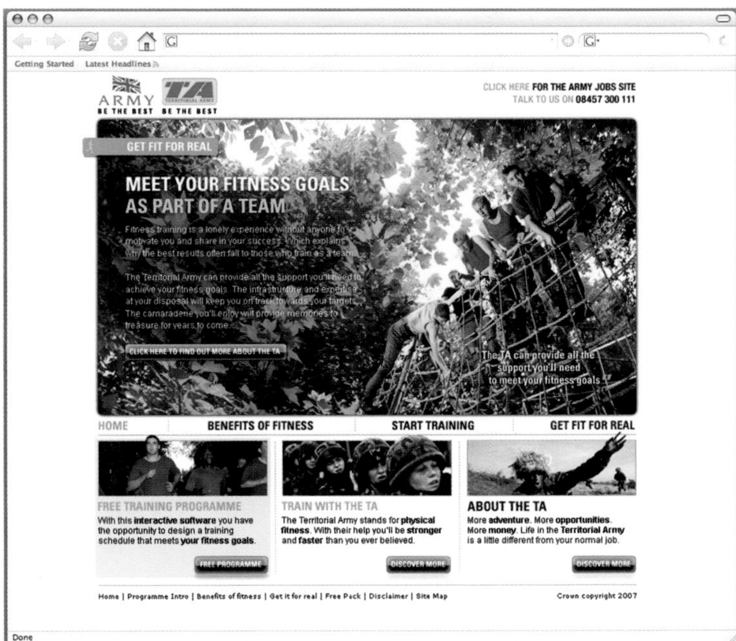
Getting Started
Latest Headlines
ARMY
BE THE BEST
TA
BE THE BEST
CLICK HERE FOR THE ARMY JOBS SITE
TALK TO US ON 08457 300 111
GET FIT FOR REAL
MEET YOUR FITNESS GOALS
AS PART OF A TEAM
Fitness training is a lonely experience without anyone to motivate you and share in your success. Which explains why the best results often fall to those who train as a team.
The Territorial Army can provide all the support you'll need to achieve your fitness goals. The infrastructure and expertise at your disposal will keep you on track towards your targets. The camaraderie you'll enjoy will provide memories to treasure for years to come.
CLICK HERE TO FIND OUT MORE ABOUT THE TA
The TA can provide all the support you'll need to meet your fitness goals
HOME
BENEFITS OF FITNESS
START TRAINING
GET FIT FOR REAL
FREE TRAINING PROGRAMME
With this interactive software you have the opportunity to design a training schedule that meets your fitness goals.
FREE PROGRAMME
TRAIN WITH THE TA
The Territorial Army stands for physical fitness. With their help you'll be stronger and faster than you ever believed.
DISCOVER MORE
ABOUT THE TA
More adventure. More opportunities. More money. Life in the Territorial Army is a little different from your normal job.
DISCOVER MORE
Home | Programme Intro | Benefits of fitness | Get it for real | Free Pack | Disclaimer | Site Map
Crown copyright 2007
Done

BEUSEFUL
BUGABOO
Agency: 72&Sunny
Netherlands – 2006

Bugaboo, the company behind the funky baby strollers, created Bugaboo Daytrips, downloadable itineraries that allow parents and children to enjoy the city together. The company has maps for about twenty cities worldwide, and each of the trips contains surprising, inspiring, kid-friendly tips and activities. Bugaboo has teamed up with local celebrated graphic designers to transform the standard city map into a visually impressive artwork, with each artist interpreting the city in his own unique way.

The maps are downloadable from a dedicated website (www.bugaboodaytrips.com) that is open to everyone. Bugaboo's free Daytrip service perfectly complements their core offering, and also highlights the company's original, design-friendly approach.

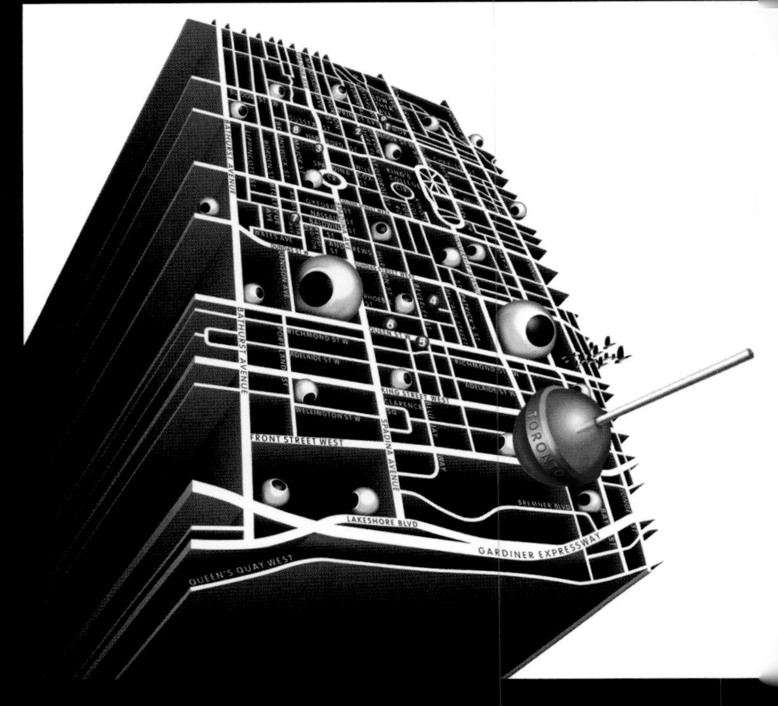

bugaboodaytrips.com

bugaboo

BEUSEFUL
BUGABOO
Agency: 72&Sunny
Netherlands – 2006

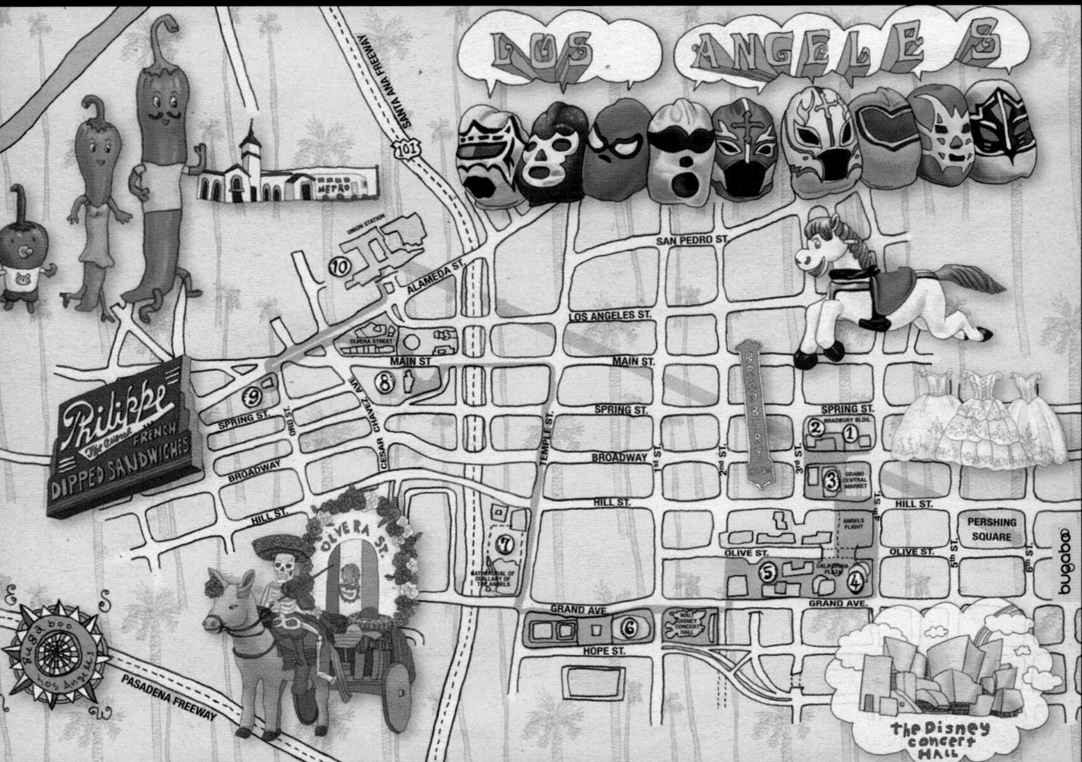

TUTTI
FRUTTI
MARTIN LUTHER KING JR DR.
LINCOLN WAY
NINTH
IRVING
bugaboo

HET IJ
STOPERA
HORTUS BOTANICUS
ARTIS
NATURA
MAGISTRA
AMSTELSTRAAT

E. HOUSTON ST.
STANTON ST.
RIVINGTON ST.
DELANCEY ST.
ALLEN ST.
ORCHARD ST.
LUDLOW ST.
ESSEX ST.
NORFOLK ST.
SUFFOLK ST.
CLINTON ST.
SEWARD PARK
bugaboo
N

HRADCANY
The Castle
MALASTRANA
CHOTKOVA
NERUDOVA
KARLUV MOST (THE CHARLES BRIDGE)
MANESUV MOST
MOST LEGII
KAMPA ISLAND
FUNICULAR RAILWAY
PRAGUE

The original Evian Spa was built in 1829 at the foot of the French Alps, in Evian-Les Baines where the source was discovered. The 'Thermes Evian' used Evian water for a full range of hydrotherapy treatments and quickly became one of the most fashionable European destinations at the turn of the century.

In the 1990s, building on its rich thermal heritage, Evian opened the Evian Royal Spa, which in 2005 was chosen as the number one spa in Europe. Almost two hundred years after the original spa was founded, the mineral water brand expanded this side of the business by establishing a series of spas around the world, the ideal antidote to today's indulgent and stressful lifestyle. Evian Spas turn the values of the Evian brand heritage – purity and rejuvenation – into a effective luxury experience. They are quite overtly branded, with the iconic Evian bottles on full display.

The Evian Spa in Shanghai opened its doors in 2006 at Three on the Bund, an urban sanctuary offering state-of-the-art treatments, and Shanghai's premier lifestyle destination. Barbers by Three is one aspect, a comfortable salon where men can relax and enjoy superb service and personalized pampering. Treatments are taken in private rooms, each equipped with a chic black leather barber's chair, a television and a CD/DVD player.

Below: As part of its Detox campaign, Evian set up a series of pop-up spas in cities such as Los Angeles and New York for thirty days only. Free detox treatments, including facials, stone massages and reflexologies, were available by appointment only, but passers-by could also walk in off the street and enjoy an Evian hand massage.

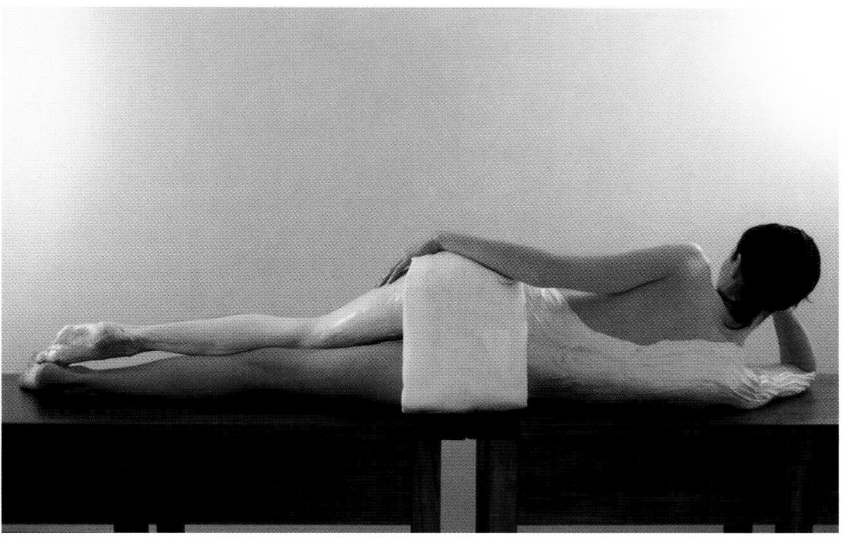

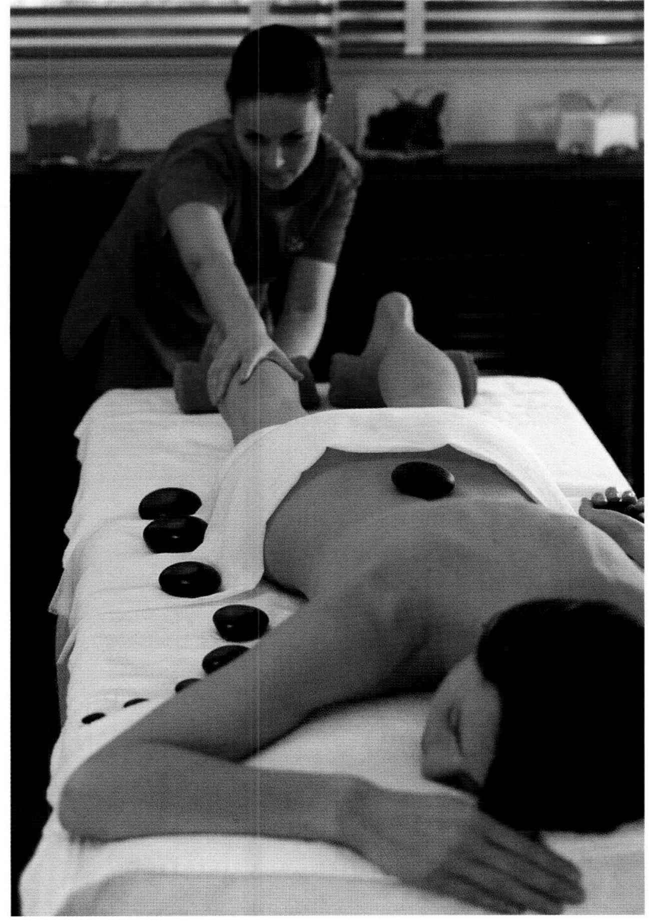

'WE FEEL THE "DETOX WITH EVIAN" PLATFORM IS A RETURN TO OUR ORIGINAL ORIGINS AS PURE AND INTEGRAL WATER AND IT TOUCHES ON OUR GOAL OF BRINGING THE EVIAN EXPERIENCE TO THE MASSES.'

MARC JACHEET, CMO OF EVIAN, NORTH AMERICA

BE USEFUL
HSBC
Agency: Renegade Marketing Group
United States – since 2003

In order to reinforce its positioning as 'the world's local bank' on the streets of New York, HSBC turned to one of the city's most familiar icons: its cabs. The bank created an HSBC-branded, vintage taxi cab that criss-crossed the streets of New York giving free rides to anyone who could present their HSBC card. As well as the free ride, customers could count on free restaurant, theatre or touring suggestions from the HSBC cab driver. In order to find New York's Most Knowledgeable Cabbie, HSBC ran a recruitment campaign, which included advertisements in *Variety* and an event with local celebrities. While the HSBC cab roamed the streets of New York, street teams dressed like cabbies distributed 80,000 HSBC-branded guides about one of four New York City neighbourhoods.

The second year of the programme brought the 'Ride Free with HSBC' concept to an even wider audience. Street teams asked the public New York City trivia questions and everyone who answered correctly received a free subway ride (25,000 in total). On top of that, for a period of twelve days the HSBC cabs opened up the free service to include all New Yorkers.

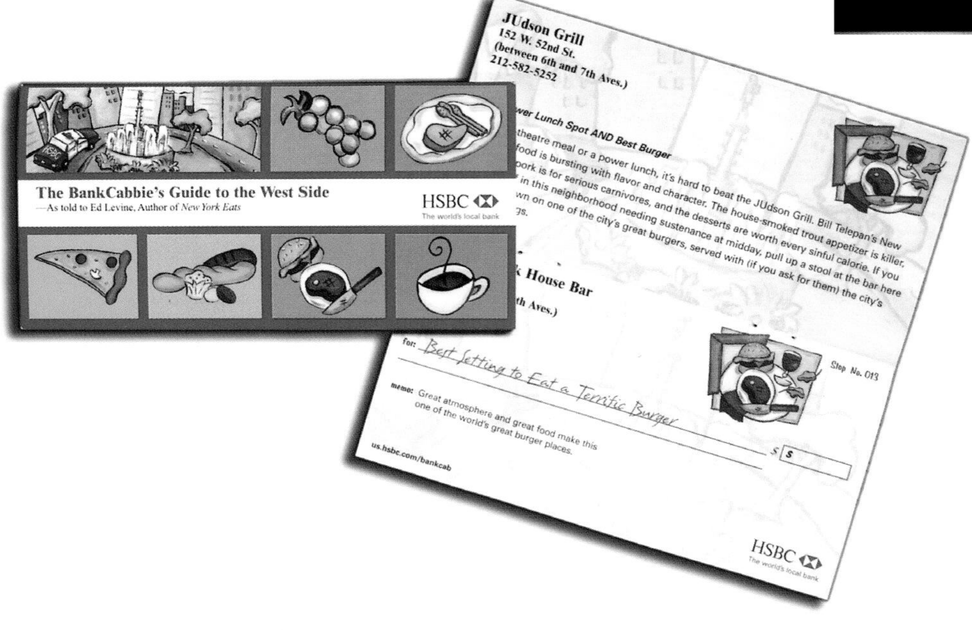

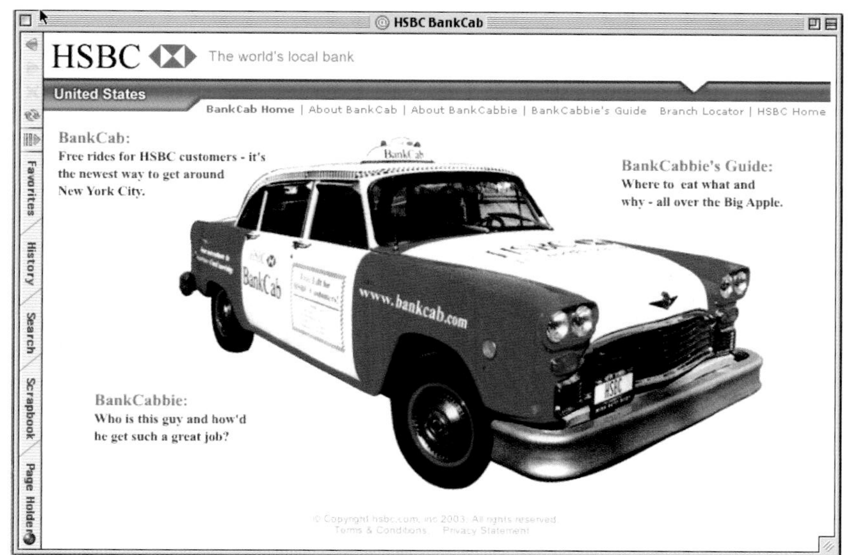
HSBC BankCab
HSBC The world's local bank
United States
BankCab Home | About BankCab | About BankCabbie | BankCabbie's Guide Branch Locator | HSBC Home
BankCab:
Free rides for HSBC customers - it's the newest way to get around New York City.
BankCabbie's Guide:
Where to eat what and why - all over the Big Apple.
BankCabbie:
Who is this guy and how'd he get such a great job?
www.bankcab.com
Favorites
History
Search
Scrapbook
Page Holder

THINK YOU KNOW THIS TOWN?
PROVE IT AND...
FREE
WITH HSBC

CNN
HSBC
BankC

HSBC
BankCab
Search for t
HSBC BankC
New York's Most Knowled
I'M FROM OUT OF TOWN
THE CITY THA DOESN'T SLEEP
MANHATTAN
DON'T BLOCK THE BOX
NEW YORK

BEUSEFUL
NIKE
Agency: BBDO Argentina
Argentina – 2006

As part of its worldwide Joga Bonito campaign, Nike transformed the tough Buenos Aires neighbourhood of La Boca into Barrio Bonito, or 'Beautiful Neighbourhood'. The brand set up football-related art installations around La Boca, an area traditionally linked with football and art and bohemian culture, thus blending the best of both worlds. Each installation was designed to enhance the core values of the Joga Bonito campaign: joy, heart, skill, honour and team spirit. All of the installations were developed by local artists, giving the entire project a local flavour. Nike also renovated and repainted rundown buildings in the area.

This project was far from an exercise in cheap branding, benefiting the local community immensely, not least by increasing the number of tourists to the area. The project took considerable effort to get off the ground, as the Argentinian government, local council, artists, police, security officials and non-governmental organizations working in the area each had to be consulted. Barrio Bonito was opened in the presence of the mayor of the city in an event that brought media, sports celebrities, artists and the community together. The campaign generated £750,000 ($1.5 m) in media coverage, and 2.2 million people visited the neighbourhood in three months. It was later included as a 'must-see' attraction in various tour guides to Buenos Aires, firmly placing the brand's image in the minds of inhabitants and visitors.

Left: A paint-soaked football was kicked against a wall to depict these Nike stars.

Above right and opposite top: To represent *alegria* (joy), giant collages of footballers were constructed from shredded newspaper (throwing handfuls of paper into the air is a football celebration in South America).

Opposite bottom: One popular feature (although probably less so with English tourists) celebrates Diego Maradona's second goal for Argentina in the 1986 World Cup quarter-final victory over England, in Mexico. Visitors can dribble around life-size statues of England players and re-enact that famous goal.

‘LA BOCA IS A FIERCELY TERRITORIAL DISTRICT, A CITY WITHIN A CITY KNOWN AS “LA REPÚBLICA DE LA BOCA”. THERE’S NO WAY WE COULD HAVE GOT AWAY WITH PLASTERING NIKE LOGOS EVERYWHERE.’ **CARLOS PEREZ**, PRESIDENT OF BBDO ARGENTINA

HE'S G

TO AN AT

JOY

OD
HEIST
TOO.

Agencies: Mountview/Alpha 69
Belgium, Netherlands, Canada – 2006

'NOKIA CREATES AT LAST THE ANSWER TO OUR PRAYERS – A SILENCE BOOTH FOR CELLPHONE USERS. NOT FOR US – FOR ALL THOSE OTHER PEOPLE WHO INSIST ON SHARING ONE-HALF OF THEIR PRIVATE CONVERSATIONS WITH US.'

TECHNOVELGY.COM

It is virtually impossible to find a moment's peace and quiet at music festivals, which is why Nokia installed a Silence Booth at venues across Belgium and the Netherlands. The transparent, soundproof chamber-within-a-chamber offered revellers an opportunity to shut out the noise and make a phone call in peace. Inside the booth, there were also Nokia phones hanging from the ceiling for people to try out. The Silence Booth later travelled to Canada for a series of similarly loud events.

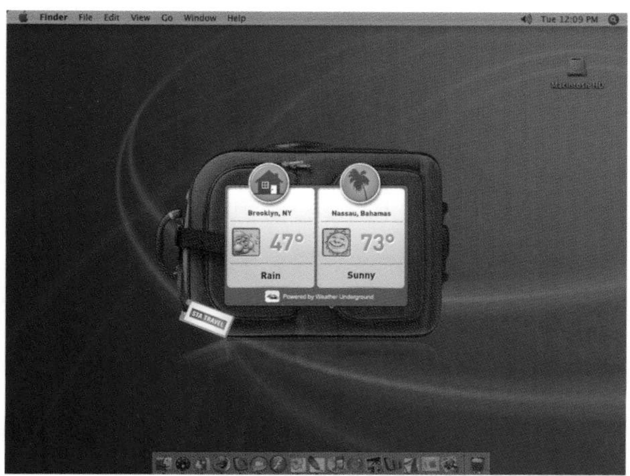

STA Travel, the travel company aimed at students, launched a whole toolbox of useful widgets to keep people updated and motivated to travel. Users can download the widgets, including a travel countdown, weather comparison, travel to-do list and a special offers device, onto their desktops and also add them to their profiles on sites such as Facebook, MySpace, Piczo and hi5. The widgets are customizable to various degrees. The colour of the weather comparison widget can be changed, for example, as can the background photo in the trip countdown.

Agency: MPM Propaganda
Brazil – 2006

São Paulo, the biggest city in Latin America with over fifteen million inhabitants, like every other big city suffers from serious congestion. To help drivers find the best route, car insurance company SulAmérica created the first local radio to broadcast traffic information 24/7. Rather than simply sponsoring the bulletins like most of its competitors, SulAmérica provided continually updated information about traffic jams, tips for alternative routes, news and discussions, all aimed at improving inner-city life.

The SulAmérica Traffic Radio has a team of more than twenty journalists and four cars that go round São Paulo getting news and information in real time. Bandeirantes, one of the leading media groups in Latin America, is responsible for the content and operation of the station. Within a few weeks, the radio became the most important source of traffic news in the city, creating a strong and relevant audience for the car insurance brand.

'NOTHING IS MORE DISCUSSED IN THIS CITY THAN THE TRAFFIC, SO ASSOCIATING THIS SUBJECT WITH A RELEVANT CATEGORY, LIKE CAR INSURANCE, CREATES A BIG PLATFORM FOR SULAMÉRICA TO ACHIEVE THE HIGHEST AWARENESS IN THEIR SEGMENT.'

AARON SUTTON, CREATIVE DIRECTOR AT MPM PROPAGANDA

Rádio
SulAmérica
Trânsito
92,1 FM
Ouça a 92,1FM para a cobertura completa do trânsito no dia da Parada Gay.
Rádio SulAmérica Trânsito. Um benefício que só o Seguro Auto SulAmérica oferece.
Realização
GRUPO
BANDEIRANTE
DE RÁDIO
SulAmérica
associada ao ING

Sintonize a Rádio SulAmérica Trânsito.

Rádio SulAmérica Trânsito 92,1 FM

Só o **Seguro SulAmérica Auto**, que protege tão bem você e o seu carro, para criar uma rádio exclusiva, 24 horas no ar com informações sobre o trânsito de São Paulo. Tudo isso com a credibilidade e o profissionalismo do jornalismo Bandeirantes. Rádio SulAmérica Trânsito 92,1 FM. Ajudando você a enfrentar o trânsito de São Paulo.

Realização GRUPO BANDEIRANTES DE RÁDIO

SulAmérica

associada ao ING

Pode me seguir.

mpm

Só o trânsito não faz greve.

O metrô entrou em greve.
Sintonize a Rádio SulAmérica Trânsito.

Para escapar dos engarrafamentos, nada melhor que uma rádio como essa. São 24 horas por dia com informações e dicas sobre o trânsito da cidade.

Rádio SulAmérica Trânsito 92,1 FM

Realização GRUPO BANDEIRANTES DE RÁDIO

SulAmérica

associada ao ING

Agency: Creature
United States – 2007

Oregon-based Umpqua bank is helping elementary school children develop the entrepreneurial mindset to start their first business – a lemonade stand. Bright yellow, handwritten application forms were printed in newspapers, instructing children to 'fill out with blue, green, blue-green or cornflower crayon and return to your local Umpqua store' and requiring the signatures of both parent and child.

After completing the application, children can pick up a free Umpqua Lemonade Starter Kit, including cups, napkins, a sticker, a yellow plastic tablecloth, a small business guide (*How to Become a Lemonaire: A Guide to Starting Your First Small Business*) and $10 (£5) in start-up capital. As well as distributing 2,100 of these kits, Umpqua held lemonade parties in its banks, where it randomly selected 105 'lemonaires'. Each of the selected candidates could borrow a deluxe, stainless-steel Umpqua lemonade stand for one week during the summer.

Dubbed 'The Lemonaire', this campaign was aimed at children in the ninety-six cities in Oregon, Washington and California where Umpqua has 144 branches. The initiative was part of a campaign targeted at small business customers.

'WE SAW BRYCE GROW IN CONFIDENCE AS HE TALKED WITH EACH CUSTOMER. IT WAS A GREAT DAY FOR HIM AND HE RECEIVED A LOT OF SUPPORT FINANCIALLY AND PERSONALLY THROUGH THIS ADVENTURE. THIS DAY WILL FOREVER BE ONE OF OUR FONDEST MEMORIES OF BRYCE'S LIFE.'

PARENTS OF BRYCE, PARTICIPANT IN THE LEMONAIRE PROGRAMME, IN A LETTER TO UMPQUA

BEUSEFUL
WAL-MART
Agency: Teknision
United States – 2006

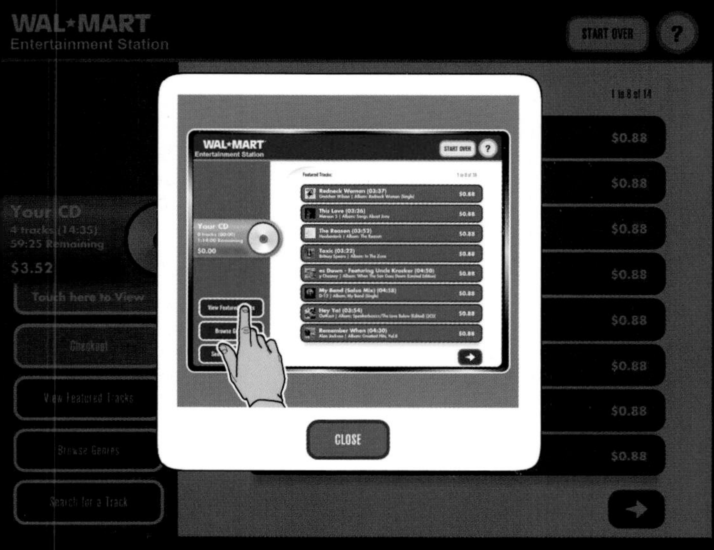

Wal-Mart made its extensive online digital library available to shoppers through an in-store touch-screen kiosk accessing the Wal-Mart music database. This meant they could choose from a far greater selection of songs than usual in store, create a personalized made-to-order CD and have it in their hands by the time they left the store. The project was implemented in several Wal-Mart stores across America, but was never rolled out on a larger scale due to the costs of staff training.

UPS
Agency: McCann Erickson London
Worldwide – 2007

In what is increasingly considered a generic market, the big three courier companies – UPS, FedEx and DHL – faced the same challenge: how to increase their share of business with additional services that would appeal to customers.

All of their customers have two basic requirements: that parcels arrive at their destination on time and that the progress of their goods can be tracked when necessary. With this in mind, UPS developed a UPS Widget, an application that users can download onto their desktop. It gives them instant access to tracking and other UPS services as well as news feeds from the integrated RSS reader.

The UPS Widget not only provides an enhanced service, but its attractive design also injects a bit of fun and entertainment into users' mundane and tedious work days. The widget offers UPS a direct messaging channel to users' desktops, and it changed the role of advertising for the company. Rather than communicating a product message, it was used to direct customers to a website where they could download the widget and learn more about how UPS can help them. The UPS Widget is an example of the changing role of branding – from communication of a brand message to delivering something useful and of intrinsic value.

Widget tracks anything, anywhere
www.ups.com/widget
Deliver more
ups

Widget gives you loads
of shipping options
For UPS services direct from your PC desktop,
download your UPS Widget.
www.ups.com/widget
Deliver more
ups

'WITH THIS CAMPAIGN, CUSTOMERS NOT ONLY LEARN MORE ABOUT HOW UPS CAN HELP VIA THE ADVERTISING AND MICROSITE, THEY ALSO HAVE SOMETHING THEY CAN DOWNLOAD, KEEP AND USE.'

JOHN WHEELER, DIRECTOR OF COMMUNICATIONS, UPS EUROPE

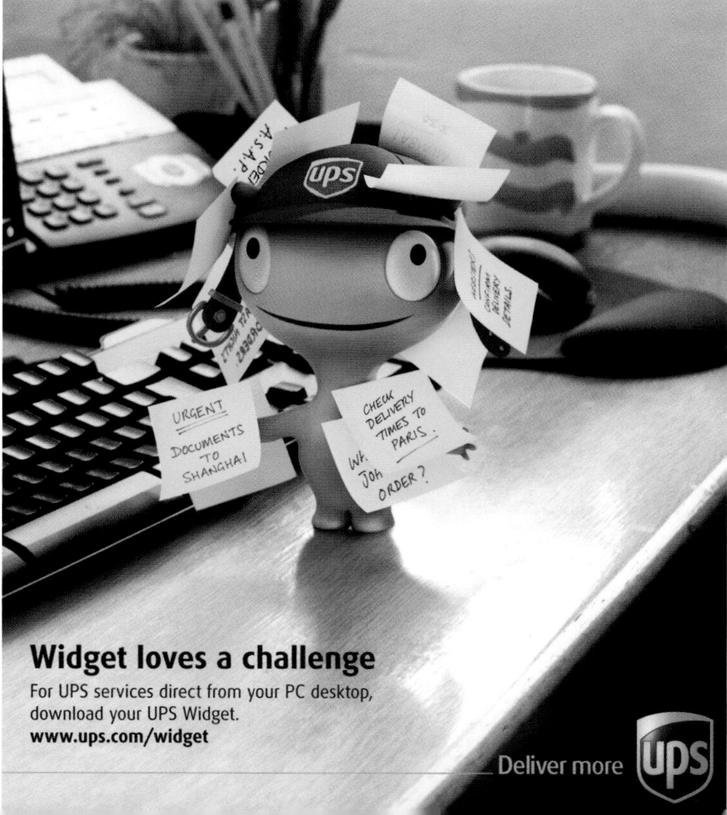

'IT'S REALLY CHARMIN'S HOLIDAY GIFT TO NEW YORK CITY AND ALL OF ITS VISITORS.'

ADAM LISOOK, ASSISTANT BRAND MANAGER FOR CHARMIN IN *THE NEW YORK TIMES*

New York has become notorious for its shocking lack of public toilets. Several attempts have been made to rectify the situation, but each time they have been thwarted by different issues. In 2000, *The New York Times* columnist Clyde Haberman wrote: 'The fact remains that this is one of the few great world cities that make no attempt to help people cope with so basic a need, a situation that constantly amazes residents and visitors alike.'

In 2005 New York City officials announced a deal with Cemusa, the North American subsidiary of a Spanish advertising conglomerate, for the installation of public toilets at newsstands and bus shelters around the city. In 2006, to mark this latest solution to the city's toilet crisis, Charmin decided to install and operate a free public toilet (with twenty cubicles) in a Times Square shop space for two months during the Christmas period. The facility was welcomed

so enthusiastically – being used close to 430,000 times over the period – that Charmin decided to repeat the initiative the following year. On the mezzanine of an office tower at 1540 Broadway, between 45th and 46th Streets, bathrooms were installed with luxurious features like white porcelain sinks and toilets, hardwood floors and of course a choice of Charmin toilet paper. About two hundred workers (with between eighteen and thirty working on each shift) were on hand to keep everything clean after each use. To make the experience more pleasurable, the space was equipped with flat-screen TVs, a fireplace, a mini-dancefloor for children and plush white couches. There was even a photo booth with the Charmin teddy bear from the TV commercials, where parents could take pictures while they waited.

The initiative was heavily promoted in various ways. A huge billboard was suspended over the door to the facility, electronic billboards were used at local airports and in the streets around Times Square, and Charmin employees walked around dressed as toilets handing out flyers.

‘THIS IS NOT JUST THE WORLD’S FIRST SOLAR-POWERED BILLBOARD, BUT A SOLAR EMPOWERMENT TOOL! BRILLIANT AS THE AFRICAN SUN!’

TRENDHUNTER.COM

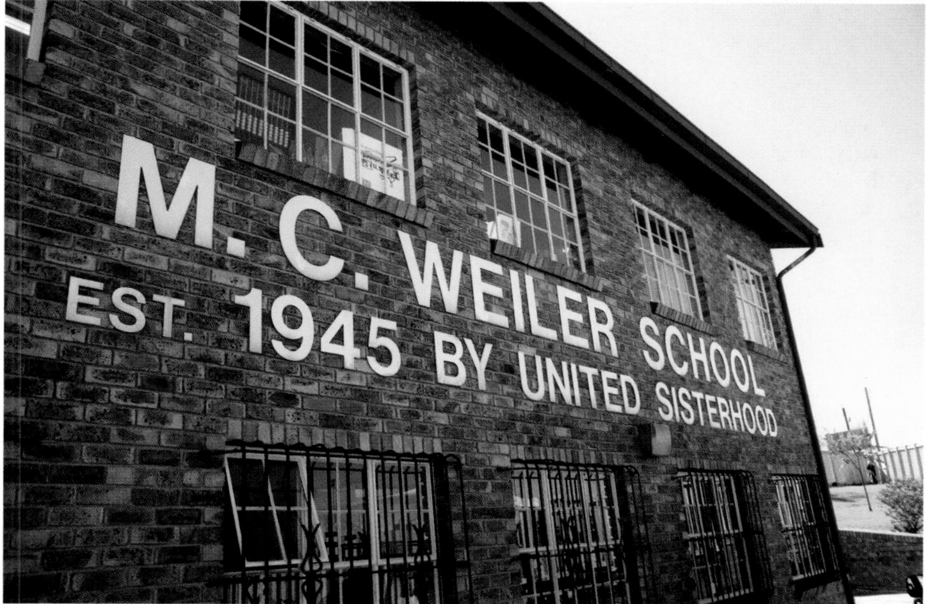

Nedbank created the world's first solar-powered billboard in South Africa. It was erected at the MC Weiler primary school in Alexandra, Johannesburg, and supplies the school kitchens with electricity, feeding 1,100 kids. In time, the initiative will grow to generate enough electricity for the entire school.

The school also makes money by renting the billboard site to Nedbank, reflecting the bank's commitment to the community and the environment. Nedbank CEO Tom Boardman, who loved the idea from the start, is eager to roll out many more of these empowering billboards in underprivileged schools all over South Africa. A patent is being explored to export this 'channel'.

BE SUPPORTIVE

One of the most famous and generous patrons of the arts was Gaius Cilnius Maecenas (70–8 BC), whose name has become a byword for a benevolent benefactor. As a confidant and political advisor to the first Emperor of Rome, Caesar Augustus, Maecenas financially supported a generation of young poets, of whom Virgil and Horace were the most famous. Throughout history, patronage has continued to play an important role in science, scholarship and philosophy, with art benefiting more than most. Virtually every major and minor artist in music, literature and the fine arts, from Leonardo da Vinci to Michelangelo, from Shakespeare to Mozart, has enjoyed the generous support of patrons.

Many brands are not unfamiliar with acts of patronage. Much like Maecenas and the many patrons throughout history, some have lent their support to individual artists or entire disciplines. In recent years, however, it has become increasingly interesting for brands to play a supportive role of this kind for creative talent. With the democratization of creative tools, content is being produced and distributed on a scale that has never before been seen, from text to video, from physical objects to websites, from music to games. For brands, there's a rising opportunity to play a supportive role in this widening creative landscape, by helping people with the exploration of their own talent and their own creative skills. Clever brands can become the mentor, the supporter, the patron of a new generation of musicians, writers, bloggers, website builders, artists, designers, product developers and entrepreneurs. These people aren't looking to be talked at from above; they're mainly looking out for help with what they're already doing.

By adopting the role of the supportive patron, brands can play a much more crucial and important function than they would by just harassing or seducing people with their own self-centred, commercial agenda. It promotes gratitude over irritation, long-term affinity over short-term interest. Motorola adopted this supportive role when it sponsored two immensely popular Chinese boys, who became notorious on YouTube for their lip-sync videos to songs by the Backstreet Boys and other pop stars. The company signed them not only as spokespeople for their mobile phones in China but also invited them to host Motorola's online lip-sync contests. Mentos, on the other hand, approached EepyBird just two weeks after their first Mentos–Diet Coke geyser video, offering to sponsor their second production. Rather than creating their own assets from scratch, Motorola and Mentos were able to recognize existing creative talent and leverage it. But support can take many forms. Iconic brand Apple not only supports creative minds by producing and selling their products, but by giving anybody free courses on how to use their products throughout the Apple retail network.

Supportive brands need to look outwards rather than inwards, embracing popular or interesting content and playing a role in its production and propagation. They need to help people with what they're already doing, rather than squeezing themselves artificially into their lives.

DIESEL
Agency: n/a
Canada, China, Denmark, Germany, Italy – since 2004

From its inception as a streetwear label, Diesel has prided itself on its creative roots. Over the years, the company has initiated several projects designed to give something back to the creative community by inspiring and supporting them to create. The Diesel Wall Award is one such project.

Diesel Wall brings contemporary art to the masses by using public spaces to define or reinterpret the surrounding territory. Young artists are asked to propose large-scale urban artwork, which, if selected by the high-profile jury, ends up on the Diesel Wall. The project has grown from just one wall in Milan in 2004 to several walls around the world in 2007, from Toronto and Beijing to Copenhagen and Berlin.

'IT'S JUST A WALL. SO GET OVER IT. GO ROUND IT. THINK OF IT. OR CLIMB ON IT. TELL US WHAT YOU SEE.'

ANNOUNCEMENT OF THE COMPETITION ON THE DIESEL WALL WEBSITE

Over the past twenty years, Beck's has sponsored contemporary art events by up-and-coming, cutting-edge artists, commissioning them to design limited-edition labels for the bottles of beer that were offered to guests at the private views. The impressive list of artists ranges from *enfant terrible* Damien Hirst to the controversial Tracey Emin. Each of the bottles instantly became a collectors' item.

Beck's also sponsored Beck's Futures, which was the UK's richest annual arts award. The award ran between 2000 and 2006 in collaboration with the Institute of Contemporary Arts with a view to showcasing the work of emerging contemporary artists. An independent jury selected artists working in a wide variety of media, including painting, film, video, installation, sculpture and photography, and the award came to rival the Turner Prize. In 2006, Beck's Futures decided to make the nomination and selection process more transparent by clearly appointing an eminent judging panel, exhibiting the artists' work at three venues across the UK, and giving the public the opportunity to vote for the winner of the prize for the first time.

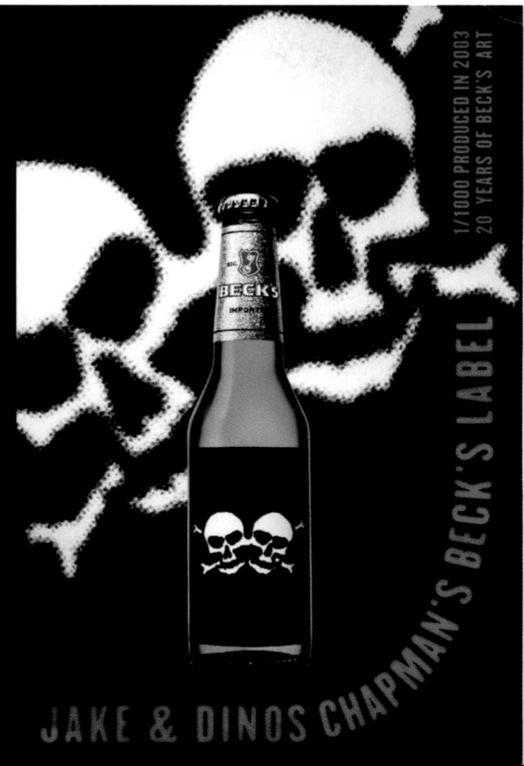
1/1000 PRODUCED IN 2003
20 YEARS OF BECK'S ART
JAKE & DINOS CHAPMAN'S BECK'S LABEL
BECK'S
IMPORTED

Beck's Art.
To the future.
Making way for new and emerging artists.
becks.co.uk
BECK'S
IMPORTED

TIM HEAD'S BECK'S LABEL
1/2000 PRODUCED IN 1992
20 YEARS OF BECK'S ART
BECK'S
IMPORTED

Beck's Art.
To the future.
Making way for new and emerging artists.
becks.co.uk
BECK'S
IMPORTED

The translucent blue glass bottle of Bombay Sapphire is instantly recognizable around the world and has prompted the brand to acknowledge and support glass as an exciting and versatile material.

The company began its association with glass design in the 1990s when it commissioned internationally acclaimed designers to create the ultimate martini cocktail glass using Bombay Sapphire as their inspiration. More than twenty martini cocktail glasses have been created to date by some of the highest-profile designers in the world and have been showcased in Bombay Sapphire's global advertising campaign as well as at international design exhibitions.

In 2001, the Bombay Sapphire Foundation was established to support and reward the use of glass in contemporary design and art. The members of the Foundation include leading international designers and some of the world's most respected figures in the glass and design industry. In 2002, the foundation launched an international glass design award, the Bombay Sapphire Prize, to support and reward international artists, designers and architects who work with this material to create stunning results. The inspiring works of the finalists in the Bombay Sapphire Prize are toured each year to exhibitions, galleries and museums worldwide to highlight the importance of glass in contemporary living.

Overleaf: Yves Béhar's Swarovski Voyage Chandelier, inspired by Bombay Sapphire.

BOMBAY SAPPHIRE
HOME
COMPETITION INFORMATION
GALLERY
BOMBAY SAPPHIRE FOUNDATION
BOMBAY SAPPHIRE BACKGROUND
PRESS
WELCOME TO
THE BOMBAY SAPPHIRE PRIZE
LAUNCH OF THE BOMBAY SAPPHIRE PRIZE
£20,000 INTERNATIONAL GLASS
DESIGN AWARD
The BOMBAY SAPPHIRE Foundation invites entries for the world's biggest annual international award for glass THE BOMBAY SAPPHIRE PRIZE.
Now in its sixth year this annual award which recognises excellence and innovation in the use of glass is open to designers, artists and architects all over the world.
RULES
JUDGES
HOW TO ENTER
2006 FINALISTS
KARIM RASHID JOINS
THE BOMBAY SAPPHIRE FOUNDATION
The Bombay Sapphire Foundation has announced that leading international designer Karim Rashid has joined the Foundation in 2007. Karim has been a
BOMBAY SAPPHIRE
Distilled
LONDON
DRY GIN

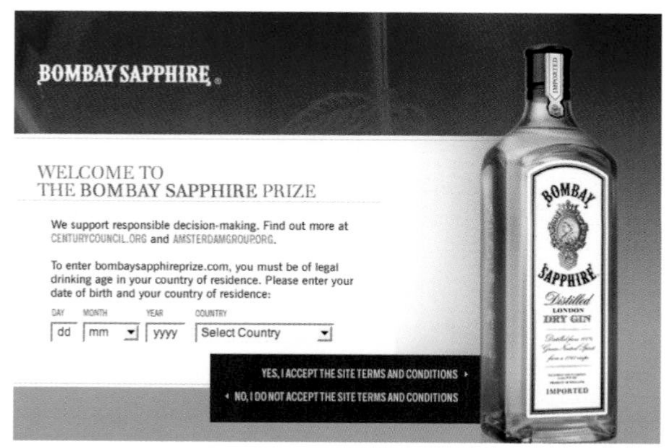
BOMBAY SAPPHIRE
WELCOME TO
THE BOMBAY SAPPHIRE PRIZE
We support responsible decision-making. Find out more at CENTURYCOUNCIL.ORG and AMSTERDAMGROUP.ORG.
To enter bombaysapphireprize.com, you must be of legal drinking age in your country of residence. Please enter your date of birth and your country of residence:
DAY
MONTH
YEAR
COUNTRY
dd
mm
yyyy
Select Country
YES, I ACCEPT THE SITE TERMS AND CONDITIONS
NO, I DO NOT ACCEPT THE SITE TERMS AND CONDITIONS
BOMBAY SAPPHIRE
Distilled
LONDON
DRY GIN
IMPORTED

Strangely enough, Cartier's involvement with the arts began as a result of counterfeiting. In 1981, the company won a court case against a Mexican national of French origin who had opened fourteen fake Cartier stores in Mexico. To make a statement, Cartier president Alain Dominique Perrin used a steamroller to smash all the fake Cartier watches into pieces.

Since he was also interested in contemporary art, he thought about creating a foundation to help protect the intellectual property of artists who, unlike Cartier, do not have the means to attack those who copy their creations. In 1983, Perrin invited César to make one of his famous 'compressions' with a pile of fake watches and the French sculptor convinced him that, rather than helping artists to defend their rights, it would be more beneficial to offer them the opportunity to 'create unusual projects, to establish an exhibition space that would be free and original'. The Fondation Cartier pour l'Art Contemporain was founded the following year.

Initially the Fondation Cartier was based near Paris, but in 1994 it moved to the heart of the city, occupying a magnificent building designed by the architect Jean Nouvel, where it has since become recognized internationally for its creativity in the contemporary art field. It has gradually put together a very large collection – more than 1,000 works from 300 artists – that retraces the major trends of artistic creation on an international level, covering all artistic disciplines, including painting, video, photography, design and fashion. Besides organizing major exhibitions of its collections both at home and abroad, since 1994 Fondation Cartier has commissioned more than seventy works or ensembles and supported budding artists in their creations from start to finish.

Perrin has imposed a clear distinction between the brand and Cartier products on the one side, and the foundation on the other. Although Cartier clearly benefits from any media coverage, Perrin wants to maintain the foundation's autonomy, independence and freedom, and views the Fondation Cartier as a work of true philanthropy.

LVMH GROUP – LOUIS VUITTON FOUNDATION
Architecture agency: Gehry Partners
France – since 2006

'THIS IS A MAJOR DECISION FOR THE WORLD OF ART AND I AM ENTHUSIASTIC ABOUT DESIGNING A MAGNIFICENT VESSEL IN PARIS THAT WILL SYMBOLIZE FRANCE'S DEVOTION TO CULTURE.'

FRANK GEHRY

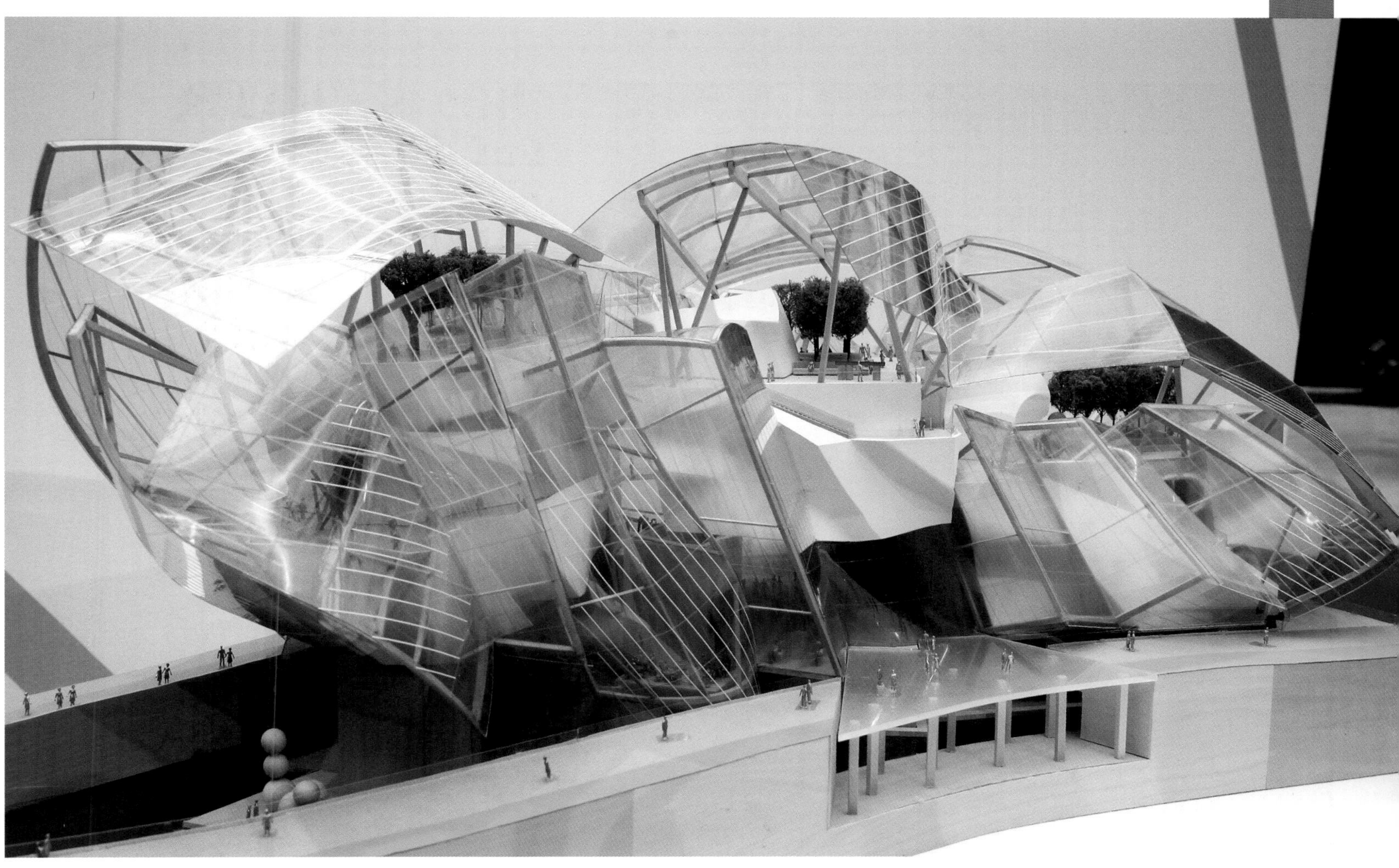

Over the past two decades, leading luxury goods group LVMH has encouraged millions of visitors to find out more about great masters of art history and their works. Between 1991 and 2006, the company was responsible for twenty-six exhibitions and renovation projects in the United States.

Group CEO Bernard Arnault took this interest to another level in 2006 when he unveiled plans for a Louis Vuitton Foundation dedicated to contemporary art. The Louis Vuitton Foundation is founded on an ambitious goal: to introduce the widest possible audience to 20th- and 21st-century art and the great masters of the past. LVMH already hosts a handful of big art exhibitions annually, but with the Foundation the company is branching out into new areas such as research and documentation, innovative teaching programmes and commissioning works.

The Californian architect Frank Gehry, best known for the Guggenheim Museum in Bilbao, is designing the glass Foundation building in the centre of Paris. The project is being funded entirely by the LVMH Group and is projected to cost € 100 m (£77 m/$154 m) over a four- to five-year period. Opening out into the lush green exterior space, the Louis Vuitton Foundation emphasizes transparency.

Diesel–U-Music is a collective of independently minded organizations and professional musicians working together to develop unsigned talent and promote creativity in music. It has been supporting the very best unsigned underground talents since 2001, coaxing them out of their bedrooms and garages and into the spotlight. The initiative is a response to the major labels' policies that endorse short-lived pop careers whilst ignoring creativity and long-term artist development.

Under the loosely bound genres of rock, urban/hip-hop and electronic, unknown artists from all over the world enter into a category, go online and upload their music, bios and photos in the hope that they will be picked as finalists by the judges, including established independent musicians, independent label heads, magazine publishers, PR agents, visual artists, journalists, and other people in the know. Diesel's support ranges from a music tour and an awards ceremony to label releases, studio time, management advice and media exposure.

Diesel-U-Music has launched the likes of Mylo, Tom Vek and We Are Scientists and has become recognized in the industry for uncovering those all-important 'ones to watch'.

'DIESEL IS THE FIRST MAJOR CLOTHING BRAND TO USE MUSIC TO MARKET ITS BRAND IN A WAY THAT ACTUALLY HELPS THOSE ARTISTS WHO NEED IT MOST.'

FASHIONWIREDAILY.COM

TUXEDO ROYALE
Dove

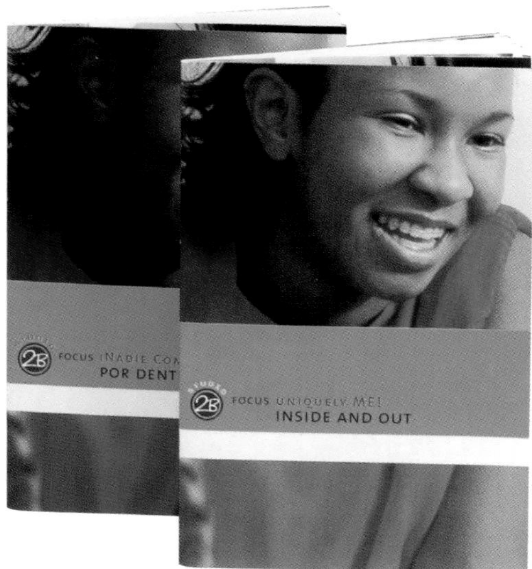

Dove's advertising campaign for real beauty has given the brand an opinionated voice, aimed at changing the current, narrow definition of beauty. The Dove Self-Esteem Fund, created in 2004, gave it further credibility. In order to make a real difference and tackle low self-esteem among women, especially young girls, the Dove Self-Esteem Fund supports different initiatives and organizations that help to educate and inspire girls on a broader definition of beauty. Causes are selected with guidance from an international advisory board, including reputed authors and medical experts.

The Dove Self-Esteem Fund is working in partnership with the Girl Scouts of the USA to raise self-esteem among girls in a venture called 'Uniquely ME!'. The programme, which uses activity booklets (*above*) and simple exercises to help build self-confidence in girls aged between eight and fourteen, has reached more than 138,000 girls in the US and Puerto Rico. The 'Real Beauty School Program' is an educational resource available to teachers and educators, designed to help young people deal with their feelings about physical appearance. In the UK, the fund supports 'Body Talk', an educational programme for schools, co-created with the Eating Disorders Association (EDA). It helps 13- and 14-year-old girls understand and deal with feelings about their physical appearance, and learn how 'idealized' images of beauty are created.

In both Canada and the Netherlands, the fund organizes a 'Beyond Compare Photo Tour', a touring exhibit showcasing interpretations of beauty by female photographers from twenty-two countries (*opposite*). The tour raises money through donations for local charities fighting against eating disorders.

BEGREEN

In recent years, no other issue has had a more dramatic impact on how companies function, produce and communicate than the environmental agenda. In the space of just a few years, green issues have moved from the background to the foreground in people's minds, impacting their attitudes and behaviours. Yet although environmental issues have become an obligatory building block for any contemporary organization, brands are still struggling to make green marketing sexy and attractive (read: accessible).

Green marketing tends to centre around serious, fact-based, corporate promises, dealing with carbon emissions, sustainable technology, recycling quotas and the like. These issues tend to be quite inward-focused, relating to how a company operates. It's the kind of stuff one would find in the environmental section of an annual report. To a certain extent, that's how it should be. Green marketing has to be more than empty promises; it has to be rooted in the products a company produces, how it produces them and how it conducts its daily business, and companies should take a holistic approach to it. As more and more companies are riding the popular green wave, the risk of 'greenwashing' is never far off. More than ever before, it's crucial that companies don't just talk green but also walk green. For those that have been green from the very start and turned it into their core asset, green marketing is a natural way of being. For those that don't have green blood running through their veins, it requires a more radical and fundamental change.

This emphasis on internal rigour and commitment shouldn't stand in the way of refreshing, outward-focused initiatives, however. As green is turning itself into a widely accepted way of thinking and way of life, companies need to communicate about green issues as they would about any other: with wit and intelligence. John Grant, author of *The Green Marketing Manifesto* (2007), claims green marketing 'is mostly about ingenuity; a different kind of creativity than communication'. True, green marketing – at least the sort that wants to make a genuine difference to this planet – requires a different kind of creativity than a standard product launch or brand campaign. It's much more about having a real impact on people's daily actions, and therefore requires ideas that are able to achieve that. But at the same time, like any other marketing domain, what green marketing really requires is the original ingredients to make the green pill digestible for a mainstream audience, one that is not necessarily that deeply involved in such issues. Creativity is also needed to steer away as much as possible from the doom-and-gloom that seems to go hand in hand with any mention of the environment. *Eco-friendly* used to be a byword for dull and worthy, but as people are becoming aware of the long-term and fundamental impact of the issues, there's a need to add some playfulness to the message.

There is definitely no shortage of green initiatives. There is, however, a shortage of clever, imaginative ways of tackling these issues. As green increasingly becomes a hygiene factor and greenwashing hits more and more people's radar, brands have to figure out how to truly stand out, rather than doing the obligatory minimum. Green marketing is maturing in much the same way as online marketing has over the last decade. While it was once sufficient to merely have a web presence, it is now a basic requirement. In much the same way, it will no longer suffice for companies to just go through the green motions. They will have to stretch themselves slightly further to stay ahead of the game. This chapter is therefore not necessarily celebrating the greenest companies, but those that have been proven to talk about their green credentials in the most consistent, original or remarkable way.

Agencies: Hill and Knowlton/FPP
United Kingdom – 2006

Research by Ariel revealed that British people's archaic washing habits are responsible for an incredible 1.6 billion kilowatt-hours of energy being wasted annually. This equates to £170 m ($340 m) – enough energy to power over 500,000 homes and 640 football stadiums for a year. With the average British household using their washing machine 274 times a year (just over five times a week), this unnecessary wastage leads to higher levels of CO_2 emissions. The figures show that British people can reduce the energy they use by nearly half (41 per cent), and reduce the negative impact of CO_2 emissions simply by turning their dials to 30°C (86°F) and washing at cooler temperatures. In comparison, Americans wash at a much cooler average temperature of 29°C (84°F).

Ariel chose to tackle this issue head-on in its advertising and on its products, simply asking its customers to rethink the way they do the laundry by washing on a lower setting. On the company's website, people can make the 'Energy Saver Promise' and compete against other regions for the accolade of the most energy-efficient town.

do a good turn
do a good turn to 30°C
make your home a green home
how energy efficient are you?
cool cleaning, and how it works
sustainability in the media
30
40
60
90
ARIEL
use your mouse to turn the dial to 30°C
Pledge to turn to 30°C with Ariel and reduce the energy per wash by up to 40%. And you could win a Toyota Prius!
Join me to do a good turn today... It's so easy... Washing your clothes at 30 degress with Ariel is a simple

save energy by doing a good turn to 30°C

step 1 do a good turn to 30°C | step 2 win a Toyota Prius | step 3 do a friend a good turn

Turn to 30° C. Save energy with every wash and you could win an energy efficient Toyota Prius!

If we're all doing little things to save energy, such as turning the temperature dial down to 30° C when washing clothes, we can all make a big difference to help live a more sustainable lifestyle. See below and look what we can achieve!

Washing at 30° C for one year saves, on average, enough energy to.

Watch around 1400 episodes of your favourite TV soap opera
Boil enough water to make 2,500 cups of tea
Equivalent to the carbon dioxide produced by driving 150 miles
Cook over 1,000 microwave ready meals

Why turning to 30° C with Ariel can make real a difference!

When washing clothes, 80 per cent of the energy is used to heat the water. By turning to 30° C with Ariel you can reduce this energy used by up to 40 per cent, while still getting your laundry as brilliantly clean as ever!

Turning to 30° C with Ariel is just one of the quick and easy ways to help reduce our energy consumption.

PS: Did you know that we are currently wasting £7.5 billion worth of energy a year in the UK alone - that's equivalent to £125 per person!

Turning to 30° C could win you a new energy saving Toyota Prius car!

By turning to 30° C with Ariel you now have the chance to win a new energy efficient Toyota Prius car! Simply enter your details and you will be automatically entered into our free prize draw.

The Toyota Prius is the car that brings us one step closer to the goal of zero CO_2 emissions.

The result of the Toyota Prius' electric motor and petrol engine is a powerful performance, outstanding fuel efficiency and exceptional environmental awareness.
WIN A TOYOTA PRIUS »

Make an even bigger difference - ask your friend's to turn to 30° C

It's really easy for you to make an even bigger difference. Simply enter the email addresses of friends and family you think will do a good turn and we'll contact them on your behalf explaining the real benefits of turning to 30° C with Ariel.

You will be able to see real energy saving facts related to the number of people in your energy saving network, so you can see exactly what a difference you and your friends are making!

PS: Did you know that if every household in London turned to 30° C, there would be enough money saved to pay 24,769 families fuel & power bills for a full year!

do a good turn to 30°C | make you home a green home | how energy efficient are you? | cool clean, and how it works | sustainability in the media

ARIEL

proud supporter of

energy saving trust®

Home | Sitemap | Privacy Statement | T&Cs | Competition T&Cs | Ariel around the World | Procter & Gamble 2007©

BEGREEN
BEN & JERRY'S/WWF
Agency: n/a
Europe – since 2005

Many years ago, Ben & Jerry's co-founder Ben Cohen said 'Business has a responsibility to give back to the community in which it operates'. Although the ice-cream company has since been taken over by Unilever, the brand's forthright attitude and social mission remain driving forces.

Because Ben & Jerry's believes that ice caps, like ice cream, are best kept frozen, the brand launched the Climate Change College in 2005 to inspire and mentor 18- to 30-year-olds who want to be part of the solution to climate change. In partnership with WWF and polar explorer Marc Cornelissen, the Climate Change College teaches talented climate campaigners about the key issues, takes them on a two-week scientific field trip to the Arctic and gives them a nine-month business mentoring programme so that they can inspire others to make a difference. In its first year, the college appointed six campaigners from the UK and the Netherlands and it has since then rolled out across Europe.

As well as the Climate Change College, Ben & Jerry's has launched many other environment-friendly initiatives, such as the creation of an anti-nuclear ice cream – known as Fossil Fuel, a Fairtrade vanilla ice cream – and the development of eco-friendly freezers.

'...ONE OF THE MOST UNIQUE AND SELECTIVE LEARNING EXPERIENCES WE'VE SEEN.'

TREEHUGGER.COM

BP took a step towards greener petrol stations by transforming a run-down asset at the corner of Olympic and Robertson in Los Angeles into a state-of-the-art, eco-conscious flagship. Helios House is described as 'a little greener' in its design and materials and in its use of water and energy, but is not a prototype 'station of the future'. It's a living lab for today, where BP can try out ideas for other stations and where people can source ideas they might want to bring into their own lives.

The green petrol station sports a futuristic metal canopy covered in shiny triangles of uncoated, recyclable stainless steel. The rooftop holds ninety solar panels and a collection system that gathers rainfall to irrigate drought-tolerant plants nearby, while the underside is outfitted with low-energy lighting. Cars roll across concrete mixed with bits of recycled glass. Visitors get a mini-crash-course in green-living, with eco-friendly tips displayed on-site, and mini-films shown at the petrol pumps, all geared to explaining how they can reduce their carbon footprint.

Staff are also specially trained to give out information and tips on green living and answer customer questions about the station. They check the tyre pressure on customers' cars, as properly inflated tyres boost petrol mileage.

BP also encourages operators of its Arco and Thrifty branded stations to adopt some of the green practices showcased at Helios House. Helios House is an extension of the company's 'Beyond Petroleum' marketing campaign that highlighted its investments in solar and alternative forms of energy.

BEGREEN
'EARTH HOUR' (WWF AUSTRALIA/FAIRFAX)
Agency: Leo Burnett Sydney
Australia – 2007–present

BEGREEN
'LIGHTS OUT LONDON' (CAPITAL 95.8FM)
Agency: n/a
United Kingdom – 2007

One of the biggest challenges facing environmental activists is the common perception that climate change is too great a problem for individuals to turn it around. Communication needs to convince people that collectively, with small changes, individuals can make a big difference. In order to show people the way, cities such as London and Sydney made a grand, symbolic statement by asking people to turn their lights off for one hour. In Sydney, the action was called 'Earth Hour', which has since become an annual event; the UK equivalent was 'Lights Out London'. Cities such as Paris and Rome have also staged similar events.

Over half of Sydney's inhabitants participated in some form in 2007. A total of 65,000 households and 2,000 businesses and landmarks switched off, including the Opera House and Sydney Harbour Bridge. The city cut energy consumption by 10.2 per cent (smashing expectations of 5 per cent), the equivalent of taking 48,000 cars off the road for one hour. Global PR coverage captured the world's attention and the story was covered in over twenty cities.

The Houses of Parliament, Buckingham Palace and Piccadilly Circus were among the London landmarks plunged into darkness to raise awareness of global warming. It was the first time the lights in Piccadilly Circus had voluntarily been switched off since the Second World War. In total around 200,000 light bulbs were switched off, resulting in a saving of around 750 MWh of electricity in just one hour – enough to run 3,000 televisions for a year.

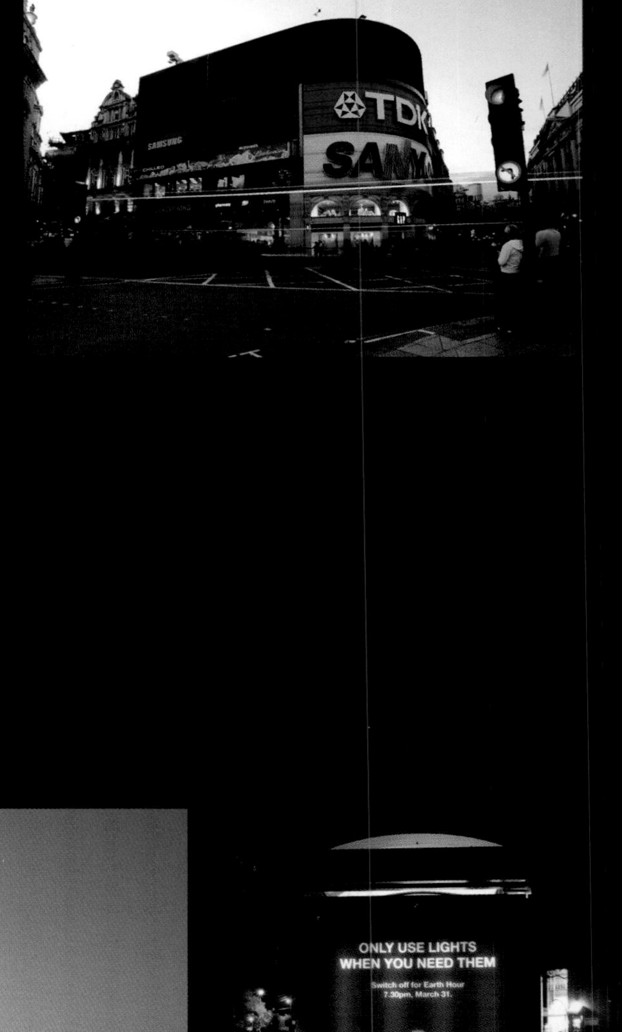

'IT'S BEEN AN AMAZING NIGHT! WATCHING THE LIGHTS GO OUT ACROSS LONDON AND KNOWING THAT SO MANY PEOPLE HAVE COME TOGETHER TO SPREAD THE WORD ABOUT CHALLENGING CLIMATE CHANGE IS REALLY EXCITING. IT JUST SHOWS THE POWER WE ALL HAVE AS INDIVIDUALS TO MAKE A DIFFERENCE.'

JOHNNY VAUGHAN, CAPITAL 95.8 BREAKFAST SHOW DJ

BEGREEN
GENERAL ELECTRIC
Agencies: BBDO New York/Syrup
Worldwide – since 2005

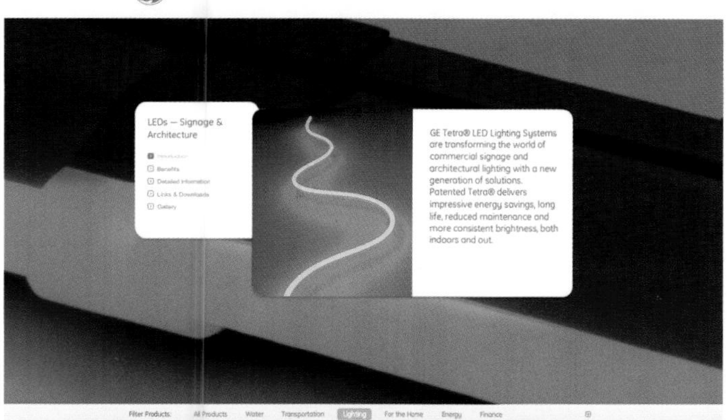

In May 2005, General Electric announced a new company-wide environmental initiative, pledging to decrease pollution from its products and to double spending on research and development for cleaner technologies. The initiative was dubbed 'ecomagination', in a play on the company's 'Imagination at Work' slogan.

According to GE chairman and chief executive Jeffrey R. Immelt, ecomagination aims to 'focus our unique energy, technology, manufacturing and infrastructure capabilities to develop tomorrow's solutions such as solar energy, hybrid locomotives, fuel cells, lower-emission aircraft engines, lighter and stronger materials, efficient lighting and water purification technology'.

The global ecomagination project has been heavily marketed through print, television and online since its conception. A series of short films was produced, narrated by Kevin Kline, in which the environmental benefits and human impact of each ecomagination product was explained. The global campaign was also supported by creative sponsorships, including Reuters' digital stories on business and the environment, and a $50,000 (£25,000) 'Environmental Business Plan Challenge' with partner Dow Jones, inviting wannabe entrepreneurs to submit eco-friendly business ideas.

In 2007, sales of forty-eight ecomagination products, including desalination technologies, high-tech windmills and super-efficient locomotives, surpassed $20 bn (£10 bn), proving the company's eco-strategy as a sound and long-term business strategy.

Agency: n/a
United Kingdom – 2007

'COMPANIES LIKE OURS NEED TO THINK OUTSIDE THE BOX AND PRESENT CUSTOMERS WITH INNOVATIONS THAT ALLOW THEM TO BUY TRULY NAKED PRODUCTS.'

MARK CONSTANTINE, FOUNDER OF LUSH

Wearing nothing but shop aprons with the challenge 'Ask me why I'm naked', Lush employees in various UK cities urged passers-by to 'go naked' by opting for goods with no packaging. For several hours brave shop workers handed out leaflets detailing the devastating environmental impact of packaged goods sold in cosmetic shops, supermarkets and other retailers.

Lush leads the cosmetics industry worldwide in its efforts to eliminate packaging by selling solid 'naked' products that do not require plastic bottles. In 2006, approximately 3 million plastic bottles were not manufactured, transported and disposed of because customers chose to buy Lush's solid shampoo bars instead of a bottled product. Lush is making further changes to improve its own green credentials, including ditching plastic bags for greaseproof paper and using popcorn as a natural filler in its gift boxes, in place of polystyrene.

The naked campaign was part of a coordinated national effort with similar events happening in thirty cities across the UK, and coincided with a Channel 4 programme presented by Lush founder Mark Constantine who is on a crusade against packaging.

CARNABY STREET
LIBERTY
SALE

BEGREEN
MARKS & SPENCER
Agency: Rainey Kelly Campbell Roalfe/Y&R
United Kingdom – since 2006

'WE'RE GLAD A COMPANY LIKE M&S HAS PROPOSALS THAT BEGIN TO MATCH THE SCALE OF THE CHALLENGE OF CLIMATE CHANGE AND PROTECTING OUR OCEANS AND FORESTS.'

BLAKE LEE-HARWOOD, CAMPAIGNS DIRECTOR OF GREENPEACE UK

We're reducing salt in our food faster than you can say 'sodium chloride'.

You don't treat your health with a pinch of salt and neither do we. That's why we are reducing salt content ahead of government targets. In the last year the salt content in our sandwiches has been reduced by 15%. And our Children's Eat Well meals were developed in line with government recommendations to contain 1g or less of salt per portion. So, the next time someone asks you to pass the salt, you'll be able to say you've already passed on it.
www.marksandspencer.com

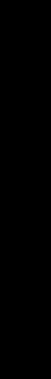
M&S
look behind the label

In 2006, Marks & Spencer launched its 'Look Behind the Label' campaign, with the aim of highlighting the company's commitment to ethical and green production and sourcing methods, including Fairtrade products, sustainable fishing and environmentally friendly textile dyes. The campaign consisted of full-page ads in national newspapers, in-store signs and window displays as well as leaflets in the larger stores. All this was supported by a 'Look Behind the Label' website providing detailed but accessible information.

At the beginning of 2007, Marks & Spencer announced its 'Plan A', a five-year business-wide £200 m ($400 m) 'eco-plan' that will have an impact on every part of M&S's operations. The 100-point plan means that by 2012 M&S will become carbon neutral, send no waste to landfill, extend sustainable sourcing, set new standards in ethical trading and help customers and employees live a healthier lifestyle. It is an ambitious agenda that will change the way the company operates forever.

MTV NETWORKS INTERNATIONAL

Agencies: Y&R/Lowe/Ogilvy/180 Amsterdam/Cake
Worldwide – 2007

MTV Switch is a first-of-its-kind, global online platform that aims to mix creativity with maximum exposure on eco issues. On the sci-fi-esque site, people can watch ads by some of the biggest advertising agencies in the business, like Y&R, Lowe, Ogilvy, 180 Amsterdam and Cake, prompting 15- to 25-year-olds to question their high-consumption lifestyles, and raising their awareness of the environment in general and the fight against global warming in particular. Users can also view messages from celebrities with tips on how to save energy.

None of the ads incurred a fee and, in an effort to reach the largest possible audience, are available rights-free and cost-free to broadcasters and content distributors around the world for use on-air, online and on mobile phones.

In a second phase, MTV Switch launched a series of ads, prompting people to unplug mobile phone chargers, turn down the thermostat by one degree, and shut down computers at night and at weekends.

Right, from top to bottom: Trees are shown panting heavily to visually demonstrate the effect that increased carbon emissions are having on the environment; This film is about a couple of guys, Brad and Earth, who live together, but unfortunately for Earth, Brad is the most inconsiderate guy to live with, and cracks in the relationship are starting to show; *(bottom two images)* The screen goes static and the station is taken over by a message from The Leader, a bizarre cult figure in a pastoral setting, as streaming words demand that you listen to his message and be green.

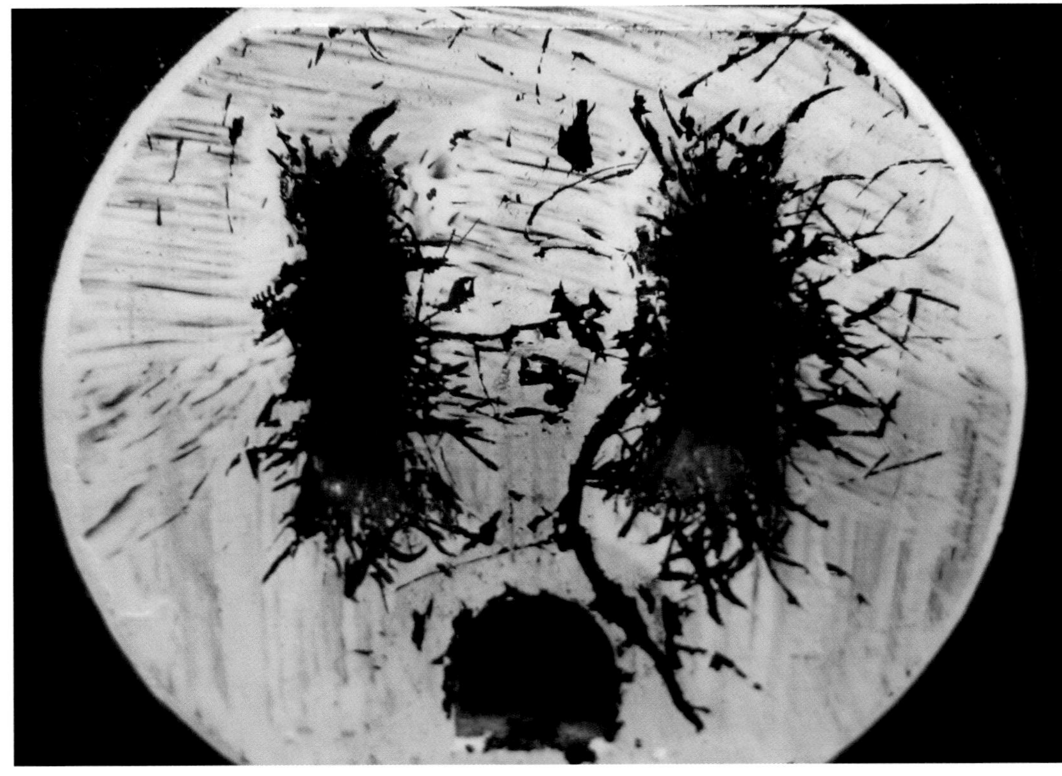

‘CLIMATE CHANGE MESSAGES TEND TO BE ABSTRACT, GLOOMY. WE TRY TO MAKE IT MORE PERSONAL, IMMEDIATE, SHOWING WHAT YOU CAN DO, WHAT THE IMPACT IS NOW, NOT IN THE FUTURE.’

BILL ROEDY, VICE CHAIRMAN OF MTV INTERNATIONAL

BEGREEN
PHILIPS
Agencies: Tribal DDB New York/Tribal DDB Amsterdam/Unit9
Worldwide – 2007

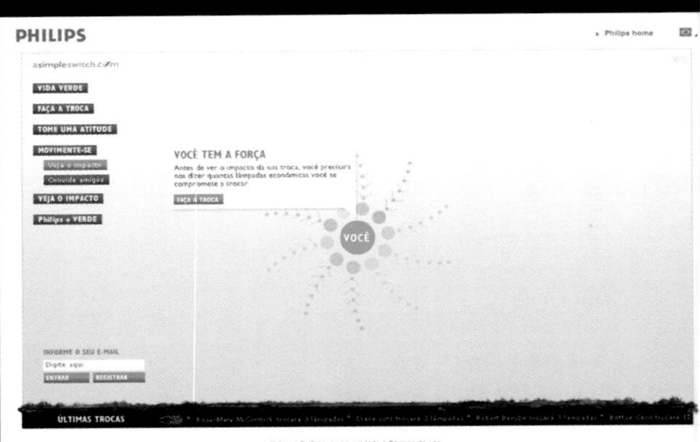

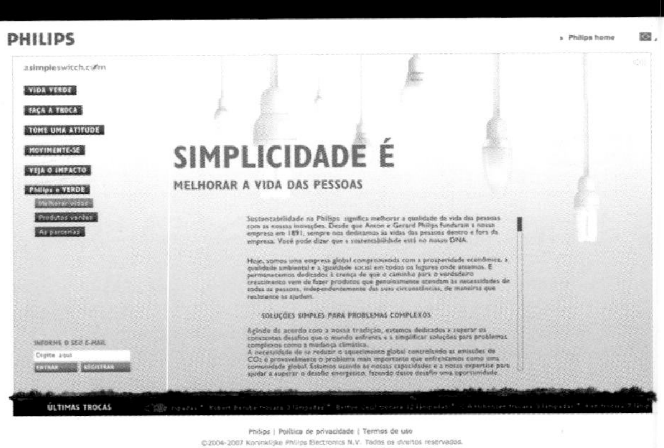

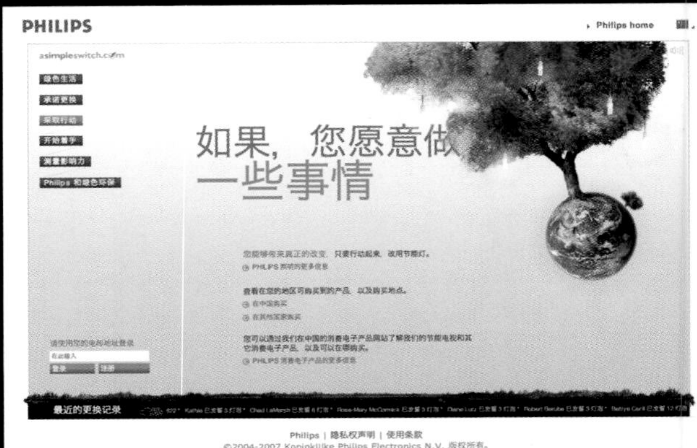

'WE ARE THRILLED THAT PHILIPS IS SUPPORTING LIVE EARTH IN OUR COMMON EFFORT TO SOLVE THE CLIMATE CRISIS.'

AL GORE, WINNER OF THE NOBEL PEACE PRIZE AND 'LIVE EARTH' SPOKESPERSON

In partnership with The Alliance for Climate Protection and the global 'Live Earth' concerts, Philips launched an educational, interactive website that challenges visitors to pledge to switch standard light bulbs in their homes for energy-efficient alternatives. Asimpleswitch.com features quizzes and tips, a glossary and lots of ideas for how to get involved in the initiative.

Visitors to the 'Live Earth' concerts and the 'Live Earth' and MSN websites were invited to record a personal 'simple switch' pledge either online or via SMS. Those who pledge have their names displayed on the site with the number of bulbs they have committed to switch. After visitors make a pledge, they can email friends through the site, inviting them to join in. Philips tracks these collective pledges and calculates the resulting energy and costs savings on the website.

Philips introduced the energy-saving light bulb back in 1980, and has put environmental improvement in product design at the heart of its business. In 2006, the Philips Green Product range accounted for more than 15 per cent of total sales.

BE GREEN
VIRGIN ATLANTIC/WE ARE WHAT WE DO
Agency: Antidote
United Kingdom – 2007

CHANGE the WORLD at 35,000 ft

Illustration: Tom Krieger at Illustration Web

we are what we do

Change the World for a Fiver was the first book created and published by We Are What We Do, the global social movement behind the best-selling 'I'm not a plastic bag' label, produced in collaboration with Anya Hindmarch. It is full of practical actions that we can all take to make the world a better place to live in. Some are eco-friendly and others are just common sense, but they are all practical and humanitarian.

Inspired by the book, Virgin Atlantic wanted to give its passengers an in-flight version. Joining forces with We Are What We Do and design agency Antidote, it created *Change the World at 35,000ft*, which contains simple actions to help passengers think about the part they could play in changing the world. The book featured like-minded brands, such as Nokia, Puma, Shell Foundation, Dermalogica and Honda, who brought their own actions to the publication, making the content much richer and more diverse.

The book coincides with and underlines the practical steps that Virgin Atlantic is already taking to make the business as sustainable as possible.

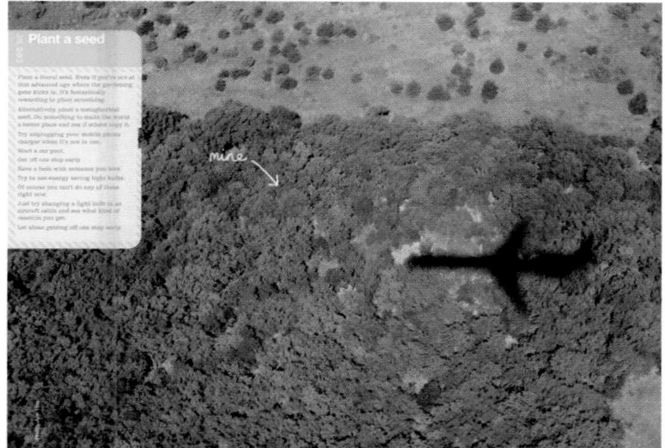

35,007

Learn plane etiquette

It's a funny thing, etiquette. We're not talking about which knife to use for the soup course, for an obvious reason. Namely, that airline catering rarely provides soup. We're just talking about 'treating others as you'd like to be treated yourself.'

A little consideration on the shared armrest jostling.
A keeping-your-voice-down if someone else is trying to sleep.
An "after you, Cuthbert" when you finally leave the plane.

If you like your partner to blow softly into your armpits while humming a selection of past Eurovision Song winners, then please don't take the second paragraph too literally.

FRAGILE!!!
TOILET

INDEX OF ADVERTISERS

INDEX OF AGENCIES

INDEX OF PEOPLE

PICTURE CREDITS

Illustrations are used with the kind permission of the relevant companies/advertisers, agencies or artists; these are listed in the running heads, unless specified below.

MINI, PP. 82–3

Photographs by Armando Rebatto

Photographs courtesy of Jim Sulley with Newscast and MINI

RED BULL, PP. 84–7

p. 84: (*top right*) Barcelona, Spain © balazsgardi.com/Red Bull Photofiles; (*bottom left*) River Thames, London, UK © balazsgardi.com/Red Bull Photofiles

p. 85: (*top left*) Abu Dhabi, U.A.E. © Schaad/Red Bull Photofiles; (*top right*) Budapest, Hungary © balazsgardi.com/Red Bull Photofiles; (*bottom*) Monument Valley, USA © balazsgardi.com/Red Bull Photofiles

pp. 86–87: Urca Bay, Rio de Janeiro, Brazil © Gregg Newton/Red Bull Photofiles

TELECOM NEW ZEALAND, PP. 92–3

Photographs by Rod Schofield

GOOGLE, PP. 120–1

© Google Inc. Used with permission

ILLY, P. 148

Left: Il primogenito by Raul Montanari. Cover by Norma Esparza Cervantez

Right, from top to bottom: In vacanza by Panos Karnezis. Cover by Maja Babic Kosir; *Ma le farfalle mangiano le ceneri?* by Chimamanda Ngozi Adichie. Cover by Patrizia Schopf; *Vigilie* by Gianrico Carofiglio. Cover by Luciano Lozano. All cover designers are from Eina, escola de disseny i art (Barcelona), working under the supervision of Miguel Gallardo.

VOLKSWAGEN, PP. 160–1

Celebrity consultant: Special Key Ltd (Birmingham, Düsseldorf)

VIRGIN ATLANTIC/TEA & SYMPATHY, PP. 206–7

Posters, photographs by Martin Parr

Picture of Kiefer Sutherland by Rodney Charters

NOKIA, PP. 248–9

Photographs by Tuomas Marttila

STORMHOEK, PP. 250–1

Flickr pictures from edublogger, kamichat, Frank Gruber of Somewhat Frank (for his pictures taken at TECH cocktail: techcocktail.com), heathervescent (heathervescent.com), Nikchick (reemer.com), mrs deedop (belly-timber.com/2006/06/24/geeking-out-in-seattle), laughing squid, frank Patrick, almsmack.

7-ELEVEN & 20TH CENTURY FOX, PP. 264–5

Flickr pictures from Soo-Mahn, Michelle Ngo, Whistling in the Dark, unsure shot

MUJI, PP. 290–1

Source: 'Design with markets! Leveraging knowledge for innovation', *Design Management Journal*, Spring 2002, by Patrick Reinmoeller

NIKON, PP. 294–5

Photographs by Sam Bayer

RED BULL, PP. 298–9

p. 298 *Left, from top to bottom: F1 Car* © Jurgen Skarwan/Red Bull Photofiles; *Together*, object from Gunther Eicher © Jurgen Skarwan/Red Bull Photofiles; Karina Padgett, *Rock Hard with Red Bull II* © Francois Portmann/Red Bull Photofiles

p. 298 *Bottom right:* Dale Busta, *Mapbull Tree* © Townley Paton/Red Bull Photofiles

p. 299, Kevin J. Arruda, *Bulls of a feather merged together* © Jurgen Skarwan/Red Bull Photofiles

ADIDAS, PP. 308–9

Photographs by Ross Brown

Repro house: Voodoo & Cake

BECK'S, PP. 358–9

Courtesy of the artists

FONDATION CARTIER, PP. 364–5

Photographs by Philippe Ruault and Patrick Gries

LVMH GROUP – LOUIS VUITTON FOUNDATION, PP. 366–7

Pictures courtesy of Gehry Partners, LLP

p. 366 *Bottom left:* by Didier Ghislain, after project by Frank Gehry

BP CORPORATION OF NORTH AMERICA, PP. 378–9

Photographs by Eric Staudenmaier.

MTV NETWORKS INTERNATIONAL, PP. 388–9

Website design by Sam Gilbey

First published in the United States in 2008 by Chronicle Books LLC.

First published in the United Kingdom in 2008 by Thames & Hudson Ltd.

Library of Congress Cataloging-in-Publication Data available.

ISBN: 978-0-8118-6539-5

Manufactured in Singapore

Design by Isambard Thomas, London
Cover design by Andrew Schapiro

10 9 8 7 6 5 4 3 2 1

Chronicle Books LLC
680 Second Street
San Francisco, CA 94107

www.chroniclebooks.com

ACKNOWLEDGMENTS

Thanks to: everyone at Naked Communications for being such brilliant misfits; Dan Burgess for teaching me to say people instead of consumers; Geoff Gray for his analogy of communication campaigns and architecture; Charlie, Alastair, Katharina, Brice and Clare and the others at C Squared Communications for the great ongoing collaboration, which has helped in shaping this book; Ed Tam, Frank Striefler, Max Kennedy, Tom Theys, Joost van de Loo, Jens Mortier, the people at Thames & Hudson, and many others for their direct and indirect support and inspiration; Jean-François Carly for supplying some of the superbly lit images in this book; *Contagious Magazine* for being a continuous source of inspiration; all the agencies, advertisers, photographers and designers who have given their consent to be a part of this book; and finally to my brothers and parents for being such awesome people.